LONGMAN
Preparation Course
for the
TOEFL® Test

iBT
READING

DEBORAH PHILLIPS

PEARSON
Longman

TOEFL® is the registered trademark of Educational Testing Service (ETS). This publication is not endorsed or approved by ETS. No endorsement of this publication by Educational Testing Service should be inferred.

Longman Preparation Course for the TOEFL® Test: iBT Reading

Pearson Education, 10 Bank Street, White Plains, NY 10606

Staff credits: The people who made up the *Longman Preparation Course for the TOEFL Test: iBT Reading* team, representing editorial, production, design, and manufacturing, are: Rhea Banker, Angela M. Castro, Dave Dickey, Warren Fischbach, Pam Fishman, Nancy Flaggman, Patrice Fraccio, Lester Holmes, Katherine Keyes, Melissa Leyva, Lise Minovitz, Linda Moser, Michael Mone, Mary Rich, and Ken Volcjak.

Project editor: Helen B. Ambrosio
CD-ROM technical manager: Evelyn Fella
Text design adaptation: Page Designs International
Text composition: Page Designs International

Library of Congress Cataloging-in-Publication Data

Phillips, Deborah,
   Longman preparation course for the TOEFL(r) test : iBT reading /
Deborah Phillips. — [2nd ed.]
      p. cm.
   Previously ed. published as: Longman preparation course for the
TOEFL(r) test, 1st ed. 2006.
   Longman preparation course for the TOEFL(r): iBT will be published in
four separate volumes: writing, reading, speaking, and listening.
   Includes bibliographical references.
   ISBN 978-0-13-612659-1 (SB Reading split)
   1. English language—Textbooks for foreign speakers. 2. Test of
English as a Foreign Language—Study guides. 3. English
language—Examination—Study guides. 4. Reading—Ability testing. I.
Title.
   PE1128.P4456 2007
   428.0076--dc22

                                          2007027705

Printed in the United States of America
2 3 4 5 6 7 8 9 10—BAH—12 11 10 09 08

CONTENTS

READING INTRODUCTION

ABOUT THIS COURSE

PURPOSE OF THE COURSE

This course is intended to prepare students for the Reading section of the TOEFL® iBT (Internet-Based Test). It is based on the most up-to-date information available on the TOEFL iBT.

Longman Preparation Course for the TOEFL Test: iBT Reading can be used in a variety of ways, depending on the needs of the reader:

- It can be used as the *primary classroom text* in a course emphasizing preparation for the TOEFL iBT.
- It can be used as a *supplementary text* in a more general ESL/EFL course.
- It can be used as a tool for *individualized study* by students preparing for the TOEFL iBT outside of the ESL/EFL classroom.

WHAT IS IN THE BOOK

The book contains a variety of materials that together provide a comprehensive preparation course for the Reading section of the TOEFL iBT:

- A **Reading Diagnostic Pre-Test** for the Reading section of the TOEFL iBT measures students' level of performance and allows students to determine specific areas of weakness.
- **Language Skills** for the Reading section of the test provide students with a thorough understanding of the language skills that are regularly tested in the Reading section of the TOEFL iBT.
- **Test-Taking Strategies** for the Reading section of the test provide students with clearly defined steps to maximize their performance in this section of the test.
- **Exercises** provide practice of one or more reading skills in a non-TOEFL format.
- **TOEFL Exercises** provide practice of one or more reading skills in a TOEFL format.
- **TOEFL Review Exercises** provide practice of all of the reading skills taught up to that point in a TOEFL format.
- A **Reading Post-Test** for the Reading section of the test measures the progress that students have made after working through the skills and strategies in the text.
- Eight **Reading Mini-Tests** allow students to simulate the experience of taking actual Reading test sections using shorter versions (approximately 20 minutes each) of the Reading section of the test.
- Two **Complete Tests** allow students to simulate the experience of taking actual Reading test sections using full-length versions (approximately 1 hour each) of the Reading section of the test.
- **Scoring Information** allows students to determine their approximate TOEFL scores on the Reading Diagnostic Pre-Tests, Reading Post-Tests, Reading Mini-Tests, and Reading Complete Tests.
- **Diagnostic Charts** allow students to monitor their progress in specific language skills on the Reading Pre-Tests, Reading Post-Tests, Reading Mini-Tests, and Reading Complete Tests so that they can determine which skills have been mastered and which skills require further study.

WHAT IS ON THE CD-ROM

The CD-ROM, with test items that are completely different from the questions in this book, includes a variety of materials that contribute to an effective preparation program for the Reading section of the TOEFL iBT.

- An **Overview** describes the features of the CD-ROM.
- **Skills Practice** for the Reading section provides students with the opportunity to review and master each of the reading language skills on the test.
- Eight **Reading Mini-Tests** allow students to simulate the experience of taking actual Reading test sections using shorter versions (approximately 20 minutes each) of the Reading section of the test.
- Two **Reading Complete Tests** allow students to simulate the experience of taking actual Reading test sections using full-length versions (approximately 1 hour each) of the Reading section of the test.
- **Answers** and **Explanations** for all Reading skills practice and test items allow students to understand their errors and learn from their mistakes.
- **Skills Reports** relate the Reading test items on the CD-ROM to the Reading language skills presented in the book.
- **Results Reports** enable students to record and print out charts that monitor their progress on all reading skills practice and test items.
- A **Send Data** feature allows students to send their reading results to the teacher.

The following chart describes the contents of the CD-ROM:

SKILLS PRACTICE		TESTS	
Reading Skills 1–2	39 questions	Reading Mini-Test 1	12 questions
Reading Skills 3–4	33 questions	Reading Mini-Test 2	13 questions
Reading Skills 5–6	39 questions	Reading Mini-Test 3	13 questions
Reading Skills 7–8	33 questions	Reading Mini-Test 4	12 questions
Reading Skills 9–10	15 questions	Reading Mini-Test 5	13 questions
		Reading Mini-Test 6	13 questions
		Reading Mini-Test 7	13 questions
		Reading Mini-Test 8	12 questions
		Reading Complete Test 1	38 questions
		Reading Complete Test 2	38 questions

OTHER AVAILABLE MATERIALS

Longman publishes a full suite of materials for TOEFL preparation: materials for the paper TOEFL test and the iBT (Internet-Based Test), at both intermediate and advanced levels. Please contact Longman's website at www.longman.com for a complete list of available TOEFL products.

ABOUT THE TOEFL iBT

OVERVIEW OF THE TOEFL iBT

The TOEFL iBT is a test to measure the English proficiency and academic skills of nonnative speakers of English. It is required primarily by English-language colleges and universities. Additionally, institutions such as government agencies, businesses, or scholarship programs may require this test.

DESCRIPTION OF THE TOEFL iBT

The TOEFL iBT currently has the following four sections:

- The **Reading** section consists of three long passages and questions about the passages. The passages are on academic topics; they are the kind of material that might be found in an undergraduate university textbook. Students answer questions about stated details, inferences, sentence restatements, sentence insertion, vocabulary, pronoun reference function, and overall ideas.

- The **Listening** section consists of six long passages and questions about the passages. The passages consist of two student conversations and four academic lectures or discussions. The questions ask the students to determine main ideas, details, function, stance, inferences, and overall organization.

- The **Speaking** section consists of six tasks, two independent tasks and four integrated tasks. In the two independent tasks, students must answer opinion questions about some aspect of academic life. In the two integrated reading, listening, and speaking tasks, students must read a passage, listen to a passage, and speak about how the ideas in the two passages are related. In the two integrated listening and speaking tasks, students must listen to long passages and then summarize and offer opinions on the information in the passages.

- The **Writing** section consists of two tasks, one integrated task and one independent task. In the integrated task, students must read an academic passage, listen to an academic passage, and write about how the ideas in the two passages are related. In the independent task, students must write a personal essay.

The probable format of a TOEFL iBT is outlined in the following chart:

	iBT	APPROXIMATE TIME
READING	3 passages and 39 questions	60 minutes
LISTENING	6 passages and 34 questions	60 minutes
SPEAKING	6 tasks and 6 questions	20 minutes
WRITING	2 tasks and 2 questions	60 minutes

It should be noted that at least one of the sections of the test will include extra, uncounted material. Educational Testing Service (ETS) includes extra material to try out material for future tests. If you are given a longer section, you must work hard on all of the materials because you do not know which material counts and which material is extra. (For example, if there are four reading passages instead of three, three of the passages will count and one of the passages will not count. It is possible that the uncounted passage could be any of the four passages.)

REGISTRATION FOR THE TEST

It is important to understand the following information about registration for the TOEFL test:

- The first step in the registration process is to obtain a copy of the *TOEFL Information Bulletin*. This bulletin can be obtained by downloading it or ordering it from the TOEFL website at www.toefl.org.
- From the bulletin, it is possible to determine when and where the TOEFL iBT will be given.
- Procedures for completing the registration form and submitting it are listed in the *TOEFL Information Bulletin*. These procedures must be followed exactly.

HOW THE TEST IS SCORED

Students should keep the following information in mind about the scoring of the TOEFL iBT:

- The TOEFL iBT is scored on a scale of 0 to 120 points.
- Each of the four sections (Reading, Listening, Speaking, and Writing) receives a scaled score from 0 to 30. The scaled scores from the four sections are added together to determine the overall score.
- Speaking is initially given a score of 0 to 4, and writing is initially given a score of 0 to 5. These scores are converted to scaled scores of 0 to 30.
- After students complete the Reading Pre-Test, Reading Post-Test, Reading Mini-Tests, and Reading Complete Tests in the book, it is possible for them to estimate their scaled scores. A description of how to determine the scaled scores of the various Reading tests is included on pages 185–188.
- After students complete the Reading Mini-Tests and Reading Complete Tests on the CD-ROM, scaled scores are provided.

HOW iBT SCORES COMPARE WITH PAPER SCORES

Both versions of the TOEFL test (the PBT or Paper-Based Test and the iBT or Internet-Based Test) have different scaled score ranges. The paper TOEFL test has scaled scores ranging from 200 to 677; the iBT has scaled scores ranging from 0 to 120. The following chart shows how the scaled scores on the two versions of the TOEFL test are related:

iBT Internet-Based Test	PBT Paper-Based Test	iBT Internet-Based Test	PBT Paper-Based Test
120	677	65	513
115	650	60	497
110	637	55	480
105	620	50	463
100	600	45	450
95	587	40	433
90	577	35	417
85	563	30	397
80	550	25	377
75	537	20	350
70	523		

TO THE STUDENTS _____

HOW TO PREPARE FOR THE TOEFL iBT

The TOEFL iBT is a standardized test of English and academic skills. To do well on this test, you should therefore work in these areas to improve your score:

- You must work to improve your knowledge of the English *language skills* that are covered on the TOEFL iBT.
- You must work to improve your knowledge of the *academic skills* that are covered on the TOEFL iBT.
- You must understand the *test-taking strategies* that are appropriate for the TOEFL iBT.
- You must take *practice tests* with the focus of applying your knowledge of the appropriate language skills and test-taking strategies.

This book can familiarize you with the English language skills, academic skills, and test-taking strategies necessary for the Reading section of the TOEFL iBT, and it can also provide you with a considerable amount of Reading test practice. A huge amount of additional practice of the English language skills, academic skills, test-taking strategies, and tests for the Reading section of the TOEFL iBT is found on the CD-ROM.

HOW TO USE THIS BOOK

This book provides a variety of materials to help you prepare for the Reading section of the TOEFL iBT. Following these steps can help you to get the most out of this book:

1. Take the Reading Diagnostic Pre-Test at the beginning of the book. When you take the Reading Pre-Test, try to reproduce the conditions and time pressure of a real TOEFL test.
   a. Take each section of the test without interruption.
   b. Time yourself for each section so that you can experience the time pressure that exists on an actual TOEFL test.

2. After you complete the Reading Diagnostic Pre-Test, you should diagnose your errors and record your results.
   a. Complete the appropriate Diagnosis and Scoring Charts on pages 185–187 to determine which language skills you have mastered and which need further study.
   b. Record your results on the Test Results chart on page 188.

3. Work through the presentations and exercises for the Reading section, paying particular attention to the skills that caused you problems in the Reading Diagnostic Pre-Test. Each time that you complete a TOEFL-format reading exercise, try to simulate the conditions and time pressure of a real TOEFL test. For reading questions, allow yourself one-and-a-half minutes for one question. (For example, if a reading passage has ten questions, you should allow yourself fifteen minutes to read the passage and answer the ten questions.)

4. When you have completed all the skills exercises for the Reading section, take the Reading Post-Test. Follow the directions above to reproduce the conditions and time pressure of a real TOEFL test. After you complete the Reading Post-Test, follow the directions above to diagnose your answers and record your results.

5. As you work through the course material, periodically schedule Reading Mini-Tests and Reading Complete Tests. There are eight Reading Mini-Tests and two Reading Complete Tests in the book. As you take each of the tests, follow the directions above to reproduce

the conditions and time pressure of a real TOEFL test. After you finish each test, follow the directions above to score it, diagnose your answers, and record your results.

HOW TO USE THE CD-ROM

The CD-ROM provides additional practice of the Reading language skills and iBT-version Reading tests to supplement the Reading language skills and Reading tests in the book. The material on the CD-ROM is completely different from the material in the book to provide the maximum amount of practice. You can now send your data from the CD-ROM to a server, and your teacher can receive this information in the form of a report. Following these steps can help you get the most out of the CD-ROM.

1. After you have completed the Reading language skills in the book, you should complete the related Reading Skills Practice exercises on the CD-ROM.

AFTER THIS IN THE BOOK	COMPLETE THIS ON THE CD-ROM
Vocabulary and Reference (Skills 1–2)	Vocabulary and Reference (Skills 1–2)
Sentences (Skills 3–4)	Sentences (Skills 3–4)
Details (Skills 5–6)	Details (Skills 5–6)
Inferences (Skills 7–8)	Inferences (Skills 7–8)
Reading to Learn (Skills 9–10)	Reading to Learn (Skills 9–10)

2. Work slowly and carefully through the Reading Skills Practice exercises. These exercises are not timed but are instead designed to be done in a methodical and thoughtful way.

   a. Answer a question on the CD-ROM using the skills and strategies that you have learned in the book.

   b. Use the *Check Answer* button to determine whether the answer to that question is correct or incorrect.

   c. If your answer is incorrect, reconsider the question, and choose a different answer.

   d. Use the *Check Answer* button to check your new response.

   e. When you are satisfied that you have figured out as much as you can on your own, use the *Explain Answer* button to see an explanation.

   f. Then move on to the next question, and repeat this process.

3. As you work your way through the Skills Practice exercises, monitor your progress on the charts included in the program.

   a. The *Results Reports* include a list of each of the exercises that you have completed and how well you have done on each of the exercises. (If you do an exercise more than once, the results of each attempt will be listed.) You can print the *Results Reports* if you would like to keep them in a notebook.

   b. The *Skills Reports* include a list of each of the reading language skills in the book, how many questions related to each reading language skill you have answered, and what percentage of the questions you have answered correctly. In this way, you can see clearly which reading language skills you have mastered and which language skills require further work. You can print the *Skills Reports* if you would like to keep them in a notebook.

4. Use the Reading Mini-Tests and Reading Complete Tests on the CD-ROM periodically throughout the course to determine how well you have learned to apply the language skills and test-taking strategies presented in the course. The CD-ROM includes eight Reading Mini-Tests and two Reading Complete Tests.

5. Take the tests in a manner that is as close as possible to the actual testing environment. Choose a time when you can work on a section without interruption.

6. Work straight through each test section. The *Check Answer* and *Explain Answer* buttons are not available during test sections.

7. After you complete a Reading test, do the following:
   a. Follow the directions to go to the *Results Report* for the test that you have just completed. A TOEFL equivalent score is given in the upper right corner of the *Results Report* for the test that you just completed.
   b. In the *Results Report,* see which reading questions you answered correctly and incorrectly, and see which reading language skills were tested in each question. Print the *Results Report* if you would like to keep it in a notebook.
   c. In the *Results Report,* review each question by double-clicking on a particular question. When you double-click on a question in the *Results Report,* you can see the question, the answer that you chose, the correct answer, and the *Explain Answer* button. You may click on the *Explain Answer* button to see an explanation.
   d. Return to the *Results Report* for a particular Reading test whenever you would like by entering through the *Results* button on the Main Menu. You do not need to review a Reading test section immediately but may instead wait to review the Reading test section.

8. After you complete any tasks on the CD-ROM, send your data to your teacher. Click on SEND DATA from the Main Menu. Your teacher will provide you with a teacher's e-mail address and a class name to fill in.

TO THE TEACHER

HOW TO GET THE MOST OUT OF THE SKILLS EXERCISES IN THE BOOK

The skills exercises are a vital part of the TOEFL preparation process presented in this book. Maximum benefit can be obtained from the exercises if the students are properly prepared for the exercises and if the exercises are carefully reviewed after completion. Here are some suggestions:

• Be sure that the students have a clear idea of the appropriate skills and strategies involved in each exercise. Before beginning each exercise, review the skills and strategies that are used in that exercise. Then, when you review the exercises, reinforce the skills and strategies that can be used to determine the correct answers.

• As you review the exercises, be sure to discuss each answer, the incorrect answers as well as the correct answers. Discuss how students can determine that each correct answer is correct and each incorrect answer is incorrect.

• The exercises are designed to be completed in class rather than assigned as homework. The exercises are short and take very little time to complete, particularly since it is important to keep students under time pressure while they are working on the exercises. Considerably more time should be spent in reviewing exercises than in actually doing them.

HOW TO GET THE MOST OUT OF THE TESTS IN THE BOOK

There are four different types of tests in this book: Reading Diagnostic Pre-Test, Reading Post-Test, Reading Mini-Tests, and Reading Complete Tests. When the tests are given, it is important that the test conditions be as similar to actual TOEFL test conditions as possible; each section of the test should be given without interruption and under the time pressure of the actual test.

Review of the tests should emphasize the function served by each of these different types of tests:

- While reviewing the Reading Diagnostic Pre-Test, you should encourage students to determine the areas where they require further practice.

- While reviewing the Reading Post-Test, you should emphasize the language skills and strategies involved in determining the correct answer to each question.

- While reviewing the Reading Mini-Tests, you should review the language skills and test-taking strategies that are applicable to the tests.

- While reviewing the Reading Complete Tests, you should emphasize the overall strategies for the Reading Complete Tests and review the variety of individual language skills and strategies taught throughout the course.

HOW TO GET THE MOST OUT OF THE CD-ROM

The CD-ROM is designed to supplement the practice that is contained in the book and to provide an alternate modality for preparation for the TOEFL iBT. Here are some ideas to consider as you decide how to incorporate the CD-ROM into your course:

- The CD-ROM is closely coordinated with the book and is intended to provide further practice of the skills and strategies that are presented in the book. This means that the overall organization of the CD-ROM parallels the organization of the book but that the exercise material and test items on the CD-ROM are different from those found in the book. It can thus be quite effective to teach and practice the language skills and strategies in the book and then use the CD-ROM for further practice and assignments.

- The CD-ROM can be used in a computer lab during class time (if you are lucky enough to have access to a computer lab during class time), but it does not need to be used in this way. It can also be quite effective to use the book during class time and to make assignments from the CD-ROM for the students to complete outside of class, either in the school computer lab or on their personal computers. Either method works quite well.

- The CD-ROM contains a Reading Skills Practice section, eight Reading Mini-Tests, and two Reading Complete Tests. In the Reading Skills Practice section, the students can practice and assess their mastery of specific skills. In the Reading Mini-Tests and Reading Complete Tests, the students can see how well they are able to apply their knowledge of the language skills and test-taking strategies to test sections.

- The CD-ROM scores the various Reading sections in different ways. The Skills Practice exercises are given a score that shows the number of points. The Reading test sections are given TOEFL-equivalent scores.

- The CD-ROM contains printable *Skills Reports* and *Results Reports* so that you can easily and efficiently keep track of your students' progress. You may want to ask your students to print the *Results Report* after they complete each reading exercise or test and compile the *Results Reports* in a notebook; you can then ask the students to turn in their notebooks periodically so that you can easily check that the assignments have been completed and monitor the progress that the students are making.

HOW MUCH TIME TO SPEND ON THE MATERIAL

You may have questions about how much time it takes to complete the materials in this course. The numbers in the following chart indicate approximately how many hours it takes to complete the material[1]:

BOOK		CD-ROM	
Reading Pre-Test	2		
Reading Skills 1–2	8	Reading Skills 1–2	2
Reading Skills 3–4	8	Reading Skills 3–4	2
Reading Skills 5–6	8	Reading Skills 5–6	2
Reading Skills 7–8	8	Reading Skills 7–8	2
Reading Skills 9–10	8	Reading Skills 9–10	1
Reading Post-Test	2		
Reading Mini-Test 1	1	Reading Mini-Test 1	1
Reading Mini-Test 2	1	Reading Mini-Test 2	1
Reading Mini-Test 3	1	Reading Mini-Test 3	1
Reading Mini-Test 4	1	Reading Mini-Test 4	1
Reading Mini-Test 5	1	Reading Mini-Test 5	1
Reading Mini-Test 6	1	Reading Mini-Test 6	1
Reading Mini-Test 7	1	Reading Mini-Test 7	1
Reading Mini-Test 8	1	Reading Mini-Test 8	1
Reading Complete Test 1	2	Reading Complete Test 1	2
Reading Complete Test 2	2	Reading Complete Test 2	2
	56 hours		**21 hours**

[1] The numbers related to the book indicate approximately how much class time it takes to introduce the material, complete the exercises, and review the exercises. The numbers related to the CD-ROM indicate approximately how much time it takes to complete the exercises and review them.

READING DIAGNOSTIC PRE-TEST

$\boxed{\text{30 minutes}}$

TOEFL Reading　　　　　　　　　　　VOLUME　HELP　OK　NEXT

PAUSE TEST　　SECTION EXIT

> **Reading**
>
> **Section Directions**

This section tests your ability to understand an English academic reading passage.

Most questions are worth one point each. Some questions are worth more than one point. The directions for these questions will state how many points each is worth.

You will now start the Reading section. You have **30 minutes** to read one passage and answer the questions about it.

Read the passage.

Paragraph

Aggression

▶1   Aggressive behavior is any behavior that is intended to cause injury, pain, suffering, damage, or destruction. While aggressive behavior is often thought of as purely physical, verbal attacks such as screaming and shouting or belittling and humiliating comments aimed at causing harm and suffering can also be a type of aggression. What is key to the definition of aggression is that whenever harm is inflicted, be it physical or verbal, it is intentional.

▶2   Questions about the causes of aggression have long been of concern to both social and biological scientists. Theories about the causes of aggression cover a broad spectrum, ranging from those with biological or instinctive emphases to those that portray aggression as a learned behavior.

▶3   Numerous theories are based on the idea that aggression is an inherent and natural human instinct. Aggression has been explained as an instinct that is directed externally toward others in a process called **displacement**, and it has been noted that aggressive impulses that are not channeled toward a specific person or group may be expressed indirectly through socially acceptable activities such as sports and competition in a process called **catharsis**. Biological, or instinctive, theories of aggression have also been put forth by **ethologists**, who study the behavior of animals in their natural environments. A number of ethologists have, based upon their observations of animals, supported the view that aggression is an innate instinct common to humans.

▶4   Two different schools of thought exist among those who view aggression as instinct. One group holds the view that aggression can build up spontaneously, with or without outside provocation, and violent behavior will thus result, perhaps as a result of little or no provocation. Another suggests that aggression is indeed an instinctive response but that, rather than occurring spontaneously and without provocation, it is a direct response to provocation from an outside source.

▶5   In contrast to instinct theories, social learning theories view aggression as a learned behavior. This approach focuses on the effect that role models and reinforcement of behavior have on the acquisition of aggressive behavior. Research has shown that aggressive behavior can be learned through a combination of modeling and positive reinforcement of the aggressive behavior and that children are influenced by the combined forces of observing aggressive behavior in parents, peers, or fictional role models and of noting either positive reinforcement for the aggressive behavior or, minimally, a lack of negative reinforcement for the behavior. While research has provided evidence that the behavior of a live model is more influential than that of a fictional model, fictional models of aggressive behavior such as those seen in movies and on television, do still have an impact on behavior. On-screen deaths or acts of violent behavior in certain television programs or movies can be counted in the tens, or hundreds, or even thousands; while some have argued that this sort of fictional violence does not in and of itself cause violence and may even have a beneficial cathartic effect, studies have shown correlations between viewing of violence and incidences of aggressive behavior in both childhood and adolescence. Studies have also shown that it is not just the modeling of aggressive behavior in either its real-life or fictional form that correlates with increased acts of violence in youths; a critical factor in increasing aggressive behaviors is the reinforcement of the behavior. If the aggressive role model is rewarded rather than punished for violent behavior, that behavior is more likely to be seen as positive and is thus more likely to be imitated.

Refer to this version of the passage to answer the questions that follow.

Paragraph   **Aggression**

▶**1**   Aggressive behavior is any behavior that is intended to cause injury, pain, suffering, damage, or destruction. While aggressive behavior is often thought of as purely physical, verbal attacks such as screaming and shouting or belittling and humiliating comments aimed at causing harm and suffering can also be a type of aggression. What is key to the definition of aggression is that whenever harm is inflicted, be it physical or verbal, it is intentional.

▶**2**   Questions about the causes of aggression have long been of concern to both social and biological scientists. Theories about the causes of aggression cover a broad spectrum, ranging from those with biological or instinctive emphases to those that portray aggression as a learned behavior.

▶**3**   Numerous theories are based on the idea that aggression is an inherent and natural human instinct. **8A** Aggression has been explained as an instinct that is directed externally toward others in a process called **displacement**, and it has been noted that aggressive impulses that are not channeled toward a specific person or group may be expressed indirectly through socially acceptable activities such as sports and competition in a process called **catharsis**. **8B** Biological, or instinctive, theories of aggression have also been put forth by **ethologists**, who study the behavior of animals in their natural environments. **8C** A number of ethologists have, based upon their observations of animals, supported the view that aggression is an innate instinct common to humans. **8D**

▶**4**   Two different schools of thought exist among those who view aggression as instinct. One group holds the view that aggression can build up spontaneously, with or without outside provocation, and violent behavior will thus result, perhaps as a result of little or no provocation. Another suggests that aggression is indeed an instinctive response but that, rather than occurring spontaneously and without provocation, it is a direct response to provocation from an outside source.

▶**5**   In contrast to instinct theories, social learning theories view aggression as a learned behavior. This approach focuses on the effect that role models and reinforcement of behavior have on the acquisition of aggressive behavior. Research has shown that aggressive behavior can be learned through a combination of modeling and positive reinforcement of the aggressive behavior and that children are influenced by the combined forces of observing aggressive behavior in parents, peers, or fictional role models and of noting either positive reinforcement for the aggressive behavior or, minimally, a lack of negative reinforcement for the behavior. While research has provided evidence that the behavior of a live model is more influential than that of a fictional model, fictional models of aggressive behavior such as those seen in movies and on television, do still have an impact on behavior. **18A** On-screen deaths or acts of violent behavior in certain television programs or movies can be counted in the tens, or hundreds, or even thousands; while some have argued that this sort of fictional violence does not in and of itself cause violence and may even have a beneficial cathartic effect, studies have shown correlations between viewing of violence and incidences of aggressive behavior in both childhood and adolescence. **18B** Studies have also shown that it is not just the modeling of aggressive behavior in either its real-life or fictional form that correlates with increased acts of violence in youths; a critical factor in increasing aggressive behaviors is the reinforcement of the behavior. **18C** If the aggressive role model is rewarded rather than punished for violent behavior, that behavior is more likely to be seen as positive and is thus more likely to be imitated. **18D**

Questions

1. Which of the following is NOT defined as aggressive behavior?
   - Ⓐ Inflicting pain accidentally
   - Ⓑ Making insulting remarks
   - Ⓒ Destroying property
   - Ⓓ Trying unsuccessfully to injure someone

2. The author mentions "belittling and humiliating comments" in paragraph 1 in order to
   - Ⓐ demonstrate how serious the problem of aggression is
   - Ⓑ clarify the difference between intentional and unintentional aggression
   - Ⓒ provide examples of verbal aggression
   - Ⓓ illustrate the nature of physical aggression

3. The word "intentional" in paragraph 1 is closest in meaning to
   - Ⓐ deliberate
   - Ⓑ estimated
   - Ⓒ forbidden
   - Ⓓ intermittent

4. Which of the sentences below best expresses the essential information in the highlighted sentence in paragraph 2? *Incorrect* choices change the meaning in important ways or leave out essential information.
   - Ⓐ Biological theories of aggression emphasize its instinctive nature.
   - Ⓑ Theories that consider aggression biological are more accepted than those that consider it learned.
   - Ⓒ Various theories about aggression attribute it to either natural or learned causes.
   - Ⓓ Various theories try to compare the idea that aggression is biological with the idea that it is learned.

5. According to paragraph 3, displacement is
   - Ⓐ internally directed aggression
   - Ⓑ a modeled type of aggression
   - Ⓒ aggression that is unintentional
   - Ⓓ aggression that is directed outward

6. It can be inferred from paragraph 3 that catharsis
   - Ⓐ is a positive process
   - Ⓑ involves channeling aggression internally
   - Ⓒ is studied by ethologists
   - Ⓓ should be negatively reinforced

7. An ethologist would be most likely to study
   - Ⓐ learned catharsis in a certain species of monkey
   - Ⓑ the evolution of a certain type of fish
   - Ⓒ the bone structure of a certain type of dinosaur
   - Ⓓ the manner in which a certain male lion fights other male lions

8. Look at the four squares [■] that indicate where the following sentence could be added to paragraph 3.

   One may, for example, release aggression by joining a football team or a debate team or even a cooking competition.

   Where would the sentence best fit? Click on a square [■] to add the sentence to the passage.

9. The phrase "schools of thought" in paragraph 4 is closest in meaning to
   - Ⓐ institutions of higher learning
   - Ⓑ lessons to improve behavior
   - Ⓒ methods of instruction
   - Ⓓ sets of shared beliefs

10. It is NOT mentioned in paragraph 4 that some believe that instinctive aggression may occur
    - Ⓐ without being provoked
    - Ⓑ in order to cause provocation
    - Ⓒ in response to minor provocation
    - Ⓓ in response to strong provocation

11. The word "it" in paragraph 4 refers to
    - Ⓐ aggression
    - Ⓑ an instinctive response
    - Ⓒ provocation
    - Ⓓ a direct response

12. The author begins paragraph 5 with the expression "In contrast to instinct theories" in order to

Ⓐ introduce the instinct theories that will be presented in paragraph 5

Ⓑ indicate that paragraph 5 will present two contrasting theories

Ⓒ contrast instinctive theories of aggression with biological theories of aggression

Ⓓ provide a transition to the idea that will be presented in paragraph 5

13. Which of the sentences below best expresses the essential information in the highlighted sentence in paragraph 5? *Incorrect* choices change the meaning in important ways or leave out essential information.

Ⓐ Research on aggression has shown that the best way to combat aggression is to model appropriate behavior and positively reinforce non-aggressive behavior.

Ⓑ Children learn to behave aggressively by witnessing aggressive behavior that is rewarded or is at least not punished.

Ⓒ When aggressive behavior is combined with modeling, it takes positive reinforcement to disrupt this type of behavior.

Ⓓ Children will model aggressive behavior even in circumstances when the aggressive behavior is negatively reinforced.

14. The word "that" in paragraph 5 refers to

Ⓐ research

Ⓑ evidence

Ⓒ the behavior

Ⓓ a live model

15. What is stated in paragraph 5 about the modeling of aggressive behavior?

Ⓐ Fictional models are as likely to cause aggressive behavior as are live models.

Ⓑ Little correlation has been found between viewing of aggressive behavior on television and acting aggressively.

Ⓒ Aggression in works of fiction may cause aggressive behavior.

Ⓓ Aggression in society has an effect on the type of violence in movies and on television.

16. The phrase "in and of itself" in paragraph 5 is closest in meaning to

Ⓐ internally

Ⓑ single-handedly

Ⓒ genuinely

Ⓓ semi-privately

17. The word "critical" in paragraph 5 could best be replaced by

Ⓐ negative

Ⓑ considerate

Ⓒ crucial

Ⓓ studied

18. Look at the four squares [■] that indicate where the following sentence could be added to paragraph 5.

Thus, it is more common for a youth to imitate aggressors who have been rewarded than those who have been punished.

Where would the sentence best fit? Click on a square [■] to add the sentence to the passage.

19.

Directions:	Select the appropriate sentences from the answer choices, and match them to the theories to which they relate. TWO of the answer choices will not be used. **This question is worth 3 points** (3 points for 5 correct answers, 2 points for 4 correct answers, 1 point for 3 correct answers, and 0 points for 2, 1, or 0 correct answers).

theories attributing aggression to <u>instinct</u>	• 6 • 2
theories attributing aggression to learned behaviors	• 7 • 5 • 4

Answer Choices (choose 5 to complete the table):

(1) Aggression occurs in response to rewards for aggressive behavior.

(2) Aggression occurs without outside provocation.

(3) Aggression occurs in order to provoke confrontations.

(4) Aggression occurs in response to observed behavior of real people.

(5) Aggression occurs in response to negative reinforcement of aggressive behavior.

(6) Aggression occurs as a natural response to provocation.

(7) Aggression occurs in response to observed behavior of fictional people.

20.

Directions:	An introductory sentence for a brief summary of the passage is provided below. Complete the summary by selecting the THREE answer choices that express the most important ideas in the passage. Some sentences do not belong in the summary because they express ideas that are not presented in the passage or are minor ideas in the passage. **This question is worth 2 points** (2 points for 3 correct answers, 1 point for 2 correct answers, and 0 points for 1 or 0 correct answers).

This passage discusses causes of aggression.

• 4
• 5
• 6

Answer Choices (choose 3 to complete the chart):

(1) Various theories indicate that learned aggression occurs as a result of observation of this type of behavior and reward for it.

(2) Various theories indicate aggression is neither instinctive nor learned.

(3) Various theories indicate that instinctively caused aggression is always cathartic.

(4) Various theories indicate that instinctively caused aggression may occur with or without provocation.

(5) Various theories indicate that aggression may be instinctive or learned.

(6) Various theories indicate that learned aggression results from displacement of anger.

> Turn to pages 185–188 to *diagnose* your errors and *record* your results.

READING OVERVIEW

The first section on the TOEFL iBT is the Reading section. This section consists of three passages, each followed by a number of questions. All of the questions accompanying a passage are worth one point each, except for the last question in the set, which is worth more than one point. You have 20 minutes to complete the first passage and 40 minutes to complete the second and third passages.

- The **passages** are lengthy readings (600 to 700 words each) on academic topics.
- The **questions** may ask about vocabulary, pronoun reference, the meanings of sentences, where sentences can be inserted, stated and unstated details, inferences, rhetorical purpose, and overall organization of ideas.

The following strategies can help you in the Reading section.

STRATEGIES FOR READING

1. **Be familiar with the directions.** The directions on every test are the same, so it is not necessary to spend time reading the directions carefully when you take the test. You should be completely familiar with the directions before the day of the test.

2. **Dismiss the directions as soon as they come up.** You should already be familiar with the directions, so you can click on Continue as soon as it appears and use your time on the passages and questions.

3. **Do not worry if a reading passage is on a topic that is not familiar to you.** All of the information that you need to answer the questions is included in the passages. You do not need any background knowledge to answer the questions.

4. **Do not spend too much time reading the passages.** You do not have time to read each passage in depth, and it is quite possible to answer the questions correctly without first reading the passages in depth.

5. **Skim each passage to determine the main idea and overall organization of ideas in the passage.** You do not need to understand every detail in each passage to answer the questions correctly. It is therefore a waste of time to read each passage with the intent of understanding every single detail before you try to answer the questions.

6. **Look at each question to determine what type of question it is.** The type of question tells you how to proceed to answer the question.
   - For *vocabulary questions,* the targeted word will be highlighted in the passage. Find the highlighted word, and read the context around it.
   - For *reference questions,* the targeted word will be highlighted in the passage. Find the targeted word, and read the context preceding the highlighted word.
   - For *sentence insertion questions,* there will be darkened squares indicating where the sentence might be inserted. Read the context around the darkened squares carefully.

- For *sentence restatement questions,* the targeted sentence will be highlighted in the passage. Read the highlighted sentence carefully. It may also be helpful to read the context around the highlighted sentence.

- For *detail questions, unstated detail questions,* and *inference questions,* choose a key word in the question, and skim for the key word (or a related idea) in order in the passage. Read the part of the passage around the key word (or related idea).

- For *rhetorical purpose questions,* the targeted word or phrase will be highlighted in the passage. Read the highlighted word or phrase and the context around it to determine the rhetorical purpose.

- For *overall ideas questions,* focus on the main ideas rather than details of the passages. The main ideas are most likely explained in the introductory paragraph and at the beginning or end of each supporting paragraph.

7. **Choose the best answer to each question.** You may be certain of a particular answer, or you may eliminate any definitely incorrect answers and choose from among the remaining answers.

8. **Do not spend too much time on a question you are completely unsure of.** If you do not know the answer to a question, simply guess and go on. You can return to this question later (while you are still working on the same passage) if you have time.

9. **Monitor the time carefully on the title bar of the computer screen.** The title bar indicates the time remaining in the section, the total number of questions in the section, and the number of the question that you are working on.

10. **Guess to complete the section before time is up.** It can only increase your score to guess the answers to questions that you do not have time to complete. (Points are not subtracted for incorrect answers.)

READING SKILLS

The following skills will help you to implement these strategies in the Reading section of the TOEFL iBT.

VOCABULARY AND REFERENCE

Reading Skill 1: UNDERSTAND VOCABULARY FROM CONTEXT

In the Reading section of the TOEFL iBT, you may be asked to determine the meaning of a word or phrase. It may be a difficult word or phrase that you have never seen before, or it may be an easier-looking word or phrase that has a number of varied meanings. In any of these cases, the passage will probably give you a clear indication of what the word or phrase means. Look at an example of a difficult word that perhaps you have never seen before; in this example, the context helps you to understand the meaning of the unknown word.

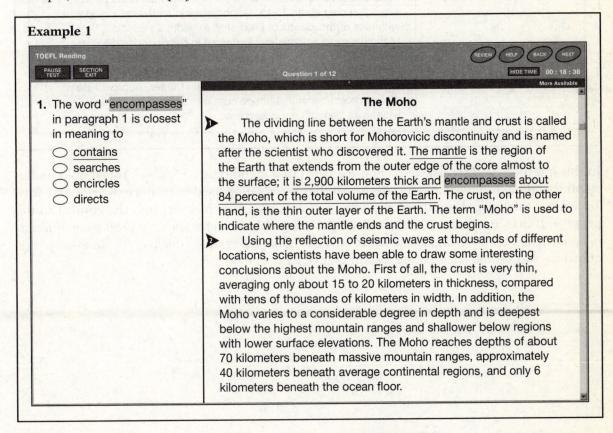

Example 1

TOEFL Reading		REVIEW HELP BACK NEXT

Question 1 of 12   HIDE TIME 00 : 18 : 38
More Available

1. The word "encompasses" in paragraph 1 is closest in meaning to

○ contains
○ searches
○ encircles
○ directs

The Moho

The dividing line between the Earth's mantle and crust is called the Moho, which is short for Mohorovicic discontinuity and is named after the scientist who discovered it. The mantle is the region of the Earth that extends from the outer edge of the core almost to the surface; it is 2,900 kilometers thick and encompasses about 84 percent of the total volume of the Earth. The crust, on the other hand, is the thin outer layer of the Earth. The term "Moho" is used to indicate where the mantle ends and the crust begins.

Using the reflection of seismic waves at thousands of different locations, scientists have been able to draw some interesting conclusions about the Moho. First of all, the crust is very thin, averaging only about 15 to 20 kilometers in thickness, compared with tens of thousands of kilometers in width. In addition, the Moho varies to a considerable degree in depth and is deepest below the highest mountain ranges and shallower below regions with lower surface elevations. The Moho reaches depths of about 70 kilometers beneath massive mountain ranges, approximately 40 kilometers beneath average continental regions, and only 6 kilometers beneath the ocean floor.

This question asks about the meaning of the word "encompasses." In this question, you are not expected to know the meaning of this word. Instead, you should see in the context that *the mantle . . . is 2,900 kilometers thick and encompasses about 84 percent of the total volume of the Earth.* From this context, you can determine that *encompasses* is closest in meaning to *contains.* To answer this question, you should click on the first answer.

Next, look at an example of a word that you often see in everyday English. In this type of question, you should *not* give the normal, everyday meaning of the word; instead, a secondary meaning is being tested, so you must study the context to determine the meaning of the word in this situation.

Example 2

TOEFL Reading

PAUSE TEST   SECTION EXIT

REVIEW   HELP   BACK   NEXT

Question 2 of 12

HIDE TIME   00 : 18 : 38

More Available

2. The word "draw" in paragraph 2 could best be replaced by
   ○ sketch
   ○ pull
   ○ draft
   ○ <u>make</u>

The Moho

➤ The dividing line between the Earth's mantle and crust is called the Moho, which is short for Mohorovicic discontinuity and is named after the scientist who discovered it. The mantle is the region of the Earth that extends from the outer edge of the core almost to the surface; it is 2,900 kilometers thick and encompasses about 84 percent of the total volume of the Earth. The crust, on the other hand, is the thin outer layer of the Earth. The term "Moho" is used to indicate where the mantle ends and the crust begins.

➤ Using the reflection of seismic waves at thousands of different locations, scientists have been able to draw some interesting conclusions about the Moho. First of all, the crust is very thin, averaging only about 15 to 20 kilometers in thickness, compared with tens of thousands of kilometers in width. In addition, the Moho varies to a considerable degree in depth and is deepest below the highest mountain ranges and shallower below regions with lower surface elevations. The Moho reaches depths of about 70 kilometers beneath massive mountain ranges, approximately 40 kilometers beneath average continental regions, and only 6 kilometers beneath the ocean floor.

In this question, you are asked to choose a word that could replace "draw." You should understand that *draw* is a normal, everyday word that is not being used in its normal, everyday way. To answer this type of question, you must see which answer best fits into the context in the passage. It does not make sense to talk about being able to *sketch, pull,* or *draft some interesting conclusions,* but it does make sense to *make some interesting conclusions.* To answer this question, you should click on the last answer.

Finally, look at an example of a phrase that perhaps you do not know; in this example, the context again helps you to understand the meaning of the unknown phrase.

Example 3

3. The phrase "to a considerable degree" in paragraph 2 is closest in meaning to
   - ◯ grandly
   - ◯ significantly
   - ◯ geometrically
   - ◯ considerately

The Moho

➊   The dividing line between the Earth's mantle and crust is called the Moho, which is short for Mohorovicic discontinuity and is named after the scientist who discovered it. The mantle is the region of the Earth that extends from the outer edge of the core almost to the surface; it is 2,900 kilometers thick and encompasses about 84 percent of the total volume of the Earth. The crust, on the other hand, is the thin outer layer of the Earth. The term "Moho" is used to indicate where the mantle ends and the crust begins.

➋   Using the reflection of seismic waves at thousands of different locations, scientists have been able to draw some interesting conclusions about the Moho. First of all, the crust is very thin, averaging only about 15 to 20 kilometers in thickness, compared with tens of thousands of kilometers in width. In addition, the Moho varies to a considerable degree in depth and is deepest below the highest mountain ranges and shallower below regions with lower surface elevations. The Moho reaches depths of about 70 kilometers beneath massive mountain ranges, approximately 40 kilometers beneath average continental regions, and only 6 kilometers beneath the ocean floor.

This question asks about the meaning of the phrase "to a considerable degree." In this question, you are again expected to determine from the context what the phrase means. The passage states that *the Moho varies to a considerable degree in depth*. From this context, you can determine that *to a considerable degree* is closest in meaning to *significantly*. To answer this question, you should click on the second answer.

The following chart outlines the key information that you should remember about questions testing vocabulary in context.

QUESTIONS ABOUT VOCABULARY IN CONTEXT	
HOW TO IDENTIFY THE QUESTION	The word (or phrase) X **is closest in meaning to . . .** The word (or phrase) X **could best be replaced by . . .**
WHERE TO FIND THE ANSWER	Information to help you to understand the meaning of an unknown word or phrase can often be found in the context surrounding the word or phrase.
HOW TO ANSWER THE QUESTION	1. Find the word or phrase in the passage. 2. Read the sentence that contains the word or phrase carefully. 3. Look for context clues to help you to understand the meaning. 4. Choose the answer that the context indicates.

READING EXERCISE 1: Study each of the passages, and choose the best answers to the questions that follow.

PASSAGE ONE *(Questions 1–5)*

Paragraph

Smog

 The oxidation of exhaust gases is one of the primary sources of the world's pollution. The brown haze that is poised over some of the world's largest cities is properly called *photochemical smog*; it results from chemical reactions that take place in the air, using the energy of sunlight. The production of smog begins when gases are created in the cylinders of vehicle engines. It is there that oxygen and nitrogen gas combine as the fuel burns to form nitric oxide (NO), a colorless gas. The nitric oxide is forced out into the air through the vehicle tailpipe along with other gases.

2 When the gas reaches the air, it comes into contact with available oxygen from the atmosphere and combines with the oxygen to produce nitrogen dioxide (NO_2), which is a gas with a brownish hue. This nitrogen dioxide plays a role in the formation of acid rain in wetter or more humid climates and tends to decompose back into nitric oxide as it releases an oxygen atom from each molecule; the released oxygen atoms quickly combine with oxygen (O_2) molecules to form ozone (O_3). The brownish colored nitrogen dioxide is partially responsible for the brown color in smoggy air; the ozone is the toxic substance that causes irritation to eyes.

1. The word "poised" in paragraph 1 is closest in meaning to
   (A) interacting
   (B) sitting
   (C) blowing
   (D) poisoning

2. The phrase "take place" in paragraph 1 is closest in meaning to
   (A) position themselves
   (B) put
   (C) are seated
   (D) occur

3. The word "forced" in paragraph 1 could best be replaced by
   (A) obliged
   (B) required
   (C) pushed
   (D) commanded

4. The word "hue" in paragraph 2 is closest in meaning to
   (A) color
   (B) odor
   (C) thickness
   (D) smoke

5. The phrase "plays a role in" in paragraph 2 is closest in meaning to
   (A) makes fun of
   (B) serves a function in
   (C) acts the part of
   (D) moves about in

PASSAGE TWO *(Questions 6–10)*

Autism

Autism is a developmental disorder that is characterized by severe behavioral abnormalities across all primary areas of functioning. Its onset is often early; it generally makes itself known by the age of two and one-half. It is not a single disease entity but is instead a syndrome defined by patterns and characteristics of behavior; it, therefore, most likely has multiple etiologies rather than a single causative factor. Autism is not fully understood and thus is controversial with respect to diagnosis, etiology, and treatment strategies.

6. The word "primary" in the passage could best be replaced by

Ⓐ elementary
Ⓑ main
Ⓒ introductory
Ⓓ primitive

7. The word "onset" in the passage is closest in meaning to

Ⓐ placement
Ⓑ arrangement
Ⓒ support
Ⓓ beginning

8. The word "syndrome" in the passage is closest in meaning to

Ⓐ concurrent set of symptoms
Ⓑ feeling of euphoria
Ⓒ mental breakdown
Ⓓ repetitive task

9. The word "etiologies" in the passage is closest in meaning to

Ⓐ symptoms
Ⓑ patterns
Ⓒ causes
Ⓓ onsets

10. The phrase "with respect to" in the passage could best be replaced by

Ⓐ with dignity toward
Ⓑ in regard to
Ⓒ irrespective of
Ⓓ out of politeness for

PASSAGE THREE (Questions 11–15)

Parasitic Plants

1   Parasitic plants are plants that survive by using food produced by host plants rather than by producing their own food from the Sun's energy. Because they do not need sunlight to survive, parasitic plants are generally found in umbrageous areas rather than in areas exposed to direct sunlight. Parasitic plants attach themselves to host plants, often to the stems or roots, by means of haustoria, which the parasite uses to make its way into the food channels of the host plant and absorb the nutrients that it needs to survive from the host plant.

2   The world's heaviest flower, a species of rafflesia, is a parasite that flourishes among, and lives off of, the roots of jungle vines. Each of these ponderous blooms can weigh up to 15 pounds (7 kilograms) and can measure up to 3 feet (1 meter) across.

11. The word "umbrageous" in paragraph 1 is closest in meaning to
    - Ⓐ moist
    - Ⓑ well lit
    - Ⓒ shaded
    - Ⓓ buried

12. "Haustoria" in paragraph 1 are most likely
    - Ⓐ offshoots from the parasite
    - Ⓑ seeds of the host plant
    - Ⓒ fruits from the host plant
    - Ⓓ food for the parasite

13. The phrase "make its way into" in paragraph 1 is closest in meaning to
    - Ⓐ develop
    - Ⓑ penetrate
    - Ⓒ outline
    - Ⓓ eat

14. The word "ponderous" in paragraph 2 is closest in meaning to
    - Ⓐ smelly
    - Ⓑ hidden
    - Ⓒ mature
    - Ⓓ heavy

15. The word "across" in paragraph 2 could best be replaced by
    - Ⓐ in diameter
    - Ⓑ on the other side
    - Ⓒ at a distance
    - Ⓓ inside and out

PASSAGE FOUR (Questions 16–24)

Paragraph

Edna Ferber

1   Edna Ferber (1887–1968) was a popular American novelist in the first half of the twentieth century. She embarked on her career by working as a newspaper reporter in Wisconsin and soon began writing novels. Her first novel, *Dawn O'Hara, the Girl Who Laughed,* was published in 1911, when she was only twenty-four years old.

2   Her big break came with the novel *So Big* (1924), which was awarded the Pulitzer Prize in Literature. The main conflict in the novel is between a mother who places a high value on hard work and honor and a son who repudiates his mother's values, instead preferring the easier path to fortune and celebrity. Like many of Ferber's novels, this novel features a tenacious female protagonist with strong character who struggles to deal with ethical dilemmas about the importance of status and money.

3   Probably the best known of Ferber's novels was *Show Boat* (1926), which tells the story of a Southern woman married to a charismatic but irresponsible man who leaves her with a daughter she must take great pains to support. In 1927, the novel was made into a musical that has endured to the present.

4   Other well-known novels by Ferber include *Cimarron* (1930) and *Giant* (1952), both of which were made into movies. These were epic novels about the settlement and growth of the West, centering on strong female lead characters who marry men lacking the same strength of character.

16. The phrase "embarked on" in paragraph 1 is closest in meaning to

Ⓐ took a trip to
Ⓑ started out on
Ⓒ improved upon
Ⓓ had an opinion about

17. The word "break" in paragraph 2 could best be replaced by

Ⓐ rupture
Ⓑ revelation
Ⓒ opportunity
Ⓓ rest

18. The word "places" in paragraph 2 could best be replaced by

Ⓐ locates
Ⓑ puts
Ⓒ recites
Ⓓ positions

19. The word "repudiates" in paragraph 2 is closest in meaning to

Ⓐ refuses to accept
Ⓑ lives up to
Ⓒ tries to understand
Ⓓ makes the best of

20. The word "protagonist" in paragraph 2 is closest in meaning to

Ⓐ arch enemy
Ⓑ voracious reader
Ⓒ skilled worker
Ⓓ lead character

21. The phrase "take great pains" in paragraph 3 is closest in meaning to

Ⓐ work diligently
Ⓑ recognize hurtfully
Ⓒ accept unequivocally
Ⓓ hurt agonizingly

22. The word "endured" in paragraph 3 is closest in meaning to

Ⓐ lasted
Ⓑ tested
Ⓒ waited
Ⓓ limited

23. The word "epic" in paragraph 4 could best be replaced by

Ⓐ lengthy narrative
Ⓑ detailed nonfictional
Ⓒ emotionally romantic
Ⓓ rousing Western

24. The phrase "centering on" in paragraph 4
could best be replaced by

Ⓐ circling around
Ⓑ pointing to
Ⓒ focusing on
Ⓓ arranging for

Reading Skill 2: RECOGNIZE REFERENTS

In the Reading section of the TOEFL iBT, you may be asked to determine the referent for a particular pronoun or adjective (the noun to which a pronoun or adjective refers). You may be asked to find the referent for a variety of words, perhaps for a third person subject pronoun (*he, she, it, they*), a third person object pronoun (*him, her, it, them*), a relative pronoun (*who, which, that*), a third person possessive adjective (*his, her, its, their*), a third person possessive pronoun (*his, hers, theirs*), a demonstrative pronoun or adjective (*this, that, these, those*), or for a quantifier (*one, some, a few, many*). A referent generally precedes the pronoun or adjective in the passage; thus, to answer this type of question, you should study the context around the pronoun or adjective carefully and look for a referent that agrees with the noun or pronoun in front of the pronoun or adjective. Look at an example of a question that asks for the referent of the subject pronoun *it*.

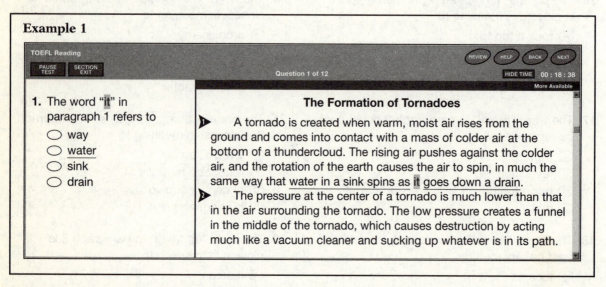

Example 1

TOEFL Reading

Question 1 of 12

1. The word "it" in paragraph 1 refers to
○ way
○ <u>water</u>
○ sink
○ drain

The Formation of Tornadoes

➊ A tornado is created when warm, moist air rises from the ground and comes into contact with a mass of colder air at the bottom of a thundercloud. The rising air pushes against the colder air, and the rotation of the earth causes the air to spin, in much the same way that <u>water in a sink spins as</u> it <u>goes down a drain.</u>

➋ The pressure at the center of a tornado is much lower than that in the air surrounding the tornado. The low pressure creates a funnel in the middle of the tornado, which causes destruction by acting much like a vacuum cleaner and sucking up whatever is in its path.

In this example, you are asked to find the referent for the subject pronoun "it." You should study the context around the singular pronoun *it* and look for a singular noun in front of *it* that fits into the context. The context around the pronoun states that *water in a sink spins as it goes down a drain*. From this context, it can be determined that *it* refers to *water* because it is *water* that *goes down a drain*. To answer this question, you should click on the second answer.

Now, look at an example of a question that asks for the referent of the demonstrative pronoun *that*.

Example 2

2. The word "that" in paragraph 2 refers to

- ○ pressure
- ○ center
- ○ tornado
- ○ air

The Formation of Tornadoes

▶ A tornado is created when warm, moist air rises from the ground and comes into contact with a mass of colder air at the bottom of a thundercloud. The rising air pushes against the colder air, and the rotation of the Earth causes the air to spin, in much the same way that water in a sink spins as it goes down a drain.

▶ The pressure at the center of a tornado is much lower than that in the air surrounding the tornado. The low pressure creates a funnel in the middle of the tornado, which causes destruction by acting much like a vacuum cleaner and sucking up whatever is in its path.

In this example, you are asked to find the referent for the demonstrative pronoun "that." You should study the context around the singular pronoun *that* and look for a singular noun in front of *that* that fits into the context. The context around the pronoun states that *the pressure at the center of a tornado is much lower than that in the air surrounding the tornado*. From this context, it can be determined that *that* refers to *pressure* because it is *pressure* at the center of a tornado that is much lower than *pressure* in the air surrounding the tornado. To answer this question, you should click on the first answer.

Finally, look at an example of a question that asks for the referent of the relative pronoun *which*.

Example 3

3. The word "which" in paragraph 2 refers to

- ○ funnel
- ○ middle
- ○ tornado
- ○ vacuum cleaner

The Formation of Tornadoes

▶ A tornado is created when warm, moist air rises from the ground and comes into contact with a mass of colder air at the bottom of a thundercloud. The rising air pushes against the colder air, and the rotation of the Earth causes the air to spin, in much the same way that water in a sink spins as it goes down a drain.

▶ The pressure at the center of a tornado is much lower than that in the air surrounding the tornado. The low pressure creates a funnel in the middle of the tornado, which causes destruction by acting much like a vacuum cleaner and sucking up whatever is in its path.

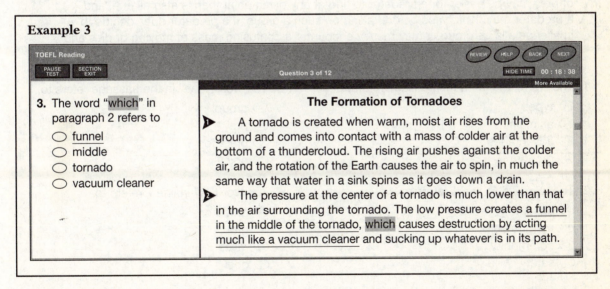

In this example, you are asked to find the referent for the relative pronoun "which." You should study the context around the relative pronoun *which* and look for a noun in front of *which* that fits into the context. The context around the pronoun mentions *a funnel in the middle of the tornado, which causes destruction by acting much like a vacuum cleaner*. From this context, it can be determined that *which* refers to *funnel* because it is a *funnel* that causes destruction by acting like a vacuum cleaner. To answer this question, you should click on the first answer.

The following chart outlines the key information that you should remember about questions testing referents.

QUESTIONS ABOUT REFERENTS	
HOW TO IDENTIFY THE QUESTION	The word X **refers** to . . .
WHERE TO FIND THE ANSWER	The pronoun or adjective is highlighted in the passage. The referent is generally in front of the highlighted word.
HOW TO ANSWER THE QUESTION	1. Locate the highlighted pronoun or adjective. 2. Look *before* the highlighted word for nouns that agree with the highlighted word. 3. Try each of the nouns in the context around the highlighted word. 4. Eliminate any definitely wrong answers, and choose the best answer from the remaining choices.

READING EXERCISE 2: Study each of the passages, and choose the best answers to the questions that follow.

PASSAGE ONE (Questions 1–4)

Animal Congregation

Many types of animals combine the advantages of family association with those conferred by membership in still larger groups. Bees congregate in hives; some fish move in schools; ants gather in mounds; wolves live in packs; deer associate in herds. The main
Line advantage of membership in a mass community is the safety that it provides. A large group
(5) of prey may be easier for a predator to find at any given point than is a small one, and a predator may think twice before taking on such a group; if a predator does decide to challenge a large group, it may merely encounter a confusing mass of moving bodies and possibly may not succeed in its primary goal.

1. The word "those" in the passage refers to
   Ⓐ types
   Ⓑ animals
   Ⓒ advantages
   Ⓓ groups

2. The word "it" in line 4 refers to
   Ⓐ advantage
   Ⓑ membership
   Ⓒ community
   Ⓓ safety

3. The word "one" in the passage refers to
   Ⓐ group
   Ⓑ prey
   Ⓒ predator
   Ⓓ point

4. The word "it" in line 7 refers to
   Ⓐ predator
   Ⓑ group
   Ⓒ mass
   Ⓓ goal

PASSAGE TWO *(Questions 5–9)*

Paragraph

Chromium Compounds

▶ **1**   Most chromium compounds have brightly colored hues, and as a result they are widely used as coloring agents, or pigments, in paints. In addition to having a pleasing color, a paint must protect the surface to which it is applied and be easy to apply in a thin, uniform coat.

▶ **2**   All paints consist of two parts. One is a powder of solid particles that is the source of the color and the opaqueness and is known as the pigment. The other, called the binder, is the liquid into which the pigment is blended. The binder used in some paints is made from oily solvents such as those derived from petroleum resources. When applied, these solvents evaporate, leaving deposits of pigment on the surface.

5. The word "they" in paragraph 1 refers to
   - Ⓐ chromium compounds
   - Ⓑ brightly colored hues
   - Ⓒ coloring agents
   - Ⓓ pigments

6. The word "it" in paragraph 1 refers to
   - Ⓐ a pleasing color
   - Ⓑ a paint
   - Ⓒ the surface
   - Ⓓ a thin, uniform coat

7. The word "that" in paragraph 2 refers to
   - Ⓐ a powder
   - Ⓑ solid particles
   - Ⓒ the source
   - Ⓓ the color

8. The word "which" in paragraph 2 refers to
   - Ⓐ powder
   - Ⓑ paint
   - Ⓒ liquid
   - Ⓓ pigment

9. The word "those" in paragraph 2 refers to
   - Ⓐ some paints
   - Ⓑ oily solvents
   - Ⓒ petroleum resources
   - Ⓓ deposits of pigment

New World Epidemics

A huge loss of life resulted from the introduction of Old World diseases into the Americas in the early sixteenth century. The inhabitants of the Americas were separated from Asia, Africa, and Europe by rising oceans following the Ice Ages, and, as a result, they were isolated by means of this watery barrier from numerous virulent epidemic diseases that had developed across the ocean, such as measles, smallpox, pneumonia, and malaria. Pre-Columbian Americans had a relatively disease-free environment but also lacked the antibodies needed to protect them from bacteria and viruses brought to America by European explorers and colonists. A devastating outbreak of disease that strikes for the first time against a completely unprotected population is known as a virgin soil epidemic. Virgin soil epidemics contributed to an unbelievable decline in the population of native inhabitants of the Americas, one that has been estimated at as much as an 80 percent decrease of the native population in the centuries following the arrival of Europeans in the Americas.

10. The word "they" in the passage refers to

   Ⓐ the inhabitants

   Ⓑ epidemic diseases

   Ⓒ rising oceans

   Ⓓ the Ice Ages

11. The word "that" in the passage refers to

   Ⓐ a disease-free environment

   Ⓑ this watery barrier

   Ⓒ virulent epidemic diseases

   Ⓓ the ocean

12. The word "them" in the passage refers to

   Ⓐ pre-Columbian Americans

   Ⓑ the antibodies

   Ⓒ bacteria and viruses

   Ⓓ European explorers and colonists

13. The word "one" in the passage refers to

   Ⓐ a virgin soil epidemic

   Ⓑ an unbelievable decline

   Ⓒ the population of native inhabitants

   Ⓓ the arrival of Europeans

PASSAGE FOUR *(Questions 14–18)*

Paragraph

Horatio Alger, Jr.

 Horatio Alger, Jr. (1832–1899) was the author of more than 100 books for boys in the second half of the nineteenth century that focused on the theme of success coming to those who work hard to achieve it. The son of a minister, Alger came from a prominent Massachusetts family. He graduated with honors from Harvard in 1852 and graduated from the Cambridge Divinity School eight years later. He served as a minister for a short time before moving to New York City in 1866 to devote his time to writing inspirational books for boys.

In many of his books, he wrote about the poor and homeless children of the slums of New York City, seeing them as unfortunate pawns of society who, if only given the opportunity, could improve their lot. A general plotline that he followed often was of a poor boy who managed to achieve a respectable and successful life by working hard and taking advantage of opportunities presented. Though his writing style was characterized by simplicity and repetition, it was well received by his target audience; his books were enormously popular, selling millions of copies well into the first few decades of the twentieth century.

14. The word "that" in paragraph 1 refers to

Ⓐ author
Ⓑ books
Ⓒ boys
Ⓓ half

15. The word "it" in paragraph 1 refers to

Ⓐ the second half
Ⓑ the nineteenth century
Ⓒ 100
Ⓓ success

16. The word "them" in paragraph 2 refers to

Ⓐ books
Ⓑ children
Ⓒ slums
Ⓓ pawns

17. The word "who" in paragraph 2 refers to

Ⓐ slums
Ⓑ society
Ⓒ pawns
Ⓓ opportunity

18. The word "it" in paragraph 2 refers to

Ⓐ style
Ⓑ simplicity
Ⓒ repetition
Ⓓ audience

READING EXERCISE (Skills 1–2): Read the passage.

Paragraph

Coral Colonies

1   Coral colonies require a series of complicated events and circumstances to develop into the characteristically intricate reef structures for which they are known. These events and circumstances involve physical and chemical processes as well as delicate interactions among various animals and plants for coral colonies to thrive.

2   The basic element in the development of coralline reef structures is a group of animals from the *Anthozoa* class, called stony corals, that is closely related to jellyfish and sea anemones. These small polyps (the individual animals that make up the coral reef), which are for the most part only a fraction of an inch in length, live in colonies made up of an immeasurable number of polyps clustered together. Each individual polyp obtains calcium from the seawater where it lives to create a skeleton around the lower part of its body, and the polyps attach themselves both to the living tissue and to the external skeletons of other polyps. Many polyps tend to retreat inside of their skeletons during hours of daylight and then stretch partially outside of their skeletons during hours of darkness to feed on minute plankton from the water around them. The mouth at the top of each body is surrounded by rings of tentacles used to grab onto food, and these rings of tentacles make the polyps look like flowers with rings of clustered petals; because of this, biologists for years thought that corals were plants rather than animals.

3   Once these coralline structures are established, they reproduce very quickly. They build in upward and outward directions to create a fringe of living coral surrounding the skeletal remnants of once-living coral. That coralline structures are commonplace in tropical waters around the world is due to the fact that they reproduce so quickly rather than the fact that they are hardy life-forms easily able to withstand external forces of nature. They cannot survive in water that is too dirty, and they need water that is at least 72° F (or 22° C) to exist, so they are formed only in waters ranging from 30° north to 30° south of the equator. They need a significant amount of sunlight, so they live only within an area between the surface of the ocean and a few meters beneath it. In addition, they require specific types of microscopic algae for their existence, and their skeletal shells are delicate in nature and are easily damaged or fragmented. They are also prey to other sea animals such as sponges and clams that bore into their skeletal structures and weaken them.

4   Coral colonies cannot build reef structures without considerable assistance. The many openings in and among the skeletons must be filled in and cemented together by material from around the colonies. The filling material often consists of fine sediments created either from the borings and waste of other animals around the coral or from the skeletons, shells, and remnants of dead plants and animals. The material that is used to cement the coral reefs comes from algae and other microscopic forms of seaweed.

5   An additional part of the process of reef formation is the ongoing compaction and cementation that occurs throughout the process. Because of the soluble and delicate nature of the material from which coral is created, the relatively unstable crystals of corals and shells break down over time and are then rearranged as a more stable form of limestone.

6   The coralline structures that are created through these complicated processes are extremely variable in form. They may, for example, be treelike and branching, or they may have more rounded and compact shapes. What they share in common, however, is the extraordinary variety of plant and animal life-forms that are a necessary part of the ongoing process of their formation.

GLOSSARY
polyps: simple sea animals with tube-shaped bodies

Refer to this version of the passage to answer the questions that follow.

Coral Colonies

Paragraph

1   Coral colonies require a series of complicated events and circumstances to develop into the characteristically intricate reef structures for which they are known. These events and circumstances involve physical and chemical processes as well as delicate interactions among various animals and plants for coral colonies to thrive.

2   The basic element in the development of coralline reef structures is a group of animals from the *Anthozoa* class, called stony corals, that is closely related to jellyfish and sea anemones. These small polyps (the individual animals that make up the coral reef), which are for the most part only a fraction of an inch in length, live in colonies made up of an immeasurable number of polyps clustered together. Each individual polyp obtains calcium from the seawater where it lives to create a skeleton around the lower part of its body, and the polyps attach themselves both to the living tissue and to the external skeletons of other polyps. Many polyps tend to retreat inside of their skeletons during hours of daylight and then stretch partially outside of their skeletons during hours of darkness to feed on minute plankton from the water around them. The mouth at the top of each body is surrounded by rings of tentacles used to grab onto food, and these rings of tentacles make the polyps look like flowers with rings of clustered petals; because of this, biologists for years thought that corals were plants rather than animals.

3   Once these coralline structures are established, they reproduce very quickly. They build in upward and outward directions to create a fringe of living coral surrounding the skeletal remnants of once-living coral. That coralline structures are commonplace in tropical waters around the world is due to the fact that they reproduce so quickly rather than the fact that they are hardy life-forms easily able to withstand external forces of nature. They cannot survive in water that is too dirty, and they need water that is at least 72° F (or 22° C) to exist, so they are formed only in waters ranging from 30° north to 30° south of the equator. They need a significant amount of sunlight, so they live only within an area between the surface of the ocean and a few meters beneath it. In addition, they require specific types of microscopic algae for their existence, and their skeletal shells are delicate in nature and are easily damaged or fragmented. They are also prey to other sea animals such as sponges and clams that bore into their skeletal structures and weaken them.

4   Coral colonies cannot build reef structures without considerable assistance. The many openings in and among the skeletons must be filled in and cemented together by material from around the colonies. The filling material often consists of fine sediments created either from the borings and waste of other animals around the coral or from the skeletons, shells, and remnants of dead plants and animals. The material that is used to cement the coral reefs comes from algae and other microscopic forms of seaweed.

5   An additional part of the process of reef formation is the ongoing compaction and cementation that occurs throughout the process. Because of the soluble and delicate nature of the material from which coral is created, the relatively unstable crystals of corals and shells break down over time and are then rearranged as a more stable form of limestone.

6   The coralline structures that are created through these complicated processes are extremely variable in form. They may, for example, be treelike and branching, or they may have more rounded and compact shapes. What they share in common, however, is the extraordinary variety of plant and animal life-forms that are a necessary part of the ongoing process of their formation.

GLOSSARY
polyps: simple sea animals with tube-shaped bodies

Questions

1. The word "they" in paragraph 1 refers to
   - (A) coral colonies
   - (B) events and circumstances
   - (C) intricate reef structures
   - (D) chemical processes

2. The word "that" in paragraph 2 refers to
   - (A) the basic element
   - (B) the development of coralline reef structures
   - (C) a group of animals
   - (D) the *Anthozoa* class

3. The phrase "an immeasurable number" in paragraph 2 is closest in meaning to
   - (A) an exact integer
   - (B) a huge quantity
   - (C) a surprising total
   - (D) a changing sum

4. The word "minute" in paragraph 2 could best be replaced by
   - (A) tiny
   - (B) light
   - (C) timely
   - (D) soft

5. The phrase "once-living" in paragraph 3 is closest in meaning to
   - (A) aging
   - (B) dead
   - (C) growing
   - (D) solitary

6. The word "hardy" in paragraph 3 is closest in meaning to
   - (A) difficult
   - (B) fragile
   - (C) scarce
   - (D) rugged

7. The word "They" in paragraph 3 refers to
   - (A) coralline structures
   - (B) upward and outward directions
   - (C) skeletal remnants
   - (D) external forces of nature

8. The word "them" in paragraph 3 refers to
   - (A) sea animals
   - (B) sponges and clams
   - (C) skeletal structures
   - (D) many openings

9. The word "borings" in paragraph 4 is closest in meaning to
   - (A) dull pieces
   - (B) strange creations
   - (C) living beings
   - (D) powdery remnants

10. The word "ongoing" in paragraph 5 is closest in meaning to
    - (A) mobile
    - (B) continuous
    - (C) increasing
    - (D) periodic

11. The phrase "break down" in paragraph 5 is closest in meaning to
    - (A) cease functioning
    - (B) interrupt
    - (C) descend
    - (D) decompose

12. The word "that" in paragraph 6 refers to
    - (A) variety
    - (B) life-forms
    - (C) part
    - (D) process

13. The word "their" in paragraph 6 refers to
    - (A) coralline structures
    - (B) complicated processes
    - (C) rounded and more compact shapes
    - (D) plant and animal life-forms

SENTENCES

Reading Skill 3: SIMPLIFY MEANINGS OF SENTENCES

In the Reading section of the TOEFL iBT, you may be asked to simplify the meaning of a long and complex sentence. In this type of question, you must choose the one answer that is closest to the meaning of a sentence that is highlighted in the passage. Look at an example from the TOEFL test that asks how to simplify the meaning of a highlighted sentence.

Example 1

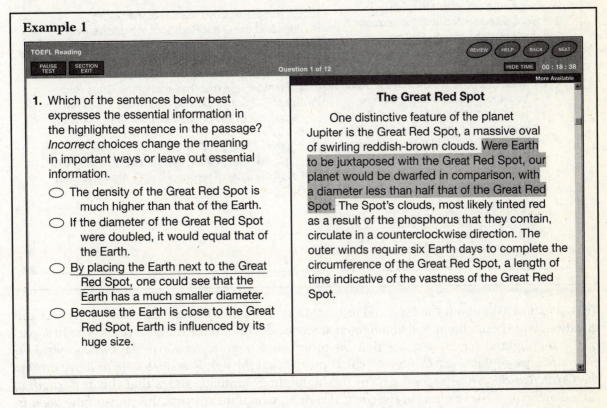

This question asks about the essential meaning of a complex sentence. To answer this question, you should break the complex sentence down into parts. The first part of the sentence says *were Earth to be juxtaposed with the Great Red Spot,* which means *by placing the Earth next to the Great Red Spot.* The next part of the sentence states that *our planet would be dwarfed in comparison, with a diameter less than half that of the Great Red Spot,* which means that *the Earth has a much smaller diameter.* To answer this question, you should click on the third answer.

Now look at another example that asks how to simplify the meaning of a highlighted sentence.

Example 2

TOEFL Reading

REVIEW HELP BACK NEXT

PAUSE TEST   SECTION EXIT

Question 2 of 12

HIDE TIME   00 : 18 : 38
More Available

2. Which of the sentences below best expresses the essential information in the highlighted sentence in the passage? *Incorrect* choices change the meaning in important ways or leave out essential information.

○ The Earth's outer winds move a distance equal to the circumference of the Great Red Spot.

○ The outer winds of the Great Red Spot move more quickly than do those on Earth.

○ The winds moving across the Great Red Spot finally change direction every six Earth days.

○ The fact that the winds take so long to move around the Great Red Spot proves how big it is.

The Great Red Spot

One distinctive feature of the planet Jupiter is the Great Red Spot, a massive oval of swirling reddish-brown clouds. Were Earth to be juxtaposed with the Great Red Spot, our planet would be dwarfed in comparison, with a diameter less than half that of the Great Red Spot. The Spot's clouds, most likely tinted red as a result of the phosphorus that they contain, circulate in a counterclockwise direction. The outer winds require six Earth days to complete the circumference of the Great Red Spot, a length of time indicative of the vastness of the Great Red Spot.

This question asks about the essential information in the highlighted sentence. To answer this question, you should break the highlighted sentence down into meaningful parts. The first part of the highlighted sentence states that *the outer winds require six Earth days to complete the circumference of the Great Red Spot,* which means that *the winds take so long to move around the Great Red Spot.* The second part of the highlighted sentence states that this is *a length of time indicative of the vastness of the Great Red Spot,* which means that this *proves how big it is.* To answer this question, you should click on the last answer.

The following chart outlines the key information that you should remember about questions testing the simplified meanings of sentences.

QUESTIONS ABOUT SIMPLIFYING THE MEANINGS OF SENTENCES	
HOW TO IDENTIFY THE QUESTION	Which of the **sentences below** best expresses the **essential information . . . ?**
WHERE TO FIND THE ANSWER	The targeted sentence is highlighted in the passage. Information to answer the question is in the highlighted sentence and may also be in the context around the highlighted sentence.
HOW TO ANSWER THE QUESTION	1. Study the highlighted sentence carefully. 2. Break the sentence down into meaningful parts by looking for punctuation and transition expressions. 3. If the highlighted sentence makes references to information outside of the highlighted sentence, read the context around the highlighted sentence. 4. Study the answer choices, and eliminate definitely wrong answers. 5. Choose the best answer from the remaining choices.

READING EXERCISE 3: Study each of the passages, and choose the best answers to the questions that follow.

PASSAGE ONE (Questions 1–2)

Camouflage

Camouflage is one of the most effective ways for animals to avoid attack in the treeless Arctic. However, the summer and winter landscapes there are so diverse that a single protective coloring scheme would, of course, prove ineffective in one season or the other. Thus, many of the inhabitants of the Arctic tundra change their camouflage twice a year. The arctic fox is a clear-cut example of this phenomenon; it sports a brownish-gray coat in the summer which then turns white as cold weather sets in, and the process reverses itself in the springtime. Its brownish-gray coat blends in with the barren tundra landscape in the months without snow, and the white coat naturally blends in with the landscape of the frozen wintertime tundra.

1. Which of the sentences below best expresses the essential information in the first highlighted sentence in the passage? *Incorrect* choices change the meaning in important ways or leave out essential information.

    Ⓐ Opposite conditions in summer and in winter necessitate different protective coloration for Arctic animals.

    Ⓑ The coloration of the summer and winter landscapes in the Arctic fails to protect the Arctic tundra.

    Ⓒ In a single season, protective coloring schemes are ineffective in the treeless Arctic.

    Ⓓ For many animals, a single protective coloring scheme effectively protects them during summer and winter months.

2. Which of the sentences below best expresses the essential information in the second highlighted sentence in the passage? *Incorrect* choices change the meaning in important ways or leave out essential information.

    Ⓐ The arctic fox is unusual in that the color of its coat changes for no reason.

    Ⓑ The arctic fox lives in an environment that is brownish gray in the summer and white in the winter.

    Ⓒ It is a phenomenon that the coat of the arctic fox turns white in the springtime and gray in the fall.

    Ⓓ The arctic fox demonstrates that protective coloration can change during different seasons.

PASSAGE TWO *(Questions 3–6)*

Paragraph

Post-it® Notes

▶**1**   Post-it® Notes were invented in the 1970s at the 3M company in Minnesota quite by accident. Researchers at 3M were working on developing different types of adhesives, and one particularly weak adhesive, a compound of acrylate copolymer microspheres, was developed. Employees at 3M were asked if they could think of a use for a weak adhesive which, provided it did not get dirty, could be reused. One suggestion was that it could be applied to a piece of paper to use as a bookmark that would stay in place in a book. Another use was found when the product was attached to a report that was to be sent to a colleague with a request for comments on the report; the colleague made his comments on the paper attached to the report and returned the report. The idea for Post-it Notes was born.

▶**2**   It was decided within the company that there would be a test launch of the product in 1977 in four American cities. Sales of this innovative product in test cities were less than stellar, most likely because the product, while innovative, was also quite unfamiliar. A final attempt was then made in the city of Boise to introduce the product. In this attempt, 3M salesmen gave demonstrations of the product in offices throughout Boise and gave away free samples of the product. When the salesmen returned a week later to the offices where the product had been demonstrated and given away, a huge percentage of the office workers, having noted how useful the simple little product could be, were interested in purchasing it. Over time, 3M came to understand the huge potential of this new product, and over the next few decades more than 400 varieties of Post-it products—in different colors, shapes, and sizes—have been developed.

3. Which of the sentences below best expresses the essential information in the first highlighted sentence in paragraph 1? *Incorrect* choices change the meaning in important ways or leave out essential information.

ⓐ Of the many adhesives that were being developed at 3M, one was not a particularly strong adhesive.

ⓑ Researchers at 3M spent many years trying to develop a really weak adhesive.

ⓒ Numerous weak adhesives resulted from a program to develop the strongest adhesive of all.

ⓓ Researchers were assigned to develop different types of uses for acrylate copolymer microspheres.

4. Which of the sentences below best expresses the essential information in the second highlighted sentence in paragraph 1? *Incorrect* choices change the meaning in important ways or leave out essential information.

ⓐ The 3M company suggested applying for a patent on the product in a report prepared by a colleague.

ⓑ One unexpectedly-discovered use for the adhesive was in sending and receiving notes attached to documents.

ⓒ A note was attached to a report asking for suggestions for uses of one of 3M's products.

ⓓ A colleague who developed the new product kept notes with suggestions by other workers.

5. Which of the sentences below best expresses the essential information in the first highlighted sentence in paragraph 2? *Incorrect* choices change the meaning in important ways or leave out essential information.

Ⓐ The 3M company was unfamiliar with the process of using test cities to introduce innovative products.

Ⓑ Sales of the product soared even though the product was quite unfamiliar to most customers.

Ⓒ The new product did not sell well because potential customers did not understand it.

Ⓓ After selling the product for a while, the company understood that the product was not innovative enough.

6. Which of the sentences below best expresses the essential information in the second highlighted sentence in paragraph 2? *Incorrect* choices change the meaning in important ways or leave out essential information.

Ⓐ The company immediately understood the potential of the product and began to develop it further.

Ⓑ The company worked overtime to develop its new product, initially creating numerous varieties to make it successful.

Ⓒ The company initially introduced 400 varieties of the product and then watched for decades as sales improved.

Ⓓ It took some time for the company to understand how important its new product was and how many variations were possible.

PASSAGE THREE (Questions 7–10)

Paragraph

The Pulitzer Prize

▶1   The Pulitzer Prize came about as part of an attempt by newspaperman Joseph Pulitzer to upgrade the profession of journalism. Pulitzer, the owner of the *New York World* and the *St. Louis Post-Dispatch,* made a proposal in 1903 to Columbia University to make a $2 million bequest to the university for the dual purposes of establishing a school of journalism at the university and also establishing prizes for exceptional work in journalism and other fields. However, the university did not initially respond as one might expect to such a seemingly generous offer.

▶2   Interestingly, Columbia University was not immediately amenable to the proposal by Pulitzer inasmuch as journalism was not held in high regard in general and Pulitzer's papers were more known for their sensationalization of the news than for the high quality of the journalism. The trustees of the university were not at all sure that they wanted a school of journalism because newspaper reporting was considered more of a trade than a profession at the time and they did not want to decrease the academic prestige of their institution. It took years of discussions and negotiations before the terms for the establishment of the school of journalism and the prizes bearing Pulitzer's name were agreed upon, and it was not actually until the year after Pulitzer's death in 1911 that construction began on the building to house Columbia's new school of journalism. The school of journalism opened in 1913, and the first prizes were awarded in 1917, for work done the previous year.

▶3   The method for selecting Pulitzer Prize winners and the categories for prizes have changed slightly over the years. Today, twenty-one different awards are given in three different areas, with the majority of awards going to journalists; fourteen of the twenty-one awards are from various aspects of journalism (i.e., news reporting, feature writing, cartoons, and photography), six awards are given in letters (in fiction, nonfiction, history, drama, poetry, and biography), and one award in music. Columbia University appoints nominating juries comprised of experts in each field, and the nominating juries submit these nominations for each category to the Pulitzer Prize Board, which makes the final decisions and awards the prizes.

7. Which of the sentences below best expresses the essential information in the highlighted sentence in paragraph 1? *Incorrect* choices change the meaning in important ways or leave out essential information.

Ⓐ Joseph Pulitzer generously offered to donate a large sum of money to Columbia University for two specific purposes.

Ⓑ In 1903, an attempt was made by Joseph Pulitzer to halt the movement of the school of journalism and the journalism prizes from Columbia University.

Ⓒ Joseph Pulitzer requested that Columbia University donate a large sum of money to the *New York World* and the *St. Louis Post-Dispatch* for the purpose of establishing journalism scholarships and prizes.

Ⓓ In 1903, Joseph Pulitzer decided to give up his position as head of two newspapers to take over the department of journalism at Columbia University.

8. Which of the sentences below best expresses the essential information in the first highlighted sentence in paragraph 2? *Incorrect* choices change the meaning in important ways or leave out essential information.

Ⓐ The university immediately appreciated Pulitzer's proposal, agreeing completely with Pulitzer as to the need for high-quality journalism.

Ⓑ University officials were unhappy when they read a sensationalized version of Pulitzer's proposal in one of Pulitzer's newspapers.

Ⓒ Initially, the university was not interested in working with Pulitzer because they did not have a high opinion of newspapers in general and Pulitzer's in particular.

Ⓓ The Pulitzer papers did not have a high regard for what was being taught in Columbia University's school of journalism.

9. Which of the sentences below best expresses the essential information in the second highlighted sentence in paragraph 2? *Incorrect* choices change the meaning in important ways or leave out essential information.

Ⓐ There were long discussions about the names that could be used in the new school of journalism and the journalism prizes, and these discussions proved quite harmful to Pulitzer.

Ⓑ It took quite some time for Pulitzer and Columbia University to reach an agreement, and the agreement was not actually implemented until after Pulitzer's death.

Ⓒ University officials spent years discussing what the new journalism building would look like and finally came to a decision about it in 1911.

Ⓓ Pulitzer's death caused university officials to rethink their decision on a school of journalism and to decide that it was a good idea to have one.

10. Which of the sentences below best expresses the essential information in the highlighted sentence in paragraph 3? *Incorrect* choices change the meaning in important ways or leave out essential information.

Ⓐ The twenty-one awards are divided equally among journalism, letters, and music.

Ⓑ Three different awards are given to journalists, while the others are given to artists and musicians.

Ⓒ Most awards are given in three different areas of journalism, while the rest are given in letters and music.

Ⓓ Two-thirds of the awards are for journalism, while the other third goes to other fields.

PASSAGE FOUR (Questions 11–14)

Paragraph

Competition and Cooperation

1   Explanations of the interrelationship between competition and cooperation have evolved over time. Early research into competition and cooperation defined each of them in terms of the distribution of rewards related to each. Competition was defined as a situation in which rewards are distributed unequally on the basis of performance; cooperation, on the other hand, was defined as a situation in which rewards are distributed equally on the basis of mutual interactive behavior among individuals. By this definition, a competitive situation requires at least one competitor to fail for each competitor that wins, while a cooperative situation offers a reward only if all members of the group receive it.

2   Researchers have found definitions of competition and cooperation based upon rewards inadequate primarily because definitions of these two concepts based upon rewards depict them as opposites. In current understanding, competition is not viewed as the opposite of cooperation; instead, cooperation is viewed as an integral component of competition. Cooperation is necessary among team members, perhaps in a sporting event or in a political race, in order to win the competition; it is equally important to understand that cooperation is of great importance between teams, in that same sporting event or political race, inasmuch as the opposing teams need to be in agreement as to the basic ground rules of the game or election in order to compete.

3   Interestingly, the word "competition" is derived from a Latin verb which means "to seek together." An understanding of the derivation of the word "competition" supports the understanding that cooperation, rather than evoking a characteristic at the opposite extreme of human nature from competition, is in reality a necessary factor in competition.

11. Which of the sentences below best expresses the essential information in the highlighted sentence in paragraph 1? *Incorrect* choices change the meaning in important ways or leave out essential information.

   Ⓐ Unequal rewards for competition should be distributed equally to achieve cooperation.

   Ⓑ Earlier definitions of competition and cooperation described them in basically the same way.

   Ⓒ Competition and cooperation were seen as opposites, with rewards distributed equally to those who competed and unequally to those who cooperated.

   Ⓓ Competition was defined in terms of unequal distribution of rewards and cooperation in terms of equal distribution of rewards.

12. Which of the sentences below best expresses the essential information in the first highlighted sentence in paragraph 2? *Incorrect* choices change the meaning in important ways or leave out essential information.

   Ⓐ It does not work well to define competition and cooperation in terms of rewards because definitions of this type incorrectly indicate that the two are opposites.

   Ⓑ Researchers tend to define competition and cooperation on the basis of rewards because this shows how the two differ.

   Ⓒ Researchers are looking for ways to define cooperation and competition in terms of rewards but have so far not been able to come up with definitions.

   Ⓓ Research has shown that the optimal definitions of competition and cooperation are those indicating that the two are opposites.

13. Which of the sentences below best expresses the essential information in the second highlighted sentence in paragraph 2? *Incorrect* choices change the meaning in important ways or leave out essential information.

Ⓐ Because sports and politics are so competitive, participants may appear to be cooperating but are not really doing so.

Ⓑ In a number of contexts, cooperation is necessary both among team members and between opposing teams.

Ⓒ When cooperation exists in contests such as games and elections, competition naturally decreases.

Ⓓ In sports, cooperation is necessary among team members but should not take place between opposing teams.

14. Which of the sentences below best expresses the essential information in the highlighted sentence in paragraph 3? *Incorrect* choices change the meaning in important ways or leave out essential information.

Ⓐ The derivation of the word "competition" indicates that competition and cooperation are clearly opposing forces.

Ⓑ The derivation of the word "competition" shows us that competition is necessary for cooperation to succeed.

Ⓒ The derivation of the word "competition" demonstrates that cooperation is an integral part of competition.

Ⓓ The derivation of the word "competition" leads to the conclusion that cooperation cannot exist without competition.

Reading Skill 4: INSERT SENTENCES INTO THE PASSAGE

In the Reading section of the TOEFL iBT, you may be asked to determine where to insert a sentence into a passage. In this type of question, you must click on one of a number of squares in a passage to indicate that the sentence should be inserted in that position. Look at an example from the TOEFL test that asks where to insert a particular sentence.

Example 1

TOEFL Reading

PAUSE TEST | SECTION EXIT

REVIEW | HELP | BACK | NEXT

Question 1 of 12

HIDE TIME 00 : 18 : 38

More Available

1. Look at the four squares [■] that indicate where the following sentence could be added to the passage.

When one brother was killed, the remaining brother had the game invented to explain the tragic events to his mother.

Where would the sentence best fit? Click on a square [■] to add the sentence to the passage.

The Origin of Chess

The origins of the game of chess are not known with certainty, and traditional stories in a number of cultures claim credit for developing the game. **1A** One legend claims that chess was invented during the Trojan Wars. **1B** According to another legend, chess was developed to depict the battle between two royal brothers for the crown of Persia. **1C** In a third legend, chess was the creation of the mythical Arab philosopher Sassa. **1D**

Whatever its origins, chess was known to exist in India as early as 500 B.C., and it eventually spread from India to Persia, where it took on much of the terminology that today is part of the game. Foot soldiers in the Persian army were called *piyadah,* which became the pawns of today's game, and the Persian chariot was a *rukh,* which became the rook. The Persian king was the *shah,* which evolved into the name *chess. Shahmat,* which means "the king is dead," became the expression "checkmate."

This question asks you to decide where a sentence could be *added* to one of the paragraphs. To answer this question, you should study the sentence to be inserted and then look at the context before and after each insertion box. The sentence mentions *one brother* and *the remaining brother,* and the context before insertion box **1C** mentions *two royal brothers*. From this, it can be determined that the sentence should be added at insertion box **1C**. You should click on **1C** to answer this question.

Now look at another example that asks where to insert a particular sentence.

Example 2

More Available

2. Look at the four squares [■] that indicate where the following sentence could be added to the passage.

This expression is used during the game to indicate that one player's king is on the verge of being captured.

Where would the sentence best fit? Click on a square [■] to add the sentence to the passage.

The Origin of Chess

The origins of the game of chess are not known with certainty, and traditional stories in a number of cultures claim credit for developing the game. One legend claims that chess was invented during the Trojan Wars. According to another legend, chess was developed to depict the battle between two royal brothers for the crown of Persia. In a third legend, chess was the creation of the mythical Arab philosopher Sassa.

Whatever its origins, chess was known to exist in India as early as 500 B.C., and it eventually spread from India to Persia, where it took on much of the terminology that today is part of the game. **2A** Foot soldiers in the Persian army were called *piyadah,* which became the pawns of today's game, and the Persian chariot was a *rukh,* which became the rook. **2B** The Persian king was the *shah,* which evolved into the name *chess.* **2C** *Shahmat,* which means "the king is dead," became the expression "checkmate." **2D**

This question asks you to decide where a sentence could be *added* to one of the paragraphs. To answer this question, you should study the sentence to be inserted and then look at the context before and after each insertion box. The sentence mentions *this expression* about the *king,* and the context before insertion box **2D** mentions the *king* and *the expression "checkmate."* From this, it can be determined that the sentence should be added at insertion box **2D**. You should click on **2D** to answer this question.

The following chart outlines the key information that you should remember about questions testing vocabulary in context.

QUESTIONS ABOUT INSERTING SENTENCES	
HOW TO IDENTIFY THE QUESTION	Look at the **four squares [■]** . . .
WHERE TO FIND THE ANSWER	The places where the sentence may be inserted are marked in the passage.
HOW TO ANSWER THE QUESTION	1. Look at the sentence to be inserted for any key words or ideas at the beginning or the end of the sentence. 2. Read the context before and after the insertion squares for any ideas that relate to the sentence to be inserted. 3. Choose the insertion square that is most related to the sentence to be inserted.

READING EXERCISE 4: Study each of the passages, and choose the best answers to the questions that follow.

PASSAGE ONE (Questions 1–2)

Paragraph

Popcorn

1. 〖1A〗 One method of popping corn involved skewering an ear of corn on a stick and roasting it until the kernels popped off the ear. 〖1B〗 Corn was also popped by first cutting the kernels off the cob, throwing them into a fire, and gathering them as they popped out of the fire. 〖1C〗 In a final method for popping corn, sand and unpopped kernels of corn were mixed together in a cooking pot and heated until the corn popped to the surface of the sand in the pot. 〖1D〗

2. 〖2A〗 This traditional Native American dish was quite a novelty to newcomers to the Americas. 〖2B〗 Columbus and his sailors found natives in the West Indies wearing popcorn necklaces, and explorer Hernando Cortés described the use of popcorn amulets in the religious ceremonies of the Aztecs. 〖2C〗 According to legendary descriptions of the celebratory meal, Quadequina, the brother of Chief Massasoit, contributed several deerskin bags of popcorn to the celebration. 〖2D〗

1. Look at the four squares [■] that indicate where the following sentence could be added to the first paragraph of the passage.

   Native Americans have been popping corn for at least 5,000 years, using a variety of different methods.

   Where would the sentence best fit? Click on a square [■] to add the sentence to the passage.

2. Look at the four squares [■] that indicate where the following sentence could be added to the second paragraph of the passage.

   A century after these early explorers, the Pilgrims at Plymouth may have been introduced to popcorn at the first Thanksgiving dinner.

   Where would the sentence best fit? Click on a square [■] to add the sentence to the passage.

PASSAGE TWO *(Questions 3–5)*

Paragraph

Lions

 1 3A Something unusual about lions is that they hunt in groups. 3B Group hunting is beneficial to lions because it means that much larger prey can be captured by the lions. 3C It also means that individual lions expend much less energy during a hunt. 3D

2 There is a standard pattern to the process of hunting in groups. 4A The process is initiated by a single female, who stations herself at a raised elevation to serve as a lookout to spot potential prey. 4B When prey is spotted, a group of young lionesses advances on the herd and pushes the herd in the direction of a different lioness who has hidden herself downwind. 4C It is up to this concealed female to choose the weakest member of the herd for the kill. 4D

3 5A As can be seen from this description of the process, it is the females rather than the male or males in the pride that take part in the kill. 5B The younger and stronger females are the ones who go on the attack. 5C While the females are on the attack, the males stay behind to protect the rest of the pride from attack by predators such as hyenas. 5D

3. Look at the four squares [■] that indicate where the following sentence could be added to the first paragraph of the passage.

Other cats do not.

Where would the sentence best fit? Click on a square [■] to add the sentence to the passage.

4. Look at the four squares [■] that indicate where the following sentence could be added to the second paragraph of the passage.

This is usually accomplished by knocking the prey to the ground and breaking its neck.

Where would the sentence best fit? Click on a square [■] to add the sentence to the passage.

5. Look at the four squares [■] that indicate where the following sentence could be added to the third paragraph of the passage.

Thus, the males have a defensive rather than an offensive role.

Where would the sentence best fit? Click on a square [■] to add the sentence to the passage.

PASSAGE THREE *(Questions 6–7)*

Paragraph

Accidental Inventions

1   A number of products that we commonly use today were developed quite by accident. Two of many possible examples of this concept are the leotard and the Popsicle, each of which came about when an insightful person recognized a potential benefit in a negative situation.

2   The first of these accidental inventions is the leotard, a close-fitting, one-piece garment worn today by dancers, gymnasts, and acrobats, among others. **6A** In 1828, a circus performer named Nelson Hower was faced with the prospect of missing his performance because his costume was at the cleaners. **6B** Instead of canceling his part of the show, he decided to perform in his long underwear. **6C** Soon, other circus performers began performing the same way. **6D** When popular acrobat Jules Leotard adopted the style, it became known as the leotard.

3   **7A** Another product invented by chance was the Popsicle. **7B** In 1905, eleven-year-old Frank Epperson stirred up a drink of fruit-flavored powder and soda water and then mistakenly left the drink, with the spoon in it, out on the back porch overnight. **7C** As the temperature dropped that night, the soda water froze around the spoon, creating a tasty treat. **7D** Years later, remembering how enjoyable the treat had been, Epperson went into business producing Popsicles.

6. Look at the four squares [■] that indicate where the following sentence could be added to the second paragraph of the passage.

They enjoyed the comfort of performing in underwear rather than costumes.

Where would the sentence best fit? Click on a square [■] to add the sentence to the passage.

7. Look at the four squares [■] that indicate where the following sentence could be added to the third paragraph of the passage.

It was a taste sensation that stayed on his mind.

Where would the sentence best fit? Click on a square [■] to add the sentence to the passage.

PASSAGE FOUR (Questions 8–9)

Paragraph

Uranium

1   Uranium, a radioactive metal named after the planet Uranus, is a primary source of energy in nuclear power plants and certain nuclear weapons. It occurs naturally in three different isotopes, which differ in their facility in undergoing nuclear fission.

2   **8A** The three naturally occurring isotopes of uranium are U-234, U-235, and U-238. **8B** Each of these isotopes has the same atomic number of 92, which is the number of protons in the nucleus. **8C** However, each has a different number of neutrons and thus has a different atomic mass, which is the sum of the number of protons and neutrons. **8D**

3   Of these three naturally occurring isotopes of uranium, U-238 is by far the most common, while U-235 is the most capable of undergoing nuclear fission. **9A** More than 99 percent of all naturally occurring uranium is U-238, while U-234 and U-235 each make up less than 1 percent. **9B** Nuclear fission can occur when a U-235 nucleus is struck by a neutron, and the nucleus splits, releasing energy and releasing two or more neutrons. **9C** However, nuclear fission rarely involves a U-238 or a U-234 nucleus because it is unusual for either of these nuclei to break apart when struck by a neutron. **9D**

8. Look at the four squares [■] that indicate where the following sentence could be added to the second paragraph of the passage.

   U-234 has 92 protons and 142 neutrons for an atomic mass of 234, U-235 has 92 protons and 143 neutrons for a total of 235, and U-238 has 92 protons and 146 neutrons for a total of 238.

   Where would the sentence best fit? Click on a square [■] to add the sentence to the passage.

9. Look at the four squares [■] that indicate where the following sentence could be added to the third paragraph of the passage.

   These neutrons can create a chain reaction by causing other U-235 nuclei to break up.

   Where would the sentence best fit? Click on a square [■] to add the sentence to the passage.

READING EXERCISE (Skills 3–4): Read the passage.

Paragraph

Theodore Dreiser

1　Theodore Dreiser, the American author best known for the novel *Sister Carrie* (1912), introduced a powerful style of writing that had a profound influence on the writers that followed him, from Steinbeck to Fitzgerald and Hemingway. It was in *Sister Carrie* that Theodore Dreiser created a fictional account that laid bare the harsh reality of life in the big city and in which Dreiser established himself as the architect of a new genre.

2　Dreiser was born in 1871 into a large family whose fortunes had in the recent past taken a dramatic turn for the worse. Before Theodore's birth, his father had built up a successful factory business only to lose it to a fire. The family was rather abruptly thrust into poverty, and Theodore spent his youth moving from place to place in the Midwest as the family tried desperately to reestablish itself financially. He left home at the age of sixteen. After earning some money, he spent a year at Indiana University but left school and returned to Chicago, yearning for the glamour and excitement that it offered. At the age of twenty-two, he began work as a reporter for a small newspaper in Chicago, the *Daily Globe,* and later worked on newspapers in Pittsburgh, Cleveland, Saint Louis, and New York City. In his work as a reporter, he was witness to the seamier side of life and was responsible for recording events that befell the less fortunate in the city, the beggars, the alcoholics, the prostitutes, and the working poor.

3　Dreiser first tried his hand at fiction by writing short stories rather than novels, and the first four short stories that he wrote were published. Based on this, he was encouraged to write a novel that would accurately depict the harsh life of the city, and the novel *Sister Carrie* was the result of his effort. This novel chronicles the life of Carrie Meeber, a small-town girl who goes to Chicago in a quest for fame and fortune. As Carrie progresses from factory worker to Broadway star by manipulating anyone in her path, Dreiser sends a clear message about the tragedy of life that is devoted purely to the quest for money.

4　*Sister Carrie,* unfortunately for Dreiser, did not achieve immediate success. The novel was accepted for publication by Doubleday, but Dreiser was immediately asked to make major revisions to the novel. When Dreiser refused to make the revisions, Doubleday published only a limited number of copies of the book and refused to promote or advertise it. Published in limited release and without the backing of the company, the novel was a dismal failure, selling fewer than 500 copies.

5　After the failure of the novel that was so meaningful to him, Dresier suffered a nervous breakdown; he was depressed, stricken with severe headaches, and unable to sleep for days on end. Having sunk to a point where he was considering suicide, he was sent by his brother to a sanatorium in White Plains, New York, where he eventually recovered. After leaving the sanatorium, he took a position as an editor for Butterick's. He was successful in this position, and was eventually able to purchase a one-third interest in a new publishing company, B. W. Dodge, which republished Dreiser's novel *Sister Carrie.* This new release of the novel proved considerably more successful than the first release had been. In its first year, the reissued version of *Sister Carrie* sold 4,500 copies, with strong reviews, and the next year it sold more than 10,000 copies. The recognition that accompanied the success of the novel was based not only on the power of the description of the perils of urban life but also on the new trend in literature that Dreiser was credited with establishing.

Refer to this version of the passage to answer the questions that follow.

Theodore Dreiser

Paragraph

1   **1A** Theodore Dreiser, the American author best known for the novel *Sister Carrie* (1912), introduced a powerful style of writing that had a profound influence on the writers that followed him, from Steinbeck to Fitzgerald and Hemingway. **1B** It was in *Sister Carrie* that Theodore Dreiser created a fictional account that laid bare the harsh reality of life in the big city and in which Dreiser established himself as the architect of a new genre. **1C**

2   Dreiser was born in 1871 into a large family whose fortunes had in the recent past taken a dramatic turn for the worse. Before Theodore's birth, his father had built up a successful factory business only to lose it to a fire. **4A** The family was rather abruptly thrust into poverty, and Theodore spent his youth moving from place to place in the Midwest as the family tried desperately to reestablish itself financially. **4B** He left home at the age of sixteen. **4C** After earning some money, he spent a year at Indiana University but left school and returned to Chicago, yearning for the glamour and excitement that it offered. **4D** At the age of twenty-two, he began work as a reporter for a small newspaper in Chicago, the *Daily Globe,* and later worked on newspapers in Pittsburgh, Cleveland, Saint Louis, and New York City. In his work as a reporter, he was witness to the seamier side of life and was responsible for recording events that befell the less fortunate in the city, the beggars, the alcoholics, the prostitutes, and the working poor.

3   **5A** Dreiser first tried his hand at fiction by writing short stories rather than novels, and the first four short stories that he wrote were published. **5B** Based on this, he was encouraged to write a novel that would accurately depict the harsh life of the city, and the novel *Sister Carrie* was the result of his effort. **5C** This novel chronicles the life of Carrie Meeber, a small-town girl who goes to Chicago in a quest for fame and fortune. **5D** As Carrie progresses from factory worker to Broadway star by manipulating anyone in her path, Dreiser sends a clear message about the tragedy of life that is devoted purely to the quest for money.

4   *Sister Carrie,* unfortunately for Dreiser, did not achieve immediate success. **7A** The novel was accepted for publication by Doubleday, but Dreiser was immediately asked to make major revisions to the novel. **7B** When Dreiser refused to make the revisions, Doubleday published only a limited number of copies of the book and refused to promote or advertise it. **7C** Published in limited release and without the backing of the company, the novel was a dismal failure, selling fewer than 500 copies. **7D**

5   After the failure of the novel that was so meaningful to him, Dreiser suffered a nervous breakdown; he was depressed, stricken with severe headaches, and unable to sleep for days on end. Having sunk to a point where he was considering suicide, he was sent by his brother to a sanatorium in White Plains, New York, where he eventually recovered. **10A** After leaving the sanatorium, he took a position as an editor for Butterick's. **10B** He was successful in this position, and was eventually able to purchase a one-third interest in a new publishing company, B. W. Dodge, which republished Dreiser's novel *Sister Carrie.* **10C** This new release of the novel proved considerably more successful than the first release had been. **10D** In its first year, the reissued version of *Sister Carrie* sold 4,500 copies, with strong reviews, and the next year it sold more than 10,000 copies. The recognition that accompanied the success of the novel was based not only on the power of the description of the perils of urban life but also on the new trend in literature that Dreiser was credited with establishing.

Questions

1. Look at the three squares [■] that indicate where the following sentence could be added to paragraph 1.

   This forceful first novel set a new path for American novels at the end of the nineteenth century.

   Where would the sentence best fit? Click on a square [■] to add the sentence to the passage.

2. Which of the sentences below best expresses the essential information in the first highlighted sentence in paragraph 2? *Incorrect* choices change the meaning in important ways or leave out essential information.

   Ⓐ Dreiser's family had formerly been rich before it had become poor.

   Ⓑ Dreiser was, unfortunately, born into an overly dramatic family.

   Ⓒ The fortunes of Dreiser's family had recently increased.

   Ⓓ Members of Dreiser's family suffered from the serious effects of a disease.

3. Which of the sentences below best expresses the essential information in the second highlighted sentence in paragraph 2? *Incorrect* choices change the meaning in important ways or leave out essential information.

   Ⓐ Dreiser served as a witness in a number of trials that involved beggars, alcoholics, and prostitutes.

   Ⓑ Dreiser observed and wrote about the poorer classes as part of his newspaper job.

   Ⓒ In New York City, during Dreiser's time, there were many people who were less fortunate than Dreiser.

   Ⓓ Dreiser's work involved working with beggars, alcoholics, and prostitutes.

4. Look at the four squares [■] that indicate where the following sentence could be added to paragraph 2.

   At this young age, he moved alone to Chicago and supported himself by taking odd jobs.

   Where would the sentence best fit? Click on a square [■] to add the sentence to the passage.

5. Look at the four squares [■] that indicate where the following sentence could be added to paragraph 3.

   It was rather unusual for a novice writer to achieve so much so quickly.

   Where would the sentence best fit? Click on a square [■] to add the sentence to the passage.

6. Which of the sentences below best expresses the essential information in the highlighted sentence in paragraph 3? *Incorrect* choices change the meaning in important ways or leave out essential information.

   Ⓐ Dreiser devoted his life primarily to trying to become rich.

   Ⓑ In Dreiser's novel, Carrie succeeds by moving from a low-level job to stardom.

   Ⓒ Dreiser used one of his characters to demonstrate the negative aspects of lust for money.

   Ⓓ Dreiser tried to warn Carrie that she was taking the wrong path in life.

7. Look at the four squares [■] that indicate where the following sentence could be added to paragraph 4.

   These changes were intended to tone down some of the starker and more scandalous descriptions.

   Where would the sentence best fit? Click on a square [■] to add the sentence to the passage.

8. Which of the sentences below best expresses the essential information in the first highlighted sentence in paragraph 5? *Incorrect* choices change the meaning in important ways or leave out essential information.

ⒶDreiser recovered from an attempted suicide at a sanatorium.

ⒷDreiser's brother went to a sanatorium after attempting suicide.

ⒸAfter being sent to a sanatorium, Dreiser considered committing suicide.

ⒹDreiser's brother stepped in to help Dreiser after Dreiser became depressed.

9. Which of the sentences below best expresses the essential information in the second highlighted sentence in paragraph 5? *Incorrect* choices change the meaning in important ways or leave out essential information.

ⒶIn Dreiser's novels, he recognized the power of urban life and new trends that existed in it.

ⒷThe success of Dreiser's novel went unrecognized because it represented such a new trend in literature.

ⒸDreiser credited his urban upbringing and literary background for the success that his novel achieved.

ⒹDreiser achieved acclaim because his writing was so powerful and because he established a new trend.

10. Look at the four squares [■] that indicate where the following sentence could be added to paragraph 5.

This company was one that published magazines to promote sewing and the sale of clothing patterns.

Where would the sentence best fit? Click on a square [■] to add the sentence to the passage.

READING REVIEW EXERCISE (Skills 1–4): Read the passage.

Paragraph

Pulsars

1 There is still much for astronomers to learn about pulsars. Based on what is known, the term **pulsar** is used to describe the phenomenon of short, precisely timed radio bursts that are emitted from somewhere in space. Though all is not known about pulsars, they are now believed in reality to emanate from spinning **neutron stars**, highly reduced cores of collapsed stars that are theorized to exist.

2 Pulsars were discovered in 1967, when Jocelyn Bell, a graduate student at Cambridge University, noticed an unusual pattern on a chart from a radio telescope. What made this pattern unusual was that, unlike other radio signals from celestial objects, this series of pulses had a highly regular period of 1.33730119 seconds. Because day after day the pulses came from the same place among the stars, Cambridge researchers came to the conclusion that they could not have come from a local source such as an Earth satellite.

3 A name was needed for this newly discovered phenomenon. The possibility that the signals were coming from a distant civilization was considered, and at that point the idea of naming the phenomenon L.G.M. (short for Little Green Men) was raised. However, after researchers had found three more regularly pulsing objects in other parts of the sky over the next few weeks, the name pulsar was selected instead of L.G.M.

4 As more and more pulsars were found, astronomers engaged in debates over their nature. It was determined that a pulsar could not be a star inasmuch as a normal star is too big to pulse so fast. The question was also raised as to whether a pulsar might be a white dwarf star, a dying star that has collapsed to approximately the size of the Earth and is slowly cooling off. However, this idea was also rejected because the fastest pulsar known at the time pulsed around thirty times per second and a white dwarf, which is the smallest known type of star, would not hold together if it were to spin that fast.

5 The final conclusion among astronomers was that only a neutron star, which is theorized to be the remaining core of a collapsed star that has been reduced to a highly dense radius of only around 10 kilometers, was small enough to be a pulsar. Further evidence of the link between pulsars and neutron stars was found in 1968, when a pulsar was found in the middle of the Crab Nebula. The Crab Nebula is what remains of the supernova of the year 1054, and inasmuch as it has been theorized that neutron stars sometimes remain following supernova explosions, it is believed that the pulsar coming from the Crab Nebula is evidently just such a neutron star.

6 The generally accepted theory for pulsars is the **lighthouse theory**, which is based upon a consideration of the theoretical properties of neutron stars and the observed properties of pulsars. According to the lighthouse theory, a spinning neutron star emits beams of radiation that sweep through the sky, and when one of the beams passes over the Earth, it is detectable on Earth. It is known as the lighthouse theory because the emissions from neutron stars are similar to the pulses of light emitted from lighthouses as they sweep over the ocean; the name lighthouse is therefore actually more appropriate than the name pulsar.

Refer to this version of the passage to answer the questions that follow.

Pulsars

Paragraph

1 There is still much for astronomers to learn about pulsars. Based on what is known, the term **pulsar** is used to describe the phenomenon of short, precisely timed radio bursts that are emitted from somewhere in space. Though all is not known about pulsars, they are now believed in reality to emanate from spinning **neutron stars**, highly reduced cores of collapsed stars that are theorized to exist.

2 Pulsars were discovered in 1967, when Jocelyn Bell, a graduate student at Cambridge University, noticed an unusual pattern on a chart from a radio telescope. What made this pattern unusual was that, unlike other radio signals from celestial objects, this series of pulses had a highly regular period of 1.33730119 seconds. Because day after day the pulses came from the same place among the stars, Cambridge researchers came to the conclusion that they could not have come from a local source such as an Earth satellite.

3 **5A** A name was needed for this newly discovered phenomenon. **5B** The possibility that the signals were coming from a distant civilization was considered, and at that point the idea of naming the phenomenon L.G.M. (short for Little Green Men) was raised. **5C** However, after researchers had found three more regularly pulsing objects in other parts of the sky over the next few weeks, the name pulsar was selected instead of L.G.M. **5D**

4 As more and more pulsars were found, astronomers engaged in debates over their nature. It was determined that a pulsar could not be a star inasmuch as a normal star is too big to pulse so fast. The question was also raised as to whether a pulsar might be a white dwarf star, a dying star that has collapsed to approximately the size of the Earth and is slowly cooling off. However, this idea was also rejected because the fastest pulsar known at the time pulsed around thirty times per second and a white dwarf, which is the smallest known type of star, would not hold together if it were to spin that fast.

5 The final conclusion among astronomers was that only a neutron star, which is theorized to be the remaining core of a collapsed star that has been reduced to a highly dense radius of only around 10 kilometers, was small enough to be a pulsar. Further evidence of the link between pulsars and neutron stars was found in 1968, when a pulsar was found in the middle of the Crab Nebula. The Crab Nebula is what remains of the supernova of the year 1054, and inasmuch as it has been theorized that neutron stars sometimes remain following supernova explosions, it is believed that the pulsar coming from the Crab Nebula is evidently just such a neutron star.

6 **13A** The generally accepted theory for pulsars is the **lighthouse theory**, which is based upon a consideration of the theoretical properties of neutron stars and the observed properties of pulsars. **13B** According to the lighthouse theory, a spinning neutron star emits beams of radiation that sweep through the sky, and when one of the beams passes over the Earth, it is detectable on Earth. **13C** It is known as the lighthouse theory because the emissions from neutron stars are similar to the pulses of light emitted from lighthouses as they sweep over the ocean; the name lighthouse is therefore actually more appropriate than the name pulsar. **13D**

Questions

1. The phrase "emanate from" in paragraph 1 is closest in meaning to
   - Ⓐ develop from
   - Ⓑ revolve around
   - Ⓒ wander away from
   - Ⓓ receive directions from

2. Which of the sentences below best expresses the essential information in the highlighted sentence in paragraph 2? *Incorrect* choices change the meaning in important ways or leave out essential information.
   - Ⓐ It was unusual for researchers to hear patterns from space.
   - Ⓑ It was unusual for celestial objects to emit radio signals.
   - Ⓒ It was unusual that the pattern of the pulsars was so regular.
   - Ⓓ It was unusual that the period of pulses was only slightly more than a second in length.

3. The word "they" in paragraph 2 refers to
   - Ⓐ day after day
   - Ⓑ the pulses
   - Ⓒ the stars
   - Ⓓ Cambridge researchers

4. The word "raised" in paragraph 3 could best be replaced by
   - Ⓐ lifted
   - Ⓑ suggested
   - Ⓒ discovered
   - Ⓓ elevated

5. Look at the four squares [■] that indicate where the following sentence could be added to paragraph 3.

   This name was selected because it indicates a regularly pulsing radio source.

   Where would the sentence best fit? Click on a square [■] to add the sentence to the passage.

6. The phrase "engaged in" in paragraph 4 could best be replaced by
   - Ⓐ became attached to
   - Ⓑ were disappointed in
   - Ⓒ made promises about
   - Ⓓ took part in

7. The word "their" in paragraph 4 refers to
   - Ⓐ weeks
   - Ⓑ pulsars
   - Ⓒ astronomers
   - Ⓓ details

8. Which of the sentences below best expresses the essential information in the highlighted sentence in paragraph 4? *Incorrect* choices change the meaning in important ways or leave out essential information.
   - Ⓐ Pulsars could not be white dwarfs because the frequency of the pulsars is too high.
   - Ⓑ Pulsars cannot spin very fast because they will fall apart if they spin fast.
   - Ⓒ White dwarfs cannot be dying stars because they cannot pulse at around thirty times per second.
   - Ⓓ White dwarfs cannot contain pulsars because white dwarfs spin much faster than pulsars.

9. The word "Further" in paragraph 5 is closest in meaning to
   - Ⓐ distant
   - Ⓑ irrelevant
   - Ⓒ additional
   - Ⓓ unreliable

10. Which of the sentences below best expresses the essential information in the highlighted sentence in paragraph 5? *Incorrect* choices change the meaning in important ways or leave out essential information.

    Ⓐ It is believed that the supernova of 1054 created the Crab Nebula, which contains a pulsing neutron star.

    Ⓑ It is believed that a pulsar created the Crab Nebula, which exploded in a supernova in 1054.

    Ⓒ It is believed that a neutron star exploded in the supernova of 1054, creating the Crab Nebula.

    Ⓓ It is believed that the Crab Nebula is a pulsar that is on the verge of becoming a supernova.

11. The word "properties" in paragraph 6 is closest in meaning to

    Ⓐ lands

    Ⓑ characteristics

    Ⓒ masses

    Ⓓ surroundings

12. The word "it" in paragraph 6 refers to

    Ⓐ a spinning neutron star

    Ⓑ the sky

    Ⓒ one of the beams

    Ⓓ the Earth

13. Look at the four squares [■] that indicate where the following sentence could be added to paragraph 6.

The periodic flashing of pulsars is related to rotation rather than pulsing, so the name pulsar is actually not very accurate.

Where would the sentence best fit? Click on a square [■] to add the sentence to the passage.

Reading Skill 5: FIND FACTUAL INFORMATION

In the Reading section of the TOEFL iBT, you may be asked questions about factual information. The answers to these multiple-choice questions are often restatements of what is given in the passage. This means that the correct answer often expresses the same idea as what is written in the passage but that the words are not exactly the same. The answers to these questions are generally given in order in the passage, and the questions generally indicate which paragraph contains the answers, so the answers are not too difficult to locate. Look at an example of a factual information question.

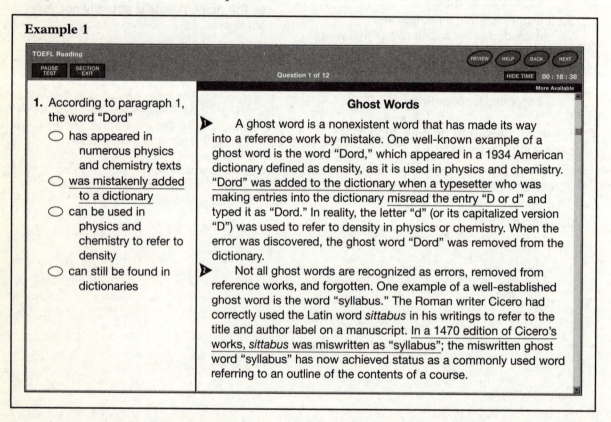

Example 1

TOEFL Reading

PAUSE TEST | SECTION EXIT

Question 1 of 12

REVIEW HELP BACK NEXT

HIDE TIME 00 : 18 : 38

More Available

1. According to paragraph 1, the word "Dord"

○ has appeared in numerous physics and chemistry texts

○ was mistakenly added to a dictionary

○ can be used in physics and chemistry to refer to density

○ can still be found in dictionaries

Ghost Words

➊ A ghost word is a nonexistent word that has made its way into a reference work by mistake. One well-known example of a ghost word is the word "Dord," which appeared in a 1934 American dictionary defined as density, as it is used in physics and chemistry. "Dord" was added to the dictionary when a typesetter who was making entries into the dictionary misread the entry "D or d" and typed it as "Dord." In reality, the letter "d" (or its capitalized version "D") was used to refer to density in physics or chemistry. When the error was discovered, the ghost word "Dord" was removed from the dictionary.

➋ Not all ghost words are recognized as errors, removed from reference works, and forgotten. One example of a well-established ghost word is the word "syllabus." The Roman writer Cicero had correctly used the Latin word _sittabus_ in his writings to refer to the title and author label on a manuscript. In a 1470 edition of Cicero's works, _sittabus_ was miswritten as "syllabus"; the miswritten ghost word "syllabus" has now achieved status as a commonly used word referring to an outline of the contents of a course.

The question asks you to answer a question _according to paragraph 1,_ which means that the correct answer is factual information from the first paragraph. It is stated in the first paragraph that _"Dord" was added to the dictionary when a typesetter . . . misread the entry "D or d."_ This means that the word _"Dord"_ was mistakenly added to a dictionary. To answer this question, you should click on the second answer.

Now look at another example of a factual information question.

Example 2

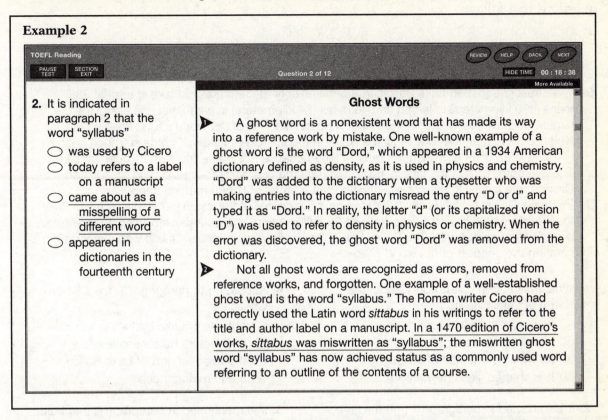

The question asks about what is *indicated in paragraph 2,* which means that you are being asked about factual information in the second paragraph. It is stated in paragraph 2 that *in a 1470 edition of Cicero's works,* sittabus *was miswritten as "syllabus."* This means that the word *"syllabus"* came about as a misspelling of a different word. To answer this question, you should click on the third answer.

The following chart outlines the key information that you should remember about questions testing details.

QUESTIONS ABOUT FACTUAL DETAILS	
HOW TO IDENTIFY THE QUESTION	**According to** paragraph X . . . It is **stated** in paragraph X . . . It is **indicated** in paragraph X . . . It is **mentioned** in paragraph X . . .
WHERE TO FIND THE ANSWER	These answers are generally found in order in the passage, and the paragraph where the answer is found is generally indicated in the question.
HOW TO ANSWER THE QUESTION	1. Choose a key word or idea in the question. 2. Scan the appropriate paragraph for the key word or idea. 3. Read the sentence that contains the key word or idea carefully. 4. Choose the best answer.

READING EXERCISE 5: Study each of the passages and choose the best answers to the questions that follow.

PASSAGE ONE *(Questions 1–5)*

Paragraph
Lake Baikal

1   Crescent-shaped Lake Baikal, in Siberia, is only the ninth largest lake in area at 385 miles (620 kilometers) in length and 46 miles (74 kilometers) in width, yet it is easily the largest body of fresh water in the world. It holds one-fifth of the world's total fresh water, which is more than the total of all the water in the five Great Lakes; it holds so much fresh water in spite of its less-than-impressive area because it is by far the world's deepest lake. The average depth of the lake is 1,312 feet (400 meters) below sea level, and the Olkhon Crevice, the lowest known point, is more than 5,250 feet (1,600 meters) deep.

2   Lake Baikal, which today is located near the center of the Asian peninsula, is most likely the world's oldest lake. It began forming 25 million years ago as Asia started splitting apart in a series of great faults. The Baikal Valley dropped away, eventually filling with water and creating the deepest of the world's lakes.

1. What is stated in paragraph 1 about the shape of Lake Baikal?
   - Ⓐ It is wider than it is long.
   - Ⓑ It is circular in shape.
   - Ⓒ Its width is one-half of its length.
   - Ⓓ It is shaped like a new moon.

2. It is indicated in paragraph 1 that the area of Lake Baikal
   - Ⓐ is less than the area of eight other lakes
   - Ⓑ is one-ninth the area of Siberia
   - Ⓒ is greater than the area of any other freshwater lake
   - Ⓓ is equal to the area of the five Great Lakes

3. According to paragraph 1, Lake Baikal
   - Ⓐ holds one-fifth of the world's water
   - Ⓑ holds five times the water of the Great Lakes
   - Ⓒ holds one-ninth of the world's water
   - Ⓓ holds 20 percent of the world's fresh water

4. According to paragraph 1, the Olkhon Crevice is
   - Ⓐ outside of Lake Baikal
   - Ⓑ 400 meters below sea level
   - Ⓒ the deepest part of Lake Baikal
   - Ⓓ 5,000 meters deep

5. It is mentioned in paragraph 2 that Lake Baikal
   - Ⓐ is not as old as some other lakes
   - Ⓑ formed when sections of the Earth were moving away from each other
   - Ⓒ was fully formed 25 million years ago
   - Ⓓ is today located on the edge of the Asian peninsula

PASSAGE TWO *(Questions 6–10)*

The Postage Stamp

▶1   The postage stamp has been around for only a relatively short period of time. The use of stamps for postage was first proposed in England in 1837, when Sir Rowland Hill published a pamphlet entitled "Post Office Reform: Its Importance and Practicability" to put forth the ideas that postal rates should not be based on the distance that a letter or package travels but should instead be based on the weight of the letter or package and that fees for postal services should be collected in advance of the delivery, rather than after, through the use of postage stamps.

▶2   The ideas proposed by Hill went into effect in England almost immediately, and other countries soon followed suit. The first English stamp, which featured a portrait of then Queen Victoria, was printed in 1840. This stamp, the "penny black," came in sheets that needed to be separated with scissors and provided enough postage for a letter weighing 14 grams or less to any destination. In 1843, Brazil was the next nation to produce national postage stamps, and various areas in what is today Switzerland also produced postage stamps later in the same year. Postage stamps in five- and ten-cent denominations were first approved by the U.S. Congress in 1847, and by 1860 postage stamps were being issued in more than ninety governmental jurisdictions worldwide.

6. According to paragraph 1, postage stamps were first suggested
   - Ⓐ in the first half of the eighteenth century
   - Ⓑ in the second half of the eighteenth century
   - Ⓒ in the first half of the nineteenth century
   - Ⓓ in the second half of the nineteenth century

7. It is indicated in paragraph 1 that Sir Rowland Hill believed that postage fees
   - Ⓐ should be paid by the sender
   - Ⓑ should be related to distance
   - Ⓒ should have nothing to do with how heavy a package is
   - Ⓓ should be collected after the package is delivered

8. What is stated in paragraph 2 about the first English postage stamp?
   - Ⓐ It was designed by Queen Victoria.
   - Ⓑ It contained a drawing of a black penny.
   - Ⓒ It was produced in sheets of fourteen stamps.
   - Ⓓ It could be used to send a lightweight letter.

9. According to paragraph 2, Brazil introduced postage stamps
   - Ⓐ before England
   - Ⓑ before Switzerland
   - Ⓒ after the United States
   - Ⓓ after Switzerland

10. It is mentioned in paragraph 2 that in 1847
   - Ⓐ postage stamps were in use in ninety different countries
   - Ⓑ it cost fifteen cents to mail a letter in the United States
   - Ⓒ two different denominations of postage stamps were introduced in the United States
   - Ⓓ the U.S. Congress introduced the "penny black" stamp

PASSAGE THREE *(Questions 11–15)*

Paragraph

The Clovis Culture

1   Archeologists have found sites all over North America that contain similar tools dating from a period about 12,000 years ago. The culture that developed these tools has been named Clovis after the site near Clovis, New Mexico, where the first tools of this sort were discovered in 1932. The tools are quite sophisticated and are unlike any tools that have been found in the Old World.

2   In the years since the first tools of this sort were discovered in New Mexico, archeologists have discovered Clovis tools in areas ranging from Mexico to Montana in the United States and Nova Scotia in Canada. All of the Clovis finds date from approximately the same period, a fact which suggests that the Clovis spread rapidly throughout the North American continent.

3   From the evidence that has been discovered, archeologists have concluded that the Clovis were a mobile culture. They traveled in groups of forty to fifty individuals, migrating seasonally and returning to the same hunting camps each year. Their population increased rapidly as they spread out over the continent, and they were quite possibly motivated to develop their sophisticated hunting tools to feed their rapidly expanding populace.

11. What is stated in paragraph 1 about Clovis tools?

Ⓐ They date from around 10,000 B.C.

Ⓑ They have been in use for 12,000 years.

Ⓒ They have been found at only one location.

Ⓓ They were discovered by archeologists hundreds of years ago.

12. According to paragraph 1, the town of Clovis

Ⓐ is in Mexico

Ⓑ was founded in 1932

Ⓒ is where all members of the Clovis culture lived

Ⓓ is where the first remnants of an ancient culture were found

13. It is indicated in paragraph 1 that the tools found near Clovis, New Mexico, were

Ⓐ very rudimentary

Ⓑ similar to others found prior to 1932

Ⓒ rather advanced

Ⓓ similar to some found in Africa and Europe

14. According to paragraph 2, what conclusion have archeologists drawn from the Clovis finds?

Ⓐ That the Clovis tended to remain in one place

Ⓑ That the Clovis expanded relatively quickly

Ⓒ That the Clovis lived throughout the world

Ⓓ That the Clovis were a seafaring culture

15. It is mentioned in paragraph 3 that it is believed that the Clovis

Ⓐ lived in familial groups of four or five people

Ⓑ had a relatively stable population

Ⓒ lived only in New Mexico

Ⓓ spent summers and winters in different places

PASSAGE FOUR *(Questions 16–22)*

Brown Dwarfs

Paragraph

 1   A brown dwarf is a celestial body that has never quite become a star. A typical brown dwarf has a mass that is 8 percent or less than that of the Sun. The mass of a brown dwarf is too small to generate the internal temperatures capable of igniting the nuclear burning of hydrogen to release energy and light.

2   A brown dwarf contracts at a steady rate, and after it has contracted as much as possible, a process that takes about 1 million years, it begins to cool off. Its emission of light diminishes with the decrease in its internal temperature, and after a period of 2 to 3 billion years, its emission of light is so weak that it can be difficult to observe from Earth.

3   Because of these characteristics of a brown dwarf, it can be easily distinguished from stars in different stages of formation. A brown dwarf is quite distinctive because its surface temperature is relatively cool and because its internal composition—approximately 75 percent hydrogen—has remained essentially the same as it was when first formed. A white dwarf, in contrast, has gone through a long period when it burns hydrogen, followed by another long period in which it burns the helium created by the burning of hydrogen and ends up with a core that consists mostly of oxygen and carbon with a thin layer of hydrogen surrounding the core.

4   It is not always as easy, however, to distinguish brown dwarfs from large planets. Though planets are not formed in the same way as brown dwarfs, they may in their current state have some of the same characteristics as a brown dwarf. The planet Jupiter, for example, is the largest planet in our solar system with a mass 317 times that of our planet and resembles a brown dwarf in that it radiates energy based on its internal energy. It is the mechanism by which they were formed that distinguishes a high-mass planet such as Jupiter from a low-mass brown dwarf.

16. It is stated in the passage that the mass of an average brown dwarf
    - Ⓐ is smaller than the mass of the Sun
    - Ⓑ generates an extremely high internal temperature
    - Ⓒ is capable of igniting nuclear burning
    - Ⓓ causes the release of considerable energy and light

17. According to paragraph 2, a brown dwarf cools off
    - Ⓐ within the first million years of its existence
    - Ⓑ after its contraction is complete
    - Ⓒ at the same time that it contracts
    - Ⓓ in order to begin contracting

18. What is stated in paragraph 2 about a brown dwarf that has cooled off for 2 to 3 billion years?
    - Ⓐ Its weak light makes it difficult to see from Earth.
    - Ⓑ It no longer emits light.
    - Ⓒ Its weak light has begun the process of restrengthening.
    - Ⓓ Scientists are unable to study it.

19. It is indicated in paragraph 3 that
    - Ⓐ the amount of hydrogen in a brown dwarf has increased dramatically
    - Ⓑ a brown dwarf had far more hydrogen when it first formed
    - Ⓒ three-quarters of the core of a brown dwarf is hydrogen
    - Ⓓ the internal composition of a brown dwarf is always changing

20. According to paragraph 3, a white dwarf
    - Ⓐ is approximately 75 percent hydrogen
    - Ⓑ still burns a considerable amount of hydrogen
    - Ⓒ creates hydrogen from helium
    - Ⓓ no longer has a predominantly hydrogen core

21. What is mentioned in paragraph 4 about brown dwarfs?

Ⓐ They are quite different from large planets.

Ⓑ They are formed in the same way as large planets.

Ⓒ They can share some similarities with large planets.

Ⓓ They have nothing in common with large planets.

22. It is indicated in paragraph 4 that Jupiter

Ⓐ radiates far less energy than a brown dwarf

Ⓑ is a brown dwarf

Ⓒ formed in the same way as a brown dwarf

Ⓓ is in at least one respect similar to a brown dwarf

Reading Skill 6: UNDERSTAND NEGATIVE FACTS

In the Reading section of the TOEFL iBT, you will sometimes be asked to find an answer that is *not stated,* or *not mentioned,* or *not true* in the passage. This type of question really means that three of the answers are *stated, mentioned,* or *true* in the passage, while one answer is not.

You should note that there are two kinds of answers to this type of question: (1) there are three answers that are true and one that is *not true* according to the passage, or (2) there are three true answers and one that is *not stated or mentioned* in the passage. Look at an example that asks you to find the one answer that is *not true.*

Example 1

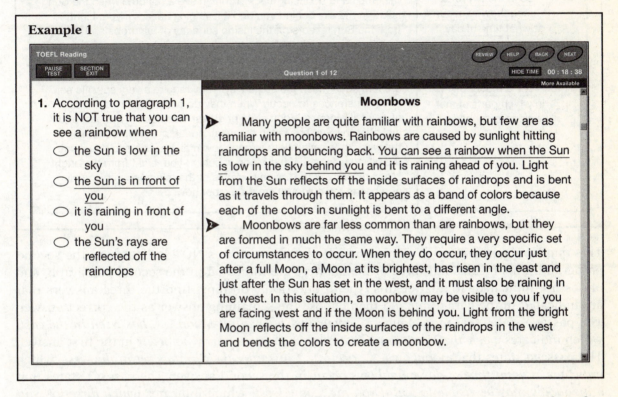

| TOEFL Reading | | REVIEW HELP BACK NEXT |

PAUSE TEST SECTION EXIT

Question 1 of 12   HIDE TIME 00 : 18 : 38

More Available

Moonbows

1. According to paragraph 1, it is NOT true that you can see a rainbow when

○ the Sun is low in the sky

○ the Sun is in front of you

○ it is raining in front of you

○ the Sun's rays are reflected off the raindrops

1 Many people are quite familiar with rainbows, but few are as familiar with moonbows. Rainbows are caused by sunlight hitting raindrops and bouncing back. You can see a rainbow when the Sun is low in the sky behind you and it is raining ahead of you. Light from the Sun reflects off the inside surfaces of raindrops and is bent as it travels through them. It appears as a band of colors because each of the colors in sunlight is bent to a different angle.

2 Moonbows are far less common than are rainbows, but they are formed in much the same way. They require a very specific set of circumstances to occur. When they do occur, they occur just after a full Moon, a Moon at its brightest, has risen in the east and just after the Sun has set in the west, and it must also be raining in the west. In this situation, a moonbow may be visible to you if you are facing west and if the Moon is behind you. Light from the bright Moon reflects off the inside surfaces of the raindrops in the west and bends the colors to create a moonbow.

This question asks you to determine which of the answers is NOT true according to the information in the first paragraph. This means that three of the answers are true according to the passage, and one is not true. To answer this type of question, you must find the one answer that is not true according to the information in the first paragraph. It is stated in the first paragraph that *you can see a rainbow when the Sun is . . . behind you.* This means that it is NOT true that you can see a rainbow when *the Sun is in front of you.* To answer this question, you should click on the second answer.

The next example asks you to find the one answer that is *not mentioned.*

Example 2

TOEFL Reading

PAUSE TEST   SECTION EXIT

REVIEW   HELP   BACK   NEXT

Question 2 of 12

HIDE TIME   00 : 18 : 38

More Available

2. It is NOT indicated in paragraph 2
- ⬤ where the Moon must be in the sky for a moonbow to occur
- ⬤ at what time of day moonbows occur
- ⬤ which direction you must be facing to see a moonbow
- ⬤ in which parts of the world moonbows occur

Moonbows

➤ Many people are quite familiar with rainbows, but few are as familiar with moonbows. Rainbows are caused by sunlight hitting raindrops and bouncing back. You can see a rainbow when the Sun is low in the sky behind you and it is raining ahead of you. Light from the Sun reflects off the inside surfaces of raindrops and is bent as it travels through them. It appears as a band of colors because each of the colors in sunlight is bent to a different angle.

➤ Moonbows are far less common than are rainbows, but they are formed in much the same way. They require a very specific set of circumstances to occur. When they do occur, they occur just after a full Moon, a Moon at its brightest, has risen in the east and just after the Sun has set in the west, and it must also be raining in the west. In this situation, a moonbow may be visible to you if you are facing west and if the Moon is behind you. Light from the bright Moon reflects off the inside surfaces of the raindrops in the west and bends the colors to create a moonbow.

This question asks you to determine which of the answers is NOT indicated in the second paragraph. This means that three of the answers are indicated in the second paragraph, and one is not indicated. To answer this type of question, you must find the three answers that are indicated in the paragraph and then choose the remaining answer as the correct answer. The passage states that *moonbows . . . occur just after a full Moon . . . has risen in the east,* which indicates *where the Moon must be in the sky for a moonbow to occur* in the first answer. The passage states that *moonbows . . . occur . . . just after the Sun has set in the west,* which indicates *at what time of day moonbows occur* in the second answer. The passage states that *a moonbow may be visible to you if you are facing west,* which indicates *which direction you must be facing to see a moonbow* in the third answer. The last answer is the one that is NOT indicated in the passage and is therefore the best answer to this question. To answer this question, you should click on the last answer.

The following chart outlines the key information that you should remember about questions testing negative facts.

QUESTIONS ABOUT NEGATIVE FACTS	
HOW TO IDENTIFY THE QUESTION	It is **NOT stated . . .** It is **NOT mentioned . . .** It is **NOT discussed . . .** It is **NOT true . . .** It is **NOT indicated . . .** All of the following are **true EXCEPT . . .**
WHERE TO FIND THE ANSWER	These answers are generally found in order in the passage, and the paragraph where the answer is found is generally indicated in the question.
HOW TO ANSWER THE QUESTION	1. Choose a key word in the question. 2. Scan the appropriate place in the passage for the key word (or related idea). 3. Read the sentence that contains the key word carefully. 4. Look for the answers that are definitely true according to the passage. Eliminate those answers. 5. Choose the answer that is not true or not discussed in the passage.

READING EXERCISE 6: Study each of the passages, and choose the best answers to the questions that follow.

PASSAGE ONE *(Questions 1–5)*

Flatfish

Members of the flatfish family, sand dabs and flounders, have an evolutionary advantage over many colorfully decorated ocean neighbors in that they are able to adapt their body coloration to different environments. These aquatic chameleons have flattened bodies that are well-suited to life along the ocean floor in the shallower areas of the continental shelf that they inhabit. They also have remarkably sensitive color vision that registers the subtlest gradations on the sea bottom and in the sea life around them. Information about the coloration of the environment is carried through the nervous system to chromatophores, which are pigment-carrying skin cells. These chromatophores are able to accurately reproduce not only the colors but also the texture of the ocean floor. Each time that a sand dab or flounder finds itself in a new environment, the pattern on the body of the fish adapts to fit in with the color and texture around it.

1. It is NOT stated in the passage that sand dabs
   Ⓐ are a type of flatfish
   Ⓑ are in the same family as flounders
   Ⓒ have evolved
   Ⓓ are colorfully decorated

2. According to the passage, it is NOT true that sand dabs and flounders
   Ⓐ have flattened bodies
   Ⓑ live along the ocean floor
   Ⓒ live in the deepest part of the ocean
   Ⓓ live along the continental shelf

3. All of the following are stated about the vision of sand dabs and flounders EXCEPT that they are
   Ⓐ overly sensitive to light
   Ⓑ able to see colors
   Ⓒ able to see the sea bottom
   Ⓓ aware of their surroundings

4. It is NOT true that chromatophores
   Ⓐ are skin cells
   Ⓑ carry pigment
   Ⓒ adapt to surrounding colors
   Ⓓ change the ocean floor

5. It is NOT mentioned in the passage that sand dabs and flounders
   Ⓐ move to new environments
   Ⓑ adapt their behavior
   Ⓒ can change color
   Ⓓ adapt to textures around them

PASSAGE TWO *(Questions 6–10)*

Paragraph

Limestone Caves

1   Limestone caves can be spectacular structures filled with giant stalactites and stalagmites. These caves are formed when rainwater, which is a weak acid, dissolves calcite, or lime, out of limestone. Over time, the lime-laden water drips down into cracks, enlarging them into caves. Some of the lime is then redeposited to form stalactites and stalagmites.

2   Stalactites, which grow down from cave ceilings, are formed in limestone caves when groundwater containing dissolved lime drips from the roof of the cave and leaves a thin deposit as it evaporates. Stalactites generally grow only a fraction of an inch each year, but over time a considerable number may grow to be several yards long. In cases where the supply of water is seasonal, they may actually have growth rings resembling those on tree trunks that indicate how old the stalactites are.

3   Stalagmites are formed on the floor of a limestone cave where water containing dissolved lime has dripped either from the cave ceiling or from a stalactite above. They develop in the same way as stalactites, when water containing dissolved limestone evaporates. In some limestone caves with mature limestone development, stalactites and stalagmites grow together, creating limestone pillars that stretch from the cave floor to the cave ceiling.

6. It is indicated in paragraph 1 that all of the following are part of the process of forming limestone caves EXCEPT that
   Ⓐ rainwater dissolves lime from limestone
   Ⓑ the lime-filled water seeps into breaks in the ground
   Ⓒ the lime in the water evaporates
   Ⓓ the cracks in the ground develop into caves

7. According to paragraph 2, it is NOT true that stalactites
   Ⓐ enlarge cave ceilings
   Ⓑ are found in limestone caves
   Ⓒ grow in a downward direction
   Ⓓ grow quite slowly

8. It is NOT mentioned in paragraph 2
   Ⓐ how long stalactites may grow
   Ⓑ how the age of a stalactite is determined
   Ⓒ what one of the effects of a limited water supply is
   Ⓓ what causes stalactites to disappear

9. According to paragraph 3, stalagmites are NOT formed
   Ⓐ on cave floors
   Ⓑ from lime dissolved in water
   Ⓒ above stalactites
   Ⓓ as water containing lime evaporates

10. It is NOT indicated in paragraph 3 that limestone pillars
   Ⓐ result when a stalactite and a stalagmite grow together
   Ⓑ are attached to both the floor and the ceiling of a cave
   Ⓒ are relatively aged limestone formations
   Ⓓ are more durable than stalactites and stalagmites

PASSAGE THREE *(Questions 11–15)*

Paragraph

Wrigley's Chewing Gum

▶**1**   Wrigley's chewing gum was actually developed as a premium to be given away with other products rather than as a primary product for sale. As a teenager, William Wrigley Jr. was working for his father in Chicago selling soap that had been manufactured in his father's factory. The soap was not very popular with merchants because it was priced at five cents, and this selling price did not leave a good profit margin for the merchants. Wrigley convinced his father to raise the price to ten cents and to give away cheap umbrellas as a premium for the merchants. This worked successfully, confirming to Wrigley that the use of premiums was an effective sales tool.

▶**2**   Wrigley then established his own company; in his company he was selling soap as a wholesaler, giving baking soda away as a premium, and using a cookbook to promote each deal. Over time, the baking soda and cookbook became more popular than the soap, so Wrigley began a new operation selling baking soda. He began hunting for a new premium item to give away with sales of baking soda; he soon decided on chewing gum. Once again, when Wrigley realized that demand for the premium was stronger than the demand for the original product, he created the Wm. Wrigley Jr. Company to produce and sell chewing gum.

▶**3**   Wrigley started out with two brands of gum, Vassar and Lotta Gum, and soon introduced Juicy Fruit and Spearmint. The latter two brands grew in popularity, while the first two were phased out. Juicy Fruit and Spearmint are two of Wrigley's main brands to this day.

11. It is NOT indicated in paragraph 1 that young William was working

  (A) in Chicago
  (B) for his father
  (C) as a soap salesman
  (D) in his father's factory

12. According to paragraph 1, it is NOT true that the soap that young Wrigley was selling

  (A) was originally well-liked
  (B) was originally priced at five cents
  (C) originally provided little profit for merchants
  (D) eventually became more popular with merchants

13. According to paragraph 2, it is NOT true that, when Wrigley first founded his own company, he was

  (A) selling soap
  (B) selling chewing gum
  (C) giving away cookbooks
  (D) using baking soda as a premium

14. It is NOT mentioned in paragraph 2 that Wrigley later

  (A) sold baking soda
  (B) used chewing gum as a premium to sell baking soda
  (C) sold chewing gum
  (D) used baking soda as a premium to sell chewing gum

15. According to paragraph 3, the Wm. Wrigley Jr. Company did all of the following EXCEPT

  (A) begin with two brands of gum
  (B) add new brands to the original two
  (C) phase out the last two brands
  (D) phase out the first two brands

PASSAGE FOUR (Questions 16–22)

Paragraph

Dissociative Identity Disorder

1 ▶ Dissociative identity disorder is a psychological condition in which a person's identity dissociates, or fragments, thereby creating distinct independent identities within one individual. Each separate personality can be distinct from the other personalities in a number of ways, including posture, manner of moving, tone and pitch of voice, gestures, facial expressions, and use of language. A person suffering from dissociative identity disorder may have a large number of independent personalities or perhaps only two or three.

2 ▶ Two stories of actual women suffering from dissociative identity disorder have been extensively recounted in books and films that are familiar to the public. One of them is the story of a woman with twenty-two separate personalities known as Eve. In the 1950s, a book by Corbett Thigpen and a motion picture starring Joanne Woodward, each of which was titled *The Three Faces of Eve,* presented her story; the title referred to three faces, when the woman known as Eve actually experienced twenty-two different personalities, because only three of the personalities could exist at one time. Two decades later, Carolyn Sizemore, Eve's twenty-second personality, wrote about her experiences in a book entitled *I'm Eve.* The second well-known story of a woman suffering from dissociative personality disorder is the story of Sybil, a woman whose sixteen distinct personalities emerged over a period of forty years. A book describing Sybil's experiences was written by Flora Rheta Schreiber and was published in 1973; a motion picture based on the book and starring Sally Field followed.

16. It is NOT stated in paragraph 1 that someone suffering from dissociative identity disorder has
  Ⓐ a psychological condition
  Ⓑ a fragmented identity
  Ⓒ a number of independent identities
  Ⓓ some violent and some nonviolent identities

17. It is indicated in paragraph 1 that distinct personalities can differ in all of the following ways EXCEPT
  Ⓐ manner of dressing
  Ⓑ manner of moving
  Ⓒ manner of speaking
  Ⓓ manner of gesturing

18. It is indicated in paragraph 2 that it is NOT true that Eve
  Ⓐ suffered from dissociative identity disorder
  Ⓑ starred in the movie about her life
  Ⓒ had twenty-two distinct personalities
  Ⓓ had only three distinct personalities at any one time

19. It is NOT stated in paragraph 2 that *The Three Faces of Eve*
  Ⓐ was based on the life of a real woman
  Ⓑ was the title of a book
  Ⓒ was the title of a movie
  Ⓓ was made into a movie in 1950

20. All of the following are mentioned in paragraph 2 about Carolyn Sizemore EXCEPT that she
  Ⓐ wrote *I'm Eve*
  Ⓑ was one of Eve's personalities
  Ⓒ wrote a book in the 1970s
  Ⓓ was familiar with all twenty-two personalities

21. According to paragraph 2, it is NOT true that Sybil
  Ⓐ was a real person
  Ⓑ suffered from dissociative identity disorder
  Ⓒ developed all her personalities over sixteen years
  Ⓓ developed sixteen distinctive personalities over a long period of time

22. It is NOT indicated in paragraph 2 that the book describing Sybil's experiences
  Ⓐ took forty years to write
  Ⓑ was written by Flora Rheta Schreiber
  Ⓒ appeared in the 1970s
  Ⓓ was made into a movie

READING EXERCISE (Skills 5–6): Study the passage, and choose the best answers to the questions that follow.

Paragraph

John Muir

1   John Muir (1838–1914), a Scottish immigrant to the United States, is today recognized for his vital contributions in the area of environmental protection and conservation of the wilderness. As such, he is often referred to as the unofficial "Father of National Parks."

2   Muir came to his role as an environmentalist in a rather circuitous way. Born in Dunbar, Scotland, Muir came to the United States with his family at the age of eleven. The family settled on a Wisconsin farm, where Muir was educated at home rather than in public school because his father felt that participation in an education in a public school would violate his strict religious code. Young Muir did read considerably at home and also developed some interesting mechanical devices by whittling them from wood; when some of his inventions were put on display at a state fair, they were noted by officials from the University of Wisconsin, and Muir was invited to attend the university in spite of his lack of formal education. He left the university after two and a half years; later, while working in a carriage factory, he suffered an injury to his eye. His vision did recover, but following the accident he decided that he wanted to spend his life studying the beauty of the natural world rather than endangering his health working in a factory. He set out on a 1,000-mile walk south to the Gulf of Mexico, and from there he made his way to Yosemite, California, lured by a travel brochure highlighting the natural beauty of Yosemite.

3   He arrived in California in 1868, at the age of thirty, and once there, he took a number of odd jobs to support himself, working as a laborer, a sheepherder, and—after he had become familiar with the wilderness area—a guide. He also began a writing campaign to encourage public support for the preservation of the wilderness, particularly the area around Yosemite. He married in 1880, and for the years that followed he was more involved in family life and in running the ranch given to him and his wife by her parents than in preservation of the environment.

4   He had been away from the environmentalist movement for some time when, in 1889, he was asked by an editor of the magazine *The Century* to write some articles in support of the preservation of Yosemite. The editor, well aware of Muir's talent as a writer and his efforts in the 1870s to support the conservation of Yosemite, took Muir camping to areas of Yosemite that Muir had not seen for years, areas that had been spoiled through uncontrolled development. Because of the experience of this trip, Muir agreed to write two articles in support of the institution of a National Parks system in the United States with Yosemite as the first park to be so designated. These two articles in *The Century* initiated the Yosemite National Park campaign.

5   The campaign was indeed successful. The law creating Yosemite National Park was enacted in 1890, and three additional national parks were created soon after. A year later, a bill known as the Enabling Act was passed; this was a bill that gave U.S. presidents the right to reserve lands for preservation by the U.S. government. Pleased by this success but keenly aware of the need to continue the effort to preserve wilderness areas from undisciplined development, Muir established an organization in 1892, the Sierra Club, with the expressed goal of protecting the wilderness, particularly the area of the Sierra Nevada mountain range where Yosemite is located.

6   From then until his death in 1914, Muir worked assiduously on his writing in an effort to build recognition of the need for environmental protection. His writings from this period include *The Mountains of California* (1894), *Our National Parks* (1901), *My First Summer in the Sierra* (1911), and *My Boyhood and Youth* (1913).

7   A century later, the results of what John Muir was instrumental in initiating are remarkable. The National Park Service is now responsible for more than 350 parks, rivers, seashores, and preserves; more than 250 million people visit these parks each year, and the Sierra Club has more than 650,000 members.

Questions

1. According to paragraph 1, Muir was born
   - (A) in the first half of the eighteenth century
   - (B) in the second half of the eighteenth century
   - (C) in the first half of the nineteenth century
   - (D) in the second half of the nineteenth century

2. It is stated in paragraph 1 that Muir is known for
   - (A) his contributions to immigration reform
   - (B) his explorations of the wilderness
   - (C) his efforts to maintain natural areas
   - (D) his extensive studies of the national parks

3. It is indicated in paragraph 2 that Muir's early education
   - (A) was conducted at home
   - (B) took place in a religious school
   - (C) violated his father's wishes
   - (D) was in a public school

4. It is NOT mentioned in paragraph 2 that Muir
   - (A) whittled with wood
   - (B) was taught how to whittle by his father
   - (C) whittled mechanical devices
   - (D) was admitted to the university because of his whittling

5. According to paragraph 2, after Muir left the university, it is NOT true that he
   - (A) took a job in a factory
   - (B) suffered an unhealable injury
   - (C) made a decision to quit his job
   - (D) embarked on a long walking tour

6. All of the following are mentioned in paragraph 3 as jobs that Muir held EXCEPT
   - (A) a laborer
   - (B) an animal tender
   - (C) a wilderness guide
   - (D) a travel writer

7. It is stated in paragraph 3 that in the years after 1880, Muir
   - (A) took some odd jobs
   - (B) devoted a lot of time to his family
   - (C) gave his wife's parents a ranch
   - (D) spent most of his time preserving the environment

8. It is NOT mentioned in paragraph 4 that Muir
   - (A) had been uninvolved with environmentalists for a period of time
   - (B) was contacted by an editor for *The Century*
   - (C) worked as an editor for *The Century*
   - (D) wrote two articles for *The Century*

9. The camping trip that is discussed in paragraph 4
   - (A) occurred in the 1870s
   - (B) led Muir to areas that he had never before seen
   - (C) took place in areas that were in their natural state
   - (D) helped to convince Muir to write the articles

10. It is stated in paragraph 5 that the Enabling Act
    - (A) allowed the president to set aside lands to conserve them
    - (B) became law in 1890
    - (C) called for the establishment of the first three national parks
    - (D) preserved lands for government use

11. According to paragraph 5, it is NOT true that the Sierra Club was founded
    - (A) after the passage of the Enabling Act
    - (B) by John Muir
    - (C) before the turn of the century
    - (D) to move Yosemite to the Sierra Nevada

12. It is mentioned in paragraph 6 that, for the last decades of his life, Muir

   Ⓐ spent a considerable amount of time in Yosemite

   Ⓑ wrote a number of new laws

   Ⓒ changed his mind on the need for environmental protection

   Ⓓ devoted himself to increasing public awareness of the environment

13. It is NOT indicated in paragraph 7 that early in the twenty-first century

   Ⓐ hundreds of locations are part of the National Park Service

   Ⓑ numerous parks, rivers, seashores, and preserves are being developed

   Ⓒ a quarter of a billion people visit these parks each year

   Ⓓ more than a half a million people belong to the Sierra Club

READING REVIEW EXERCISE (Skills 1–6): Read the passage.

Caretaker Speech

1   Children learn to construct language from those around them. Until about the age of three, children tend to learn to develop their language by modeling the speech of their parents, but from that time on, peers have a growing influence as models for language development in children. It is easy to observe that, when adults and older children interact with younger children, they tend to modify their language to improve communication with younger children, and this modified language is called **caretaker speech**.

2   Caretaker speech is used often quite unconsciously; few people actually study how to modify language when speaking to young children but, instead, without thinking, find ways to reduce the complexity of language in order to communicate effectively with young children. A caretaker will unconsciously speak in one way with adults and in a very different way with young children. Caretaker speech tends to be slower speech with short, simple words and sentences which are said in a higher-pitched voice with exaggerated inflections and many repetitions of essential information. It is not limited to what is commonly called baby talk, which generally refers to the use of simplified, repeated syllable expressions such as "ma-ma," "boo-boo," "bye-bye," "wa-wa," but also includes the simplified sentence structures repeated in sing-song inflections.

3   Caretaker speech serves the very important function of allowing young children to acquire language more easily. The higher-pitched voice and the exaggerated inflections tend to focus the small child on what the caretaker is saying, the simplified words and sentences make it easier for the small child to begin to comprehend, and the repetitions reinforce the child's developing understanding. Then, as a child's speech develops, caretakers tend to adjust their language in response to the improved language skills, again quite unconsciously. Parents and older children regularly adjust their speech to a level that is slightly above that of a younger child; without studied recognition of what they are doing, these caretakers will speak in one way to a one-year-old and in a progressively more complex way as the child reaches the age of two or three.

4   An important point to note is that the function covered by caretaker speech, that of assisting a child to acquire language in small and simple steps, is an unconsciously used but extremely important part of the process of language acquisition and as such is quite universal. Studying cultures where children do not acquire language through caretaker speech is difficult because such cultures are difficult to find. The question of why caretaker speech is universal is not clearly understood; instead, proponents on either side of the nature vs. nurture debate argue over whether caretaker speech is a natural function or a learned one. Those who believe that caretaker speech is a natural and inherent function in humans believe that it is human nature for children to acquire language and for those around them to encourage their language acquisition naturally; the presence of a child is itself a natural stimulus that increases the rate of caretaker speech among those present. In contrast, those who believe that caretaker speech develops through nurturing rather than nature argue that a person who is attempting to communicate with a child will learn by trying out different ways of communicating to determine which is the most effective from the reactions to the communication attempts; a parent might, for example, learn to use speech with exaggerated inflections with a small child because the exaggerated inflections do a better job of attracting the child's attention than do more subtle inflections. Whether caretaker speech results from nature or nurture, it does play an important and universal role in child language acquisition.

Refer to this version of the passage to answer the questions that follow.

Paragraph

Caretaker Speech

1   Children learn to construct language from those around them. Until about the age of three, children tend to learn to develop their language by modeling the speech of their parents, but from that time on, peers have a growing influence as models for language development in children. It is easy to observe that, when adults and older children interact with younger children, they tend to modify their language to improve communication with younger children, and this modified language is called **caretaker speech**.

2   Caretaker speech is used often quite unconsciously; few people actually study how to modify language when speaking to young children but, instead, without thinking, find ways to reduce the complexity of language in order to communicate effectively with young children. **5A** A caretaker will unconsciously speak in one way with adults and in a very different way with young children. **5B** Caretaker speech tends to be slower speech with short, simple words and sentences which are said in a higher-pitched voice with exaggerated inflections and many repetitions of essential information. **5C** It is not limited to what is commonly called baby talk, which generally refers to the use of simplified, repeated syllable expressions such as "ma-ma," "boo-boo," "bye-bye," "wa-wa," but also includes the simplified sentence structures repeated in sing-song inflections. **5D**

3   Caretaker speech serves the very important function of allowing young children to acquire language more easily. The higher-pitched voice and the exaggerated inflections tend to focus the small child on what the caretaker is saying, the simplified words and sentences make it easier for the small child to begin to comprehend, and the repetitions reinforce the child's developing understanding. Then, as a child's speech develops, caretakers tend to adjust their language in response to the improved language skills, again quite unconsciously. Parents and older children regularly adjust their speech to a level that is slightly above that of a younger child; without studied recognition of what they are doing, these caretakers will speak in one way to a one-year-old and in a progressively more complex way as the child reaches the age of two or three.

4   **13A** An important point to note is that the function covered by caretaker speech, that of assisting a child to acquire language in small and simple steps, is an unconsciously used but extremely important part of the process of language acquisition and as such is quite universal. **13B** Studying cultures where children do not acquire language through caretaker speech is difficult because such cultures are difficult to find. **13C** The question of why caretaker speech is universal is not clearly understood; instead, proponents on either side of the nature vs. nurture debate argue over whether caretaker speech is a natural function or a learned one. **13D** Those who believe that caretaker speech is a natural and inherent function in humans believe that it is human nature for children to acquire language and for those around them to encourage their language acquisition naturally; the presence of a child is itself a natural stimulus that increases the rate of caretaker speech among those present. In contrast, those who believe that caretaker speech develops through nurturing rather than nature argue that a person who is attempting to communicate with a child will learn by trying out different ways of communicating to determine which is the most effective from the reactions to the communication attempts; a parent might, for example, learn to use speech with exaggerated inflections with a small child because the exaggerated inflections do a better job of attracting the child's attention than do more subtle inflections. Whether caretaker speech results from nature or nurture, it does play an important and universal role in child language acquisition.

Questions

1. According to paragraph 1, children over the age of three
   Ⓐ learn little language from those around them
   Ⓑ are no longer influenced by the language of their parents
   Ⓒ are influenced more and more by those closer to their own age
   Ⓓ first begin to respond to caretaker speech

2. The word "modeling" in paragraph 1 could best be replaced by
   Ⓐ demonstrating
   Ⓑ mimicking
   Ⓒ building
   Ⓓ designing

3. Which of the sentences below best expresses the essential information in the highlighted sentence in paragraph 2? *Incorrect* choices change the meaning in important ways or leave out essential information.
   Ⓐ Most people are quite aware of the use of caretaker speech because of thorough study and research about it.
   Ⓑ The unconscious use of caretaker speech involves a reduction in the complexity of language, while the conscious use of caretaker speech involves an increase in complexity.
   Ⓒ Young children tend to use caretaker speech quite unconsciously in order to reduce the complexity of their thoughts to language that they can express.
   Ⓓ People generally seem to be able to adapt their language to the level of a child's language without thinking consciously about it.

4. The word "It" in paragraph 2 refers to
   Ⓐ caretaker speech
   Ⓑ a higher-pitched voice
   Ⓒ essential information
   Ⓓ baby talk

5. Look at the four squares [■] that indicate where the following sentence could be added to paragraph 2.

   Examples of these are expressions such as "Say bye-bye" or "Where's da-da?"

   Where would the sentence best fit? Click on a square [■] to add the sentence to the passage.

6. All of the following are mentioned in paragraph 3 as characteristics of caretaker speech EXCEPT
   Ⓐ overemphasized inflections
   Ⓑ the use of rhyming sounds
   Ⓒ the tendency to repeat oneself
   Ⓓ the use of easier words and structures

7. It is indicated in paragraph 3 that parents tend to
   Ⓐ speak in basically the same way to a one-year-old and a three-year-old
   Ⓑ use language that is far above the language level of a child
   Ⓒ speak in a progressively less complex way as a child matures
   Ⓓ modify their speech according to the language development of a child

8. The word "reaches" in paragraph 3 could best be replaced by
   Ⓐ holds on to
   Ⓑ takes charge of
   Ⓒ arrives at
   Ⓓ extends out to

9. The word "that" in paragraph 4 refers to
   Ⓐ an important point
   Ⓑ the function
   Ⓒ caretaker speech
   Ⓓ a child

10. Which of the sentences below best expresses the essential information in the highlighted sentence in paragraph 4? *Incorrect* choices change the meaning in important ways or leave out essential information.

Ⓐ People who believe in nature over nurture feel that adults or older children who are around younger children will naturally make changes in their language.

Ⓑ Caretaker speech is one of many natural functions that are used to stimulate young children to develop more rapidly.

Ⓒ The natural human tendency to acquire language makes caretaker speech unimportant in improving the rate of language acquisition by children.

Ⓓ It is human nature for children to develop the use of caretaker speech in order to take part effectively in conversations around them.

11. According to paragraph 4, it is NOT expected that someone who believes in nurture over nature

Ⓐ would believe that caretaker speech is more of a learned style of language than a natural one

Ⓑ would use different styles of caretaker speech with children in response to what is working best

Ⓒ would learn to use different styles of caretaker speech with different children

Ⓓ would use less caretaker speech than do those who believe in nature over nurture

12. The phrase "trying out" in paragraph 4 is closest in meaning to

Ⓐ experimenting with

Ⓑ bringing about

Ⓒ throwing away

Ⓓ taking over

13. Look at the four squares [■] that indicate where the following sentence could be added to paragraph 4.

It is not merely a device used by English-speaking parents.

Where would the sentence best fit? Click on a square [■] to add the sentence to the passage.

INFERENCES

Reading Skill 7: MAKE INFERENCES FROM STATED FACTS

In the Reading section of the TOEFL iBT, you may sometimes be asked to answer a multiple-choice question by drawing a conclusion from a specific detail or details in the passage. Questions of this type contain the words *implied, inferred, likely,* or *probably* to let you know that the answer to the question is not directly stated. In this type of question, it is important to understand that you do not need to "pull the answer out of thin air." Instead, some information will be given in the passage, and you will draw a conclusion from that information. Look at an example of an inference question.

Example 1

TOEFL Reading   REVIEW   HELP   BACK   NEXT

PAUSE TEST   SECTION EXIT   Question 1 of 12   HIDE TIME   00 : 18 : 38

More Available

1. It can be inferred from paragraph 1 that gold came into use as a medium of exchange

- ○ before 700 B.C.
- ○ after 700 B.C.
- ○ during the reign of King Croesus
- ○ in 525 B.C.

Ancient Coins

1   Long before coins were invented, metals such as gold, silver, copper, and bronze were used as a medium of exchange for trade. However, each piece of metal had to be weighed each time it was used in trade to establish its value. The Lydians of western Anatolia were the first to begin producing metal coins in standard weights, in the seventh century B.C., impressing a seal into the coin to indicate its value.

2   One such coin minted during the time of Lydian King Croesus, who ruled from 560 B.C. to 546 B.C., has been recovered by archeologists; this coin is imprinted with the heads and forelegs of two animals, a bull and a lion, who are facing each other. It was not until 525 B.C. that coins with images on both sides came into being.

In this example, you are asked to infer when gold came into use as a medium of exchange based upon stated information in the first paragraph. To answer this question, you should refer to the information about gold in the passage and draw a conclusion from that information. The passage states that *long before coins were invented, metals such as gold . . . were used as a medium of exchange* and that *the Lydians . . . were the first to begin producing metal coins . . . in the seventh century B.C.* From this context, it can be determined that gold came into use as a medium of exchange *before 700 B.C.* To answer this question, you should click on the first answer.

Now, look at another example of an inference question.

Example 2

TOEFL Reading

PAUSE TEST   SECTION EXIT

REVIEW   HELP   BACK   NEXT

Question 2 of 12

HIDE TIME   00 : 18 : 38

More Available

2. It is implied in paragraph 2 that coins from the time of King Croesus were all
- imprinted on one side only
- made of gold
- imprinted with two animals
- imprinted on both sides

Ancient Coins

▶   Long before coins were invented, metals such as gold, silver, copper, and bronze were used as a medium of exchange for trade. However, each piece of metal had to be weighed each time it was used in trade to establish its value. The Lydians of western Anatolia were the first to begin producing metal coins in standard weights, in the seventh century B.C., impressing a seal into the coin to indicate its value.

▶   One such coin minted during the time of Lydian King Croesus, who ruled from 560 B.C. to 546 B.C., has been recovered by archeologists; this coin is imprinted with the heads and forelegs of two animals, a bull and a lion, who are facing each other. It was not until 525 B.C. that coins with images on both sides came into being.

In this example, you are asked to determine what is implied about coins from the time of King Croesus, based upon stated information in the second paragraph. To answer this question, you should refer to the information about coins and King Croesus in the second paragraph. The passage mentions *King Croesus, who ruled from 560 B.C. to 546 B.C.* and that *it was not until 525 B.C. that coins with images on both sides came into being.* From this context, it can be determined that coins from the time of King Croesus were all *imprinted on one side only.* To answer this question, you should click on the first answer.

The following chart outlines the key information that you should remember about questions testing inferences.

QUESTIONS ABOUT INFERENCES FROM STATED FACTS	
HOW TO IDENTIFY THE QUESTION	It is **implied** in paragraph X . . . It can be **inferred** from paragraph X . . . It is most **likely** that . . . What **probably** happened . . . ?
WHERE TO FIND THE ANSWER	The answers to these questions are generally found in order in the passage.
HOW TO ANSWER THE QUESTION	1. Choose a key word or phrase in the question. 2. Scan the passage for the key word or phrase (or related idea). 3. Carefully read the sentence that contains the key word or phrase.

READING EXERCISE 7: Study each of the passages, and choose the best answers to the questions that follow.

PASSAGE ONE *(Questions 1–4)*

Tiger Moths

One of the most beautiful of the 100,000 known species in the order *Lepidoptera* are the tiger moths, moths known for the striking appeal of their distinctive coloration. This type of moth is covered with highly conspicuous orange-and-black or yellow-and-black patterns of spots and stripes. Such boldly patterned color combinations are commonplace in the animal world, serving the function of forewarning potential predators of unpleasant tastes and smells. This is unquestionably the function served by the striking coloration of the garden tiger moth, which is quite visually attractive but is also poisonous to predators. Certain glands in the garden tiger moth produce strong toxins that circulate throughout the insect's bloodstream, while other glands secrete bubbles that produce a noxious warning smell. The tiger moth, indeed, is a clear example of a concept that many predators intuitively understand, that creatures with the brightest coloration are often the least suitable to eat.

1. It is implied in the passage about the order *Lepidoptera* that
   Ⓐ all members of the order are moths
   Ⓑ there may be more than 100,000 species in this order
   Ⓒ all members of the order are brightly colored
   Ⓓ there are most likely fewer than 100,000 species in this order

2. It can be inferred from the passage that the tiger moth was so named because
   Ⓐ its coloration resembles that of a tiger
   Ⓑ it is a ferocious predator, like the tiger
   Ⓒ its habitat is the same as the tiger's
   Ⓓ it is a member of the same scientific classification as the tiger

3. What would most likely happen to a predator that wanted to eat a tiger moth?
   Ⓐ The predator would be unable to catch it.
   Ⓑ The predator would capture it by poisoning it.
   Ⓒ The predator would be unable to find it.
   Ⓓ The predator would back away from it.

4. Which of the following would a predator be most likely to attack successfully?
   Ⓐ A purple and orange moth
   Ⓑ A green and blue moth
   Ⓒ A brown and grey moth
   Ⓓ A red and yellow moth

Paragraph

The Cambrian Explosion

▶ **1**   Many of the major phyla of animals arose during the Cambrian period, in what is called the Cambrian Explosion. Prior to the Cambrian period, simple one-celled organisms had slowly evolved into primitive multicellular creatures. Then, in a relatively rapid explosion during the period from 540 million years ago to 500 million years ago, there was a period of astonishing diversification in which quickly developing organisms became widely distributed and formed complex communities.

▶ **2**   One theoretical explanation for the rapid diversification that occurred during the Cambrian period is known as the theory of polar wander. According to this theory, the rapid diversification occurred because of an unusually rapid reorganization of the Earth's crust during the Cambrian period. This rapid change in the Earth's crust initiated evolutionary change inasmuch as change in the environment serves to trigger evolutionary change.

5. It can be inferred from paragraph 1 that
   - Ⓐ some major phyla developed during periods other than the Cambrian period
   - Ⓑ many other phyla of animals became extinct during the Cambrian Explosion
   - Ⓒ descriptions of various animal phyla were created during the Cambrian period
   - Ⓓ the major phyla of animals that came about during the Cambrian period died out in the Cambrian Explosion

6. It can be determined from paragraph 1 that the Cambrian Explosion most likely lasted
   - Ⓐ 40 million years
   - Ⓑ 450 million years
   - Ⓒ 500 million years
   - Ⓓ 540 million years

7. It is implied in paragraph 2 that
   - Ⓐ only one theory to explain the rapid diversification has been proposed
   - Ⓑ the polar wander explanation is accepted by all scientists
   - Ⓒ the theory of polar wander fails to adequately explain the rapid diversification
   - Ⓓ the theory of polar wander is not the only theory to explain the rapid diversification

8. It can be inferred from paragraph 2 that one basis of the theory of polar wander is that
   - Ⓐ relatively little change in the Earth's crust took place during the Cambrian period
   - Ⓑ rapid diversification was unable to take place because of the changes in the Earth's crust
   - Ⓒ the Earth's crust changed more slowly in other periods
   - Ⓓ evolutionary change is unrelated to changes in the environment

PASSAGE THREE (Questions 9–13)

Paragraph

The Golden Age of Comics

▶1   The period from the late 1930s to the middle 1940s is known as the Golden Age of comic books. The modern comic book came about in the early 1930s in the United States as a giveaway premium to promote the sales of a whole range of household products such as cereal and cleansers. The comic books, which were printed in bright colors to attract the attention of potential customers, proved so popular that some publishers decided to produce comic books that would come out on a monthly basis and would sell for a dime each. Though comic strips had been reproduced in publications prior to this time, the *Famous Funnies* comic book, which was started in 1934, marked the first occasion that a serialized book of comics was attempted.

▶2   Early comic books reprinted already existing comic strips and comics based on known characters; however, publishers soon began introducing original characters developed specifically for comic books. Superman was introduced in *Action Comics* in 1938, and Batman was introduced a year later. The tremendous success of these superhero comic books led to the development of numerous comic books on a variety of topics, though superhero comic books predominated. Astonishingly, by 1945 approximately 160 different comic books were being published in the United States each month, and 90 percent of U.S. children were said to read comic books on a regular basis.

9. It can be inferred from paragraph 1 that, at the beginning of the 1930s, comic books most likely cost

  Ⓐ nothing
  Ⓑ five cents
  Ⓒ ten cents
  Ⓓ twenty-five cents

10. Comic books would least likely have been used to promote

  Ⓐ soap
  Ⓑ cookies
  Ⓒ jewelry
  Ⓓ bread

11. It is implied in the passage that *Famous Funnies*

  Ⓐ was a promotional item
  Ⓑ appeared in a magazine
  Ⓒ had been produced prior to 1934
  Ⓓ was published on a regular basis

12. From the information in paragraph 2, it appears that Superman most likely

  Ⓐ was introduced sometime after Batman
  Ⓑ was a character that first appeared in a comic book
  Ⓒ first appeared in *Famous Funnies*
  Ⓓ first appeared in a promotional comic strip

13. It is implied in paragraph 2 that it is surprising that

  Ⓐ comic strips were more popular than comic books
  Ⓑ superheroes were not too popular
  Ⓒ 90 percent of U.S. children did not read comics
  Ⓓ comic books developed so quickly

PASSAGE FOUR *(Questions 14–19)*

Paragraph
The Filibuster

1   The term "filibuster" has been in use since the mid-nineteenth century to describe the tactic of delaying legislative action in order to prevent the passage of a bill. The word comes from the Dutch *freebooter,* or pirate, and most likely developed from the idea that someone conducting a filibuster is trying to steal away the opportunity that proponents of a bill have to make it successful.

2   In the earlier history of the U.S. Congress, filibusters were used in both the House of Representatives and in the Senate, but they are now much more a part of the culture of the Senate than of the House. Because the House is a much larger body than is the Senate, the House now has rules which greatly limit the amount of time that each member may speak, which effectively serves to eliminate the filibuster as a mechanism for delaying legislation in the House.

3   In the Senate, the smaller of the two bodies, there are now rules that can constrain but not totally eliminate filibusters. The Senate adopted its first cloture rule in 1917, a rule which requires a vote of two-thirds of the Senate to limit debate to one hour on each side. The rule was changed in 1975 and now requires a vote of three-fifths of the members to invoke cloture in most situations.

4   The longest filibuster on record occurred in 1957, when Senator Strom Thurmond of South Carolina wanted to delay voting on civil rights legislation. The filibuster was conducted for 24 hours and 18 minutes on August 28 and 29, when Thurmond held the floor of the Senate by lecturing on the law and reading from court decisions and newspaper columns. It was his hope that this filibuster would rally opponents of civil rights legislation; however, two weeks after the filibuster, the Civil Rights Act of 1957 passed.

14. It can be inferred from the information in paragraph 1 that around 1800

   Ⓐ the first filibuster took place
   Ⓑ legislative action was never delayed
   Ⓒ the term "filibuster" was not in use in the U.S. Congress
   Ⓓ the Dutch introduced the term *freebooter*

15. It can be determined from paragraph 1 that a *freebooter* was most likely someone who

   Ⓐ served in the Senate
   Ⓑ robbed passing ships
   Ⓒ enacted legislation
   Ⓓ served in the Dutch government

16. It is implied in paragraph 2 that, in its early years, the House

   Ⓐ had no rules against filibusters
   Ⓑ had few filibusters
   Ⓒ had fewer filibusters than the Senate
   Ⓓ had the longest filibuster on record

17. Based on the information in paragraph 3, a vote of cloture would most likely be used to

   Ⓐ initiate filibusters
   Ⓑ break filibusters
   Ⓒ extend filibusters
   Ⓓ encourage filibusters

18. It can be inferred from the information in paragraph 3 that the 1975 rule change

   Ⓐ increased the number of people needed to vote for cloture
   Ⓑ made it easier to limit a filibuster
   Ⓒ covered all types of Senate votes
   Ⓓ decreased the number of people in the Senate

19. It is implied in paragraph 4 that Senator Thurmond was opposed to

   Ⓐ filibusters
   Ⓑ lecturing on the law
   Ⓒ speaking in the Senate
   Ⓓ the Civil Rights Act of 1957

Reading Skill 8: INFER RHETORICAL PURPOSE

In the Reading section of the TOEFL iBT, you may be asked to explain why the author includes certain words, phrases, or sentences in a passage. The highlighted words, phrases, or sentences are included by the author to improve the rhetoric, or overall presentation of ideas, of the passage. You must decide which of four multiple-choice answers best explains why the author chose to include the highlighted information. Because you are asked about the rhetorical purpose for a certain piece of information, you must look at how the highlighted information fits into the overall presentation of ideas in the passage rather than only looking at the highlighted information itself.

Look at an example of a question that asks you to determine the rhetorical purpose of a particular phrase.

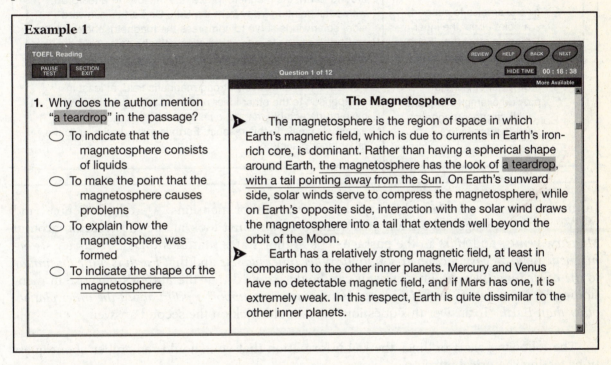

Example 1

TOEFL Reading

Question 1 of 12

HIDE TIME 00 : 18 : 38

More Available

1. Why does the author mention "a teardrop" in the passage?

○ To indicate that the magnetosphere consists of liquids

○ To make the point that the magnetosphere causes problems

○ To explain how the magnetosphere was formed

○ To indicate the shape of the magnetosphere

The Magnetosphere

The magnetosphere is the region of space in which Earth's magnetic field, which is due to currents in Earth's iron-rich core, is dominant. Rather than having a spherical shape around Earth, the magnetosphere has the look of a teardrop, with a tail pointing away from the Sun. On Earth's sunward side, solar winds serve to compress the magnetosphere, while on Earth's opposite side, interaction with the solar wind draws the magnetosphere into a tail that extends well beyond the orbit of the Moon.

Earth has a relatively strong magnetic field, at least in comparison to the other inner planets. Mercury and Venus have no detectable magnetic field, and if Mars has one, it is extremely weak. In this respect, Earth is quite dissimilar to the other inner planets.

In this question, you are asked to explain why the author mentions "a teardrop" in the passage. To answer this question, you must look at the information around *a teardrop* to see how it fits into the ideas around it. The author states that *the magnetosphere has the look of a teardrop, with a tail pointing away from the Sun.* From this, it can be determined that the author mentions *a teardrop* in order *to indicate the shape of the magnetosphere.* To answer this question, you should click on the last answer.

Now look at another example, one that asks you about the rhetorical purpose of certain words in the passage.

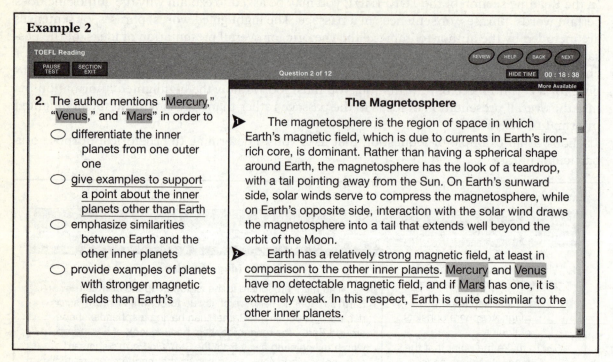

Example 2

2. The author mentions "Mercury," "Venus," and "Mars" in order to
- ○ differentiate the inner planets from one outer one
- ○ give examples to support a point about the inner planets other than Earth
- ○ emphasize similarities between Earth and the other inner planets
- ○ provide examples of planets with stronger magnetic fields than Earth's

The Magnetosphere

➊   The magnetosphere is the region of space in which Earth's magnetic field, which is due to currents in Earth's iron-rich core, is dominant. Rather than having a spherical shape around Earth, the magnetosphere has the look of a teardrop, with a tail pointing away from the Sun. On Earth's sunward side, solar winds serve to compress the magnetosphere, while on Earth's opposite side, interaction with the solar wind draws the magnetosphere into a tail that extends well beyond the orbit of the Moon.

➋   Earth has a relatively strong magnetic field, at least in comparison to the other inner planets. Mercury and Venus have no detectable magnetic field, and if Mars has one, it is extremely weak. In this respect, Earth is quite dissimilar to the other inner planets.

In this question, you are asked to explain why the author mentions "Mercury," "Venus," and "Mars" in the passage. To answer this question, you must look at the information around *Mercury, Venus,* and *Mars* in the passage. The author states that *Earth has a relatively strong magnetic field, at least in comparison to the other inner planets* and that *Earth is quite dissimilar to the other inner planets.* From this, it can be determined that the author's purpose in mentioning *Mercury, Venus,* and *Mars* is to *give examples to support a point about the inner planets other than Earth.* To answer this question, you should click on the second answer.

The following chart outlines the key information that you should remember about questions testing rhetorical purpose.

QUESTIONS ABOUT RHETORICAL PURPOSE	
HOW TO IDENTIFY THE QUESTION	**Why** does the author . . . The author mentions X **in order to** . . .
WHERE TO FIND THE ANSWER	The targeted information is highlighted in the passage.
HOW TO ANSWER THE QUESTION	1. Study the highlighted information carefully. 2. Study the context around the highlighted information, and ask yourself how the highlighted information is related to the context around it. 3. Draw a conclusion about the purpose of the highlighted information. 4. Read the answer choices, and eliminate any definitely wrong answers. 5. Choose the best answer from the remaining choices.

READING EXERCISE 8: Study each of the passages, and choose the best answers to the questions that follow.

PASSAGE ONE *(Questions 1–4)*

Paragraph

Xerography

1   One more familiar use of electrochemistry that has made its way into the mainstream is xerography, a process for replicating documents that is dependent on photoconductive materials. A photoconductive material is an insulator in the dark but becomes a conductor when exposed to bright light. When a photocopy is being made, an image of a document is projected onto the surface of a rotating drum, and bright light causes the photoconductive material on the surface of the drum to become conductive.

2   As a result of the conductivity, the drum loses its charge in the lighted areas, and toner (small grains to which dry ink adheres) attaches itself only to the darker parts of the image. The grains are then carried to a sheet of paper and fused with heat. When a laser printer is used, the image is projected by means of a laser beam, which creates a brighter light and a greater contrast between lighter and darker areas and therefore results in sharper printed images.

1. The author begins the first paragraph with "One more familiar use of electrochemistry" in order to

   (A) explain that xerography is one of the less familiar uses of electrochemistry

   (B) make it clear that electrochemistry requires photoconductive materials

   (C) show that xerography is the only known use for electrochemistry

   (D) indicate that other less familiar uses have already been discussed

2. Why does the author explain that "A photoconductive material is an insulator in the dark but becomes a conductor when exposed to bright light"?

   (A) It gives an explanation of a property that is necessary for xerography.

   (B) It indicates that bright light is required for insulation to take place.

   (C) It gives one example of a successful xerographic process.

   (D) It explains the role of insulation in xerography.

3. The author places the phrase "small grains to which dry ink adheres" in parentheses in order to

   (A) provide information that contradicts the previous statement

   (B) provide another example of conductivity

   (C) provide further detail information about toner

   (D) provide an alternate explanation for the effectiveness of toner

4. Why is "a laser printer" mentioned?

   (A) It is an alternative to xerography.

   (B) It is a way of duplicating without using electrochemistry.

   (C) It is a second example of xerography.

   (D) It is a less effective type of xerography than is a photocopier.

PASSAGE TWO *(Questions 5–9)*

Paragraph

Demographic Change

▶**1**   By the end of the 1920s, American society had undergone a long and historic demographic change. Since the 1870s, the country had been moving from a more rural mode that was based on high birthrates—as high as fifty births annually per thousand people in the early nineteenth century—to a more metropolitan mode. Prior to the 1870s, the population of the country was increasing by about a third every decade; however, by the end of the 1920s, a radical about-face had taken place.

▶**2**   One major factor to affect the demographics of the country during this period was a dramatic decrease in birthrates. The trend during this era was more pronounced in urban areas but also had an effect in rural areas. As a result of the trend toward smaller families, particularly in cities, the birthrate was down to 27.7 births annually per thousand women by 1920 and had dropped even further—to 21.3 births annually per thousand women—by 1930.

▶**3**   At the same time, the deathrate, too, was falling. Urban living led to better sanitation, refrigeration, and water purification; it also resulted in better medical care as doctors and hospitals were more readily available. Most likely as a result of these factors, there were only eleven deaths per thousand annually by the early 1920s, which was half the rate of the 1880s.

---

5. Why does the author include the phrase "as high as fifty births annually per thousand people in the early nineteenth century" in paragraph 1?

Ⓐ To show that metropolitan areas of the country had higher birthrates than rural areas

Ⓑ To provide statistical evidence of the elevated birthrate prior to the 1870s

Ⓒ To quantify what had happened with the American population in the previous century

Ⓓ To argue against the belief that the demographics of the country had changed

6. The author uses the word "however" in paragraph 1 in order

Ⓐ to make it clear that an extreme change had taken place

Ⓑ to emphasize how tremendously the population was increasing

Ⓒ to point out an alternate explanation for the change

Ⓓ to indicate a difference of opinion with other demographers

7. The author includes the word "too" in paragraph 3

Ⓐ to indicate that both the birthrate and the deathrate were holding steady

Ⓑ to show that the rural mode was similar to the metropolitan mode

Ⓒ to clarify the explanation that population trends before and after 1870 were similar

Ⓓ to emphasize that paragraph 3 discusses a second factor in the demographic change

8. Why does the author mention "better medical care" in paragraph 3?

Ⓐ It helps to explain why the birthrate is increasing.

Ⓑ It is an example of a factor that contributed to the improved birthrate.

Ⓒ It helps to explain why the deathrate is increasing.

Ⓓ It is an example of a factor that contributed to the improved deathrate.

9. The author includes the expression "Most likely" in paragraph 3 to show

Ⓐ that the data about the average number of deaths was not verified

Ⓑ that doctors and hospitals may not have actually been more available

Ⓒ that other factors may have contributed to the decreasing deathrate

Ⓓ that the deathrate may not have decreased as much as stated

PASSAGE THREE *(Questions 10–14)*

Paragraph

The Hubble Telescope

1 The Hubble telescope was launched into space with great fanfare on April 25, 1990. Although there are many powerful telescopes at various locations on Earth, the Hubble telescope was expected to be able to provide considerably better information because it would be able to operate from the vacuum of space, without interference from the Earth's atmosphere. By launching the Hubble telescope into space, NASA was, in essence, placing an observatory above the Earth's atmosphere.

2 Unfortunately, the Hubble telescope was initially delayed in relaying its first pictures back from space due to a simple mathematical miscalculation. The Hubble telescope relies upon certain stars to orient its observations, and astronomers working on the pointing instructions for the telescope used charts created in 1950, with adjustments for the movements of the stars in the ensuing period. In making these adjustments, however, astronomers added the amount of the adjustment rather than subtracting it—a simple checkbook-balancing error. The adjustment was a change of only half a degree, but by adding half a degree rather than subtracting it, the telescope's aim was misdirected by millions of miles.

10. Why does the author mention "many powerful telescopes at various locations on Earth" in paragraph 1?

   Ⓐ To emphasize the need for telescopes at various locations on Earth
   Ⓑ To show that the Hubble telescope was different from existing telescopes
   Ⓒ To indicate how the atmosphere improves the quality of information from space
   Ⓓ To emphasize the similarities between the Hubble telescope and other telescopes

11. The author uses the phrase "in essence" in paragraph 2 in order to indicate that the information that follows the phrase

   Ⓐ provides a simplified description of a previously stated situation
   Ⓑ indicates the cause of a previously stated effect
   Ⓒ provides further details about a previously stated main idea
   Ⓓ indicates the classification to which previously stated examples belong

12. Why does the author begin paragraph 2 with "Unfortunately"?

   Ⓐ It indicates that NASA has been unhappy with all of Hubble's photographs.
   Ⓑ It shows that NASA's plan to use stars to orient the Hubble telescope was misguided.
   Ⓒ It emphasizes the need to have telescopes on Earth.
   Ⓓ It indicates that high expectations were not initially met.

13. The author mentions "a simple checkbook-balancing error" in paragraph 2 in order to suggest that

   Ⓐ the astronomers must have difficulties with their checkbooks
   Ⓑ the adjustment made by the astronomers should have been more than half a degree
   Ⓒ a more balanced approach was needed when making adjustments
   Ⓓ the mistake made by the astronomers was a simple, everyday error

14. Why does the author mention the detail "millions of miles" in paragraph 2?

   Ⓐ It reinforces the idea that the mistake had a huge effect.
   Ⓑ It emphasizes the wide range of the Hubble telescope.
   Ⓒ It demonstrates that the Hubble telescope travels long distances.
   Ⓓ It helps the reader to understand how powerful the Hubble telescope is.

PASSAGE FOUR (Questions 15–19)

Paragraph

Territoriality

1 In many species, members of the species exhibit aggressive behavior toward one another, often with a focus on territoriality, the fight for exclusive control of a particular area. The level of violence in territorial aggression varies widely from species to species, though few species fight other members of the species to death and instead rely on non-lethal contests for control of territory that involves noise-making maneuvers such as roaring or hissing or aggressive posturing or gestures.

2 Most bird species are known to be territorial to some degree, though the territorial behaviors exhibited by most species are limited to singing contests, which can go on for days, or threatening postures with wings lifted or extended. The swan, on the other hand, is quite unlike other birds in this respect. The swan may seem particularly elegant and serene as it glides across the surface of a lake; however, male swans are, in reality, quite territorial and will fight other male swans for the exclusive use of a lake no matter how large the lake is. Males will engage in ferocious contests, with their necks entwined as they attempt to cause mortal injury to each other.

15. Why does the author include "the fight for exclusive control of a particular area" in paragraph 1?

  Ⓐ It presents an argument against a previously stated point.
  Ⓑ It provides a definition of a previously stated term.
  Ⓒ It presents a second area of focus of aggressive behavior.
  Ⓓ It introduces a new idea to be further developed in the paragraph.

16. The author uses the word "instead" in paragraph 1 to show that the information that follows

  Ⓐ contradicts what precedes it
  Ⓑ expands upon what precedes it
  Ⓒ provides an example of what precedes it
  Ⓓ explains an effect of what precedes it

17. Why does the author mention "singing contests" in paragraph 2?

  Ⓐ To demonstrate that birds create beautiful sounds
  Ⓑ To provide an example of unusual behavior by birds
  Ⓒ To show how violently aggressive some bird behavior is
  Ⓓ To demonstrate that some types of territorial behaviors are not very aggressive

18. The author discusses the "swan" in paragraph 2 to provide an example of

  Ⓐ a bird that makes threatening postures with its wings
  Ⓑ a bird whose territorial behavior is extremely aggressive
  Ⓒ non-lethal contests for control of territory
  Ⓓ the limited aggressive behavior generally exhibited by birds

19. The author mentions "their necks entwined" in paragraph 2 in order

  Ⓐ to indicate that swans are really rather affectionate
  Ⓑ to emphasize how long swans' necks are
  Ⓒ to make the point that the swans are only pretending to hurt one another
  Ⓓ to create a mental image for the reader of fighting swans

READING EXERCISE (Skills 7–8): Read the passage.

Paragraph
Ella Deloria

1   It was not until her posthumous novel *Waterlily* was published in 1988 that Ella C. Deloria became known for her literary ability in addition to her already-established reputation in the academic arena of linguistics and ethnology. During her lifetime, she was recognized for the linguistic ability and cultural sensitivity that went into the production of a collection of traditional short stories entitled *Dakota Texts* (1932). After her death, her versions of a number of longer traditional stories and the novel *Waterlily* were published; with the publication of *Waterlily* came the recognition of her true literary ability and the awareness that it was the strength of her literary ability, in addition to her linguistic expertise and her deep cultural understanding, that had made her versions of traditional stories so compelling.

2   Ella Cara Deloria was born into a Nakota-speaking family in 1889; however, she grew up among the Lakota people in North Dakota, where her father was a leader in the Episcopal Church. Her father, the son of a traditional Nakota medicine man, valued both the cultural traditions of his family and those of the country of his citizenship. As a result, Deloria primarily spoke Nakota at home and Lakota when she was out in the community, and she was well versed there in the cultural traditions of her Sioux ancestors (with a complex kinship structure in which all of a child's father's brothers are also considered fathers, all of a child's mother's sisters are also considered mothers, and all of the children of all these mothers and fathers are considered siblings). Her education, however, was in English, at the Episcopalian Saint Elizabeth Mission School and the All Saints School. After high school, she attended Oberlin College in Ohio for one year, and then she transferred to Columbia University to study linguistics under Franz Boas, the founder of American Indian linguistics.

3   After graduating from Columbia, she was encouraged by Boas to collect and record traditional Lakota stories. She was in a unique position to take on this task because of her fluency in the Lakota language as well as in English, her understanding from childhood of the complexities and subtleties of Lakota culture, and her linguistic training from Columbia. The result of her research was the *Dakota Texts,* a bilingual collection of sixty-four short stories. To create this remarkable work, Deloria was able to elicit stories from venerable Sioux elders, without need for translators and with an awareness of appropriately respectful behavior. She listened to the stories as numerous generations had before her, and then, unlike previous generations, recorded them in writing—initially in Lakota and later in English. She transcribed them essentially as they were told but with her own understanding of the nuances of what was being told.

4   In addition to the shorter stories that were published in *Dakota Texts,* Deloria spent 1937 working on transcribing a number of longer and more complicated texts, which were not published until after her death. "Iron Hawk: Oglala Culture Hero" (1993) presents the diverse elements of the culture-hero genre; "The Buffalo People" (1994) focuses on the importance of tribal education in building character; "A Sioux Captive" (1994) tells the story of a Lakota woman who rescued her husband from the Crow; "The Prairie Dogs" (1994) describes the sense of hope offered by the Sioux warrior-society ceremonies and dances.

5   Her novel *Waterlily,* which was first published forty years after it was completed and seventeen years after her death, reflects her true literary talent as well as her accumulated understanding of traditional culture and customs. The novel recounts the fictional story of the difficult life of the title character, with a horrendous childhood experience as witness to a deadly enemy raid and a first marriage terminated by the untimely death of her husband in a smallpox epidemic, and comes to a close with the hopeful expectations of an impending second marriage. At the same time, it presents a masterful account of life in a nineteenth-century Sioux community with its detailed descriptions of interpersonal relationships and attitudes, everyday tasks and routines, and special ceremonies and celebrations.

GLOSSARY
The *Lakota, Nakota,* and *Dakota* are related groups of people who are part of the Sioux nation.

Refer to this version of the passage to answer the questions that follow.

Ella Deloria

1   It was not until her posthumous novel *Waterlily* was published in 1988 that Ella C. Deloria became known for her literary ability in addition to her already-established reputation in the academic arena of linguistics and ethnology. During her lifetime, she was recognized for the linguistic ability and cultural sensitivity that went into the production of a collection of traditional short stories entitled *Dakota Texts* (1932). After her death, her versions of a number of longer traditional stories and the novel *Waterlily* were published; with the publication of *Waterlily* came the recognition of her true literary ability and the awareness that it was the strength of her literary ability, in addition to her linguistic expertise and her deep cultural understanding, that had made her versions of traditional stories so compelling.

2   Ella Cara Deloria was born into a Nakota-speaking family in 1889; however, she grew up among the Lakota people in North Dakota, where her father was a leader in the Episcopal Church. Her father, the son of a traditional Nakota medicine man, valued both the cultural traditions of his family and those of the country of his citizenship. As a result, Deloria primarily spoke Nakota at home and Lakota when she was out in the community, and she was well versed there in the cultural traditions of her Sioux ancestors (with a complex kinship structure in which all of a child's father's brothers are also considered fathers, all of a child's mother's sisters are also considered mothers, and all of the children of all these mothers and fathers are considered siblings). Her education, however, was in English, at the Episcopalian Saint Elizabeth Mission School and the All Saints School. After high school, she attended Oberlin College in Ohio for one year, and then she transferred to Columbia University to study linguistics under Franz Boas, the founder of American Indian linguistics.

3   After graduating from Columbia, she was encouraged by Boas to collect and record traditional Lakota stories. She was in a unique position to take on this task because of her fluency in the Lakota language as well as in English, her understanding from childhood of the complexities and subtleties of Lakota culture, and her linguistic training from Columbia. The result of her research was the *Dakota Texts,* a bilingual collection of sixty-four short stories. To create this remarkable work, Deloria was able to elicit stories from venerable Sioux elders, without need for translators and with an awareness of appropriately respectful behavior. She listened to the stories as numerous generations had before her, and then, unlike previous generations, recorded them in writing—initially in Lakota and later in English. She transcribed them essentially as they were told but with her own understanding of the nuances of what was being told.

4   In addition to the shorter stories that were published in *Dakota Texts,* Deloria spent 1937 working on transcribing a number of longer and more complicated texts, which were not published until after her death. "Iron Hawk: Oglala Culture Hero" (1993) presents the diverse elements of the culture-hero genre; "The Buffalo People" (1994) focuses on the importance of tribal education in building character; "A Sioux Captive" (1994) tells the story of a Lakota woman who rescued her husband from the Crow; "The Prairie Dogs" (1994) describes the sense of hope offered by the Sioux warrior-society ceremonies and dances.

5   Her novel *Waterlily,* which was first published forty years after it was completed and seventeen years after her death, reflects her true literary talent as well as her accumulated understanding of traditional culture and customs. The novel recounts the fictional story of the difficult life of the title character, with a horrendous childhood experience as witness to a deadly enemy raid and a first marriage terminated by the untimely death of her husband in a smallpox epidemic, and comes to a close with the hopeful expectations of an impending second marriage. At the same time, it presents a masterful account of life in a nineteenth-century Sioux community with its detailed descriptions of interpersonal relationships and attitudes, everyday tasks and routines, and special ceremonies and celebrations.

GLOSSARY
The *Lakota, Nakota,* and *Dakota* are related groups of people that are part of the Sioux nation.

Questions

1. It can be inferred from paragraph 1 that, while she was alive, Ella Deloria
   - Ⓐ did little to make use of her education in linguistics
   - Ⓑ achieved acclaim more for her transcriptions than for her novel
   - Ⓒ was the published author of a number of types of fiction and nonfiction
   - Ⓓ was recognized for the literary maturity of her novel

2. Why does the author use the word "however" in paragraph 2?
   - Ⓐ To emphasize that she was born in an earlier century
   - Ⓑ To clarify the differences between the Lakota and the Dakota
   - Ⓒ To show that she was raised in a different environment from the one where she was born
   - Ⓓ To demonstrate that she was very different from other members of her family

3. Why does the author include in paragraph 2 the information "with a complex kinship structure in which all of a child's father's brothers are also considered fathers, all of a child's mother's sisters are also considered mothers, and all of the children of all these mothers and fathers are considered siblings" in parentheses?
   - Ⓐ To provide details to emphasize how the Nakota and the Lakota differed
   - Ⓑ To introduce the idea that Deloria's education in English was completely different from her home life
   - Ⓒ To provide an alternate explanation for Deloria's use of Nakota at home and Lakota in the community
   - Ⓓ To provide an example of one cultural tradition of the Sioux

4. Why does the author begin paragraph 3 with "After graduating from Columbia"?
   - Ⓐ To indicate that paragraph 3 follows paragraph 2 in chronological order
   - Ⓑ To clarify that paragraph 3 describes Deloria's education at Columbia
   - Ⓒ To recognize the importance of education throughout Deloria's life
   - Ⓓ To demonstrate that paragraph 3 provides examples of a concept presented in paragraph 2

5. It is implied in paragraph 3 that *Dakota Texts* was written
   - Ⓐ only in English
   - Ⓑ only in Dakota
   - Ⓒ in Dakota and Lakota
   - Ⓓ in Lakota and English

6. Why does the author mention "an awareness of appropriately respectful behavior" in paragraph 3?
   - Ⓐ To show one way that Deloria was qualified to elicit stories from Sioux elders
   - Ⓑ To show that Deloria's linguistic training had been effective
   - Ⓒ To show the difference between Deloria's transcriptions and her novel
   - Ⓓ To show why Deloria needed to work with a translator

7. It can be inferred from paragraph 4 that "Iron Hawk: Oglala Culture Hero" was published
   - Ⓐ in the same year that it was written
   - Ⓑ just prior to Deloria's death
   - Ⓒ long after it was transcribed
   - Ⓓ long before *Waterlily* was published

8. Why does the author discuss "The Prairie Dogs" in paragraph 4?
   - Ⓐ It was written by Deloria.
   - Ⓑ It describes Deloria's own life story.
   - Ⓒ It provides insight into rituals and dances.
   - Ⓓ It was one of the earliest short stories that Deloria transcribed.

9. It can be inferred from the passage that *Waterlily* was completed

Ⓐ in 1937

Ⓑ in 1948

Ⓒ in 1954

Ⓓ in 1988

10. Why does the author mention "the untimely death of her husband in a smallpox epidemic" in paragraph 5?

Ⓐ It provides a harsh example of Waterlily's difficult life.

Ⓑ It provides evidence of the historical existence of Waterlily.

Ⓒ It demonstrates how unusual Waterlily's life in a nineteenth-century Sioux community was.

Ⓓ It reinforces the overall message of hopelessness of *Waterlily*.

READING REVIEW EXERCISE (Skills 1–8): Read the passage.

Paragraph   **Early Autos**

▶ **1**   America's passion for the automobile developed rather quickly in the beginning of the twentieth century. At the turn of that century, there were few automobiles, or horseless carriages, as they were called at the time, and those that existed were considered frivolous playthings of the rich. They were rather fragile machines that sputtered and smoked and broke down often; they were expensive toys that could not be counted on to get one where one needed to go; they could only be afforded by the wealthy class, who could afford both the expensive upkeep and the inherent delays that resulted from the use of a machine that tended to break down time and again. These early automobiles required repairs so frequently both because their engineering was at an immature stage and because roads were unpaved and often in poor condition. Then, when breakdowns occurred, there were no services such as roadside gas stations or tow trucks to assist drivers needing help in their predicament. Drivers of horse-drawn carriages considered the horseless mode of transportation foolhardy, preferring instead to rely on their four-legged "engines," which they considered a tremendously more dependable and cost-effective means of getting around.

▶ **2**   Automobiles in the beginning of the twentieth century were quite unlike today's models. Many of them were electric cars, even though the electric models had quite a limited range and needed to be recharged frequently at electric charging stations; many others were powered by steam, though it was often required that drivers of steam cars be certified steam engineers due to the dangers inherent in operating a steam-powered machine. The early automobiles also lacked much emphasis on body design; in fact, they were often little more than benches on wheels, though by the end of the first decade of the century they had progressed to leather-upholstered chairs or sofas on thin wheels that absorbed little of the incessant pounding associated with the movement of these machines.

▶ **3**   In spite of the rather rough and undeveloped nature of these early horseless carriages, something about them grabbed people's imagination, and their use increased rapidly, though not always smoothly. In the first decade of the last century, roads were shared by the horse-drawn and horseless variety of carriages, a situation that was rife with problems and required strict measures to control the incidents and accidents that resulted when two such different modes of transportation were used in close proximity. New York City, for example, banned horseless vehicles from Central Park early in the century because they had been involved in so many accidents, often causing injury or death; then, in 1904, New York state felt that it was necessary to control automobile traffic by placing speed limits of 20 miles per hour in open areas, 15 miles per hour in villages, and 10 miles per hour in cities or areas of congestion. However, the measures taken were less a means of limiting use of the automobile and more a way of controlling the effects of an invention whose use increased dramatically in a relatively short period of time. Under 5,000 automobiles were sold in the United States for a total cost of approximately $5 million in 1900, while considerably more cars, 181,000, were sold for $215 million in 1910, and by the middle of the 1920s, automobile manufacturing had become the top industry in the United States and accounted for 6 percent of the manufacturing in the country.

Refer to this version of the passage to answer the questions that follow.

Early Autos

Paragraph

▶1   America's passion for the automobile developed rather quickly in the beginning of the twentieth century. At the turn of that century, there were few automobiles, or horseless carriages, as they were called at the time, and those that existed were considered frivolous playthings of the rich. **5A** They were rather fragile machines that sputtered and smoked and broke down often; they were expensive toys that could not be counted on to get one where one needed to go; they could only be afforded by the wealthy class, who could afford both the expensive upkeep and the inherent delays that resulted from the use of a machine that tended to break down time and again. **5B** These early automobiles required repairs so frequently both because their engineering was at an immature stage and because roads were unpaved and often in poor condition. **5C** Then, when breakdowns occurred, there were no services such as roadside gas stations or tow trucks to assist drivers needing help in their predicament. **5D** Drivers of horse-drawn carriages considered the horseless mode of transportation foolhardy, preferring instead to rely on their four-legged "engines," which they considered a tremendously more dependable and cost-effective means of getting around.

▶2   Automobiles in the beginning of the twentieth century were quite unlike today's models. Many of them were electric cars, even though the electric models had quite a limited range and needed to be recharged frequently at electric charging stations; many others were powered by steam, though it was often required that drivers of steam cars be certified steam engineers due to the dangers inherent in operating a steam-powered machine. The early automobiles also lacked much emphasis on body design; in fact, they were often little more than benches on wheels, though by the end of the first decade of the century they had progressed to leather-upholstered chairs or sofas on thin wheels that absorbed little of the incessant pounding associated with the movement of these machines.

▶3   In spite of the rather rough and undeveloped nature of these early horseless carriages, something about them grabbed people's imagination, and their use increased rapidly, though not always smoothly. In the first decade of the last century, roads were shared by the horse-drawn and horseless variety of carriages, a situation that was rife with problems and required strict measures to control the incidents and accidents that resulted when two such different modes of transportation were used in close proximity. New York City, for example, banned horseless vehicles from Central Park early in the century because they had been involved in so many accidents, often causing injury or death; then, in 1904, New York state felt that it was necessary to control automobile traffic by placing speed limits of 20 miles per hour in open areas, 15 miles per hour in villages, and 10 miles per hour in cities or areas of congestion. However, the measures taken were less a means of limiting use of the automobile and more a way of controlling the effects of an invention whose use increased dramatically in a relatively short period of time. Under 5,000 automobiles were sold in the United States for a total cost of approximately $5 million in 1900, while considerably more cars, 181,000, were sold for $215 million in 1910, and by the middle of the 1920s, automobile manufacturing had become the top industry in the United States and accounted for 6 percent of the manufacturing in the country.

Questions

1. Based on the information in paragraph 1, who would have been most likely to own a car in 1900?

    Ⓐ A skilled laborer

    Ⓑ A successful investor

    Ⓒ A scholarship student

    Ⓓ A rural farmer

2. The word "frivolous" in paragraph 1 is closest in meaning to

    Ⓐ trivial

    Ⓑ delicate

    Ⓒ essential

    Ⓓ natural

3. It is indicated in paragraph 1 that it was necessary to repair early autos because of

    Ⓐ the elaborate engines

    Ⓑ the lack of roads

    Ⓒ the immature drivers

    Ⓓ the rough roads

4. The author refers to "four-legged 'engines'" in paragraph 1 in order to indicate that

    Ⓐ early autos had little more than an engine and wheels

    Ⓑ it was foolish to travel on a four-legged animal

    Ⓒ horses were an effective mode of transportation

    Ⓓ automobile engines were evaluated in terms of their horsepower

5. Look at the four squares [■] that indicate where the following sentence could be added to paragraph 1.

    These horrendous road conditions forced drivers to use their automobiles on grooved, rutted, and bumpy roads.

    Where would the sentence best fit? Click on a square [■] to add the sentence to the passage.

6. The phrase "many others" in paragraph 2 refers to

    Ⓐ automobiles in the beginning of the twentieth century

    Ⓑ today's models

    Ⓒ electric models

    Ⓓ electric charging stations

7. It is stated in paragraph 2 that the owners of steam-powered cars

    Ⓐ sometimes had to demonstrate knowledge of steam engineering

    Ⓑ had to hire drivers to operate their cars

    Ⓒ often had to take their automobiles to charging stations

    Ⓓ were often in danger because of the limited range of their automobiles

8. Why does the author mention "benches on wheels" in paragraph 2?

    Ⓐ To show how remarkably automobile design had progressed

    Ⓑ To show that car designs of the time were neither complex nor comfortable

    Ⓒ To indicate that early automobiles had upholstered chairs or sofas

    Ⓓ To emphasize how the early automobiles were designed to absorb the pounding of the machine on the road

9. The word "incessant" in paragraph 2 is closest in meaning to

    Ⓐ heavy

    Ⓑ bothersome

    Ⓒ jolting

    Ⓓ continual

10. The phrase "rife with" in paragraph 3 could be replaced by

    Ⓐ full of

    Ⓑ surrounded by

    Ⓒ dangerous due to

    Ⓓ occurring as a result of

11. It can be inferred from paragraph 3 that the government of New York state believed that

    Ⓐ all horseless vehicles should be banned from all public parks

    Ⓑ strict speed limits should be placed on horse-drawn carriages

    Ⓒ horseless and horse-drawn vehicles should not travel on the same roads

    Ⓓ it was safer for cars to travel faster where there was less traffic and there were fewer people

12. Which of the sentences below best expresses the essential information in the highlighted sentence in paragraph 3? *Incorrect* choices change the meaning in important ways or leave out essential information.

Ⓐ It was necessary to take a measured approach in dealing with inventions such as the automobile.

Ⓑ The various laws were needed because the use of automobiles grew so fast.

Ⓒ The dramatic look of the automobile changed considerably over a short period of time.

Ⓓ It was important to lawmakers to discover the causes of the problems relating to automobiles.

13. According to paragraph 3, it is NOT true that

Ⓐ the total cost of the automobiles sold in the United States in 1900 was around $5 million

Ⓑ sales of cars increased by more than 175,000 from 1900 to 1910

Ⓒ automobile manufacturing was the top U.S. industry in 1920

Ⓓ automobile manufacturing represented more than 5 percent of total U.S. manufacturing by 1925

READING TO LEARN

Reading Skill 9: SELECT SUMMARY INFORMATION

In the Reading section of the TOEFL iBT, you may be asked to complete a summary chart in which the overall topic is given and you must determine the major supporting ideas. This kind of question has three correct answers and is worth 2 points. You will receive 2 points for 3 correct answers, 1 point for 2 correct answers, and 0 points for either 1 or 0 correct answers.

To complete this type of question successfully, you must be able to recognize the rhetorical pattern of the information in the passage (i.e., compare and contrast, cause and effect, argument supported by reasons), including the major ideas and the critical supporting information. Look at an example of a question that asks you to select summary information.

Example - Screen 1

TOEFL Reading

| PAUSE TEST | SECTION EXIT | | Question 1 of 12 | HIDE TIME 00 : 18 : 38 |

More Available

The Great Compromise

At the Constitutional Convention of 1787, numerous plans for the structure of the legislative branch of government were proposed and debated extensively. There was a great amount of disagreement over how the legislature should be structured, with the greatest amount of discord arising between the smaller states and the larger states. The smaller and less populous states wanted all states to be represented equally in the legislature, while the larger and more populous states favored representation according to population. The final decision reached at the convention, which has come to be known as the Great Compromise, was to create a bicameral legislature with a Senate and a House of Representatives: each state was given two senators so that the Senate would reflect the will of each state equally, and seats were to be apportioned to the House of Representatives according to population so that larger states would have a stronger voice in the House.

To return to the question, click on View Question.

The passage is included on one screen, and the question is included on a different screen. You can click back and forth between the question and the passage while you are answering this type of question.

Example – Screen 2

Directions: An introductory sentence for a brief summary of the passage is provided below. Complete the summary by selecting the THREE answer choices that express the most important ideas in the passage. Some sentences do not belong in the summary because they express ideas that are not presented in the passage or are minor ideas in the passage. **This question is worth 2 points** (2 points for 3 correct answers, 1 point for 2 correct answers, and 0 points for 1 or 0 correct answers).

This passage discusses how the legislative branch of the U.S. government came to be organized.
•
•
•

Answer Choices (choose 3 to complete the chart):

A compromise was reached that gave some advantages to both smaller and larger states.

Many different plans were submitted at the Constitutional Convention.

States with smaller populations preferred that each state be given equal representation.

The New Jersey Plan was a plan submitted to advance the rights of smaller states.

The number of representatives in the House of Representatives would be the same for each state.

States with larger populations wanted representation to be based on population.

The three correct answer choices should be selected because they summarize the major points in the passage. The passage states that *there was a great amount of disagreement,* that the disagreement was that *the smaller and less populous states wanted all states to be represented equally in the legislature, while the larger and more populous states favored representation according to population,* and that *the final decision . . . was . . . the Great Compromise,* in which *the Senate would reflect the will of each state equally* and *the larger states would have a stronger voice in the House.* From this, it can be determined that the most important factors in the passage are that *states with smaller populations preferred that each state be given equal representation,* that *states with larger populations wanted representation to be based on population,* and that *a compromise was reached that gave some advantages to both smaller and larger states.*

The remaining answer choices are not part of the solution for a variety of reasons. The statement that *many different plans were submitted at the Constitutional Convention* is mentioned in the passage but is *not a major factor* in support of the topic. The statement that *the New Jersey Plan was a plan submitted to advance the rights of smaller states* is not discussed in the passage. The statement that *the number of representatives in the House of Representatives would be the same for each state* is not true according to the passage, which states that *seats were to be apportioned in the House of Representatives according to population so that larger states would have a stronger voice in the House.*

The following chart outlines the key information that you should remember about answering summary information questions.

QUESTIONS ABOUT SUMMARY INFORMATION	
HOW TO IDENTIFY THE QUESTION	A summary information chart is given.
WHERE TO FIND THE ANSWER	Because the answer demonstrates an understanding of the major points and critical supporting information, the information needed to answer the question is found throughout the passage.
HOW TO ANSWER THE QUESTION	1. Read the topic stated in the summary chart carefully. 2. Read the passage, focusing on the main ideas as they relate to the topic stated in the summary chart. 3. Read each answer choice, evaluating whether it is *true* information according to the passage, *false* information according to the passage, or *not discussed* in the passage. 4. Eliminate any answers that are *false* or *not discussed*. 5. For each statement that is *true* according to the passage, evaluate whether it is a *major factor* related to the topic or is a *minor detail*. 6. Select the answers that are true and are major factors as your responses. 7. Partial credit is possible, and your answers may be in any order.
HOW TO SCORE THE RESPONSE	A summary question has 3 correct answers and is worth 2 points. 1. You get 2 points for 3 correct answers. 2. You get 1 point for 2 correct answers. 3. You get 0 points for 1 or 0 correct answers. The answers may be in any order in the chart to be correct.

READING EXERCISE 9: An introductory sentence for a brief summary of each passage is provided below each passage. Complete the summary by selecting the answer choices that express the most important ideas in the passage. Some sentences do not belong in the summary because they express ideas that are not presented in the passage or are minor ideas in the passage.

PASSAGE ONE *(Question 1)*

This question is worth 2 points (2 points for 3 correct answers, 1 point for 2 correct answers, and 0 points for 1 or 0 correct answers).

Island Plant Life

Islands are geographical formations that are completely surrounded by water, yet many islands are covered with a rich assortment of plant life. It may seem surprising that so much plant life exists on many islands, yet there are surprisingly simple explanations as to how the vegetation has been able to establish itself there. Some islands were formerly attached to larger bodies of land, while others were created on their own. Islands that were created when flooding or rising water levels cut them off from their neighbors often still have the plant life that they had before they were cut off. In cases where islands formed out of the ocean, they may have plant life from neighboring lands even though they were never actually attached to the neighboring lands. Winds carry many seeds to islands; some plants produce extremely light seeds that can float thousands of feet above the Earth and then drift down to islands where they can sprout and develop. Birds also carry seeds to islands; as birds move over open stretches of water, they can serve as the transportation system to spread seeds from place to place.

This passage discusses the ways that plant life is able to develop on islands.
•
•
•

Answer Choices (choose 3 to complete the chart):

(1) Some seeds are able to float great distances in the air.

(2) Some plant life existed before islands were cut off from larger bodies of land.

(3) Some islands have many different varieties of plants.

(4) Birds sometimes carry seeds to islands.

(5) Some islands were created when rising water cut them off from larger bodies of land.

(6) Some plant seeds are carried to islands by the wind.

PASSAGE TWO (Question 2)

This question is worth 2 points (2 points for 3 correct answers, 1 point for 2 correct answers, and 0 points for 1 or 0 correct answers).

Paragraph   **Ben and Jerry**

1   All successful businesses are not established and run in the same way, with formal business plans, traditional organizational structures, and a strong focus on profits. Ben Cohen and Jerry Greenfield, the entrepreneurs responsible for the highly successful ice cream business that bears their names, were businessmen with a rather unconventional approach.

2   They were rather unconventional from the start, not choosing to begin their careers by attending one of the elite business schools but instead choosing to take a five-dollar correspondence course from Pennsylvania State University. They had little financial backing to start their business, so they had to cut corners wherever they could; the only location they could afford for the startup of their business was a gas station that they converted to ice cream production. Though this start-up was rather unconventional, they were strongly committed to creating the best ice cream possible, and this commitment to the quality of their product eventually led to considerable success.

3   Even though they became extremely successful, they did not convert to a more conventional style of doing business. In an era where companies were measured on every penny of profit that they managed to squeeze out, Ben and Jerry had a strong belief that business should give back to the community; thus, they donated 7.5 percent of their pretax profit to social causes that they believed in. They also lacked the emphasis on executive salary and benefits packages that so preoccupy other corporations, opting instead for a five-to-one policy in which the salary of the employee receiving the highest pay could never be more than five times the salary of the employee receiving the lowest pay.

This passage discusses Ben and Jerry's unconventional company.
•
•
•

Answer Choices (choose 3 to complete the chart):

(1) They each had a personal commitment to social causes.

(2) They began their business with little background and investment.

(3) They believed strongly in producing a very high-quality product.

(4) They had a salary structure that limits the salaries of high-level executives.

(5) They set aside a noteworthy portion of their profits for social causes.

(6) They borrowed several thousand dollars from friends to start their business.

PASSAGE THREE (Question 3)

This question is worth 2 points (2 points for 3 correct answers, 1 point for 2 correct answers, and 0 points for 1 or 0 correct answers).

Paragraph

The Bald Eagle

When the bald eagle became the national symbol of the United States in 1782, soon after the country was born, it is estimated that there were as many as 75,000 nesting pairs in North America. By the early 1960s, however, the number of nesting pairs had been reduced to only around 450.

The demise of the bald eagle is generally attributed to the effects of the pesticide DDT (dichloro-diphenyl-trichloroethane). This pesticide was used to kill insects harmful to agriculture, thereby increasing agricultural production. One unintended negative result of the use of DDT was that, while it did get rid of the undesirable insects, it also made its way along the food chain into fish, a favorite food source of the bald eagle.

The bald eagle is now protected by federal laws. It was originally protected by the Bald Eagle Act of 1940 and later by the Endangered Species Act of 1973. However, it is not just the laws directly related to endangered species that aided in the resurgence of the bald eagle; its resurgence has also been widely attributed to the banning of DDT in 1972. Today there are more than 5,000 pairs of bald eagles, a tenfold increase over the low point of 450, and the bird was removed from the list of endangered species in July, 1999.

This passage discusses radical shifts in population that the bald eagle has undergone.
•
•
•

Answer Choices (choose 3 to complete the chart):

(1) The numbers of bald eagles was greatly reduced by the 1960s, at least in part due to the effects of a pesticide.

(2) The pesticide DDT was successful in removing undesirable insects.

(3) The bald eagle was named as the national symbol of the United States in the late eighteenth century.

(4) A certain pesticide had a negative effect on the number of bald eagles.

(5) Two different pieces of legislation were enacted thirty-three years apart.

(6) Legislation was specifically designed to protect the bald eagle as well as to outlaw the pesticide DDT.

This question is worth 2 points (2 points for 3 correct answers, 1 point for 2 correct answers, and 0 points for 1 or 0 correct answers).

Paragraph

Modernism in Art

1   A proliferation of varying styles characterized the world of American art and architecture in the period between 1880 and the outbreak of World War II in 1939. In spite of the fact that these various styles often had little in common with each other, they are traditionally clustered under the label of **modernism**. It is thus rather difficult to give a precise definition of modernism, one that encompasses all the characteristics of the artists and architects who are commonly grouped under this label. What modernists do have in common is that their work contains at least one of two characteristics of modernism.

2   One fundamental characteristic of modernism is a demonstration of progressive innovation. In general, a modernist is someone who tries to develop an individual style by adding to or improving upon the style of immediate predecessors. The modernist belief was in starting with the ideas of the mainstream movement and then innovating from the mainstream to improve upon the ideas of predecessors rather than in breaking away from the mainstream to create something entirely new. However, because there were varying ideas on what constituted the mainstream and because the potential innovations emanating from the mainstream were infinite, modernism under this definition could take a myriad of directions.

3   A second fundamental characteristic of modernism was the belief that art could and should reflect the reality of modern life and would not, for example, focus on the lives of society's most privileged members or on otherworld entities such as angels and sprites. Though there was agreement among modernists as to the need for art to reflect modern life, there was far less agreement on what actually constituted modern life. Thus, modern artists and architects reflect very different aspects of modern life in their works.

Though modernism in art shares certain characteristics, these characteristics can be difficult to define precisely.
•
•
•

Answer Choices (choose 3 to complete the chart):

(1) A reflection of the reality of modern life is one aspect of modernism.

(2) There is no universal agreement as to exactly what makes up modern life.

(3) Modernism is a very specific style of art.

(4) Modernism in art improves upon the style of the mainstream.

(5) Many different styles are part of modern art.

(6) It can be difficult to define what the mainstream is.

Reading Skill 10: COMPLETE SCHEMATIC TABLES

In the Reading section of the TOEFL iBT, you may be asked to complete a schematic table. A schematic table is a table that outlines the key information from a passage. This kind of question may have 5 or 7 correct answers. A question that has 5 correct answers is worth 3 points; in this type of question you will receive 3 points for 5 correct answers, 2 points for 4 correct answers, 1 point for 3 correct answers, and 0 points for either 2, 1, or 0 correct answers. A question that has 7 correct answers is worth 4 points; in this type of question you will receive 4 points for 7 correct answers, 3 points for 6 correct answers, 2 points for 5 correct answers, 1 point for 4 correct answers, and 0 points for 3, 2, 1, or 0 correct answers.

To complete this type of question successfully, you must be able to recognize overall organization of the information in the passage, including the major points and the critical supporting information. Look at an example of a question that asks you to complete a schematic table.

Example - Screen 1

TOEFL Reading		REVIEW HELP BACK NEXT
PAUSE TEST SECTION EXIT	Question 1 of 12	HIDE TIME 00 : 18 : 38

More Available

To return to the question, click on View Question.

Pterosaurs

The largest flying reptiles ever to exist were the pterosaurs. These close relatives of dinosaurs, with lightweight frames of hollow bone, could have wingspans up to 40 feet (12 meters) and could weigh up to 220 pounds (100 kilograms). There are two kinds of pterosaurs. The earlier of the two were the long-tailed and short-headed rhamphorhynchoids, which first appeared in the Triassic period and had become extinct by the end of the Jurassic period. The short-tailed and long-headed pterodactyloids appeared shortly before the rhamphorhynchoids disappeared and survived until the end of the Cretaceous period.

The passage is included on one screen, and the question is included on a different screen. You can click back and forth between the question and the passage while you are answering this type of question.

Example – Screen 2

Directions: Select the appropriate phrases from the answer choices, and match them to the type of reptile to which they relate. TWO of the answer choices will not be used. **This question is worth 3 points** (3 points for 5 correct answers, 2 points for 4 correct answers, 1 point for 3 correct answers, and 0 points for 2, 1, or 0 correct answers).

rhamphorhynchoids	• •
pterodactyloids	• • •

Answer Choices (choose 5 to complete the table):

Had short tails and short heads

Had short tails and long heads

Existed from the Triassic period to the Jurassic period

Existed later than the other kind of pterosaur

Existed from the Jurassic period to the Cretaceous period

Had long tails and short heads

Were dinosaurs

The passage discusses *two kinds of pterosaurs.* One is *the long-tailed and short-headed rhamphorhynchoids, which first appeared in the Triassic period and had become extinct by the end of the Jurassic period.* From this, it can be determined that the rhamphorhynchoids *had long tails and short heads* and that they *existed from the Triassic period to the Jurassic period,* so these are the two correct answers that describe rhamphorhynchoids.

The passage goes on to state that *the short-tailed and long-headed pterodactyloids appeared shortly before the rhamphorhynchoids disappeared and survived until the end of the Cretaceous period.* From this, and from the information about rhamphorhynchoids, it can be determined that pterodactyloids *had short tails and long heads,* that they *existed from the Jurassic period to the Cretaceous period,* and that they *existed later than the other kind of pterosaur.*

The remaining answer choices are not a part of the correct solution. The description that they *had short tails and short heads* does not describe either of the types of pterosaurs described in the passage. The description that they *were dinosaurs* describes pterosaurs in general and is not a factor that differentiates rhamphorhynchoids and pterodactyloids.

The following chart outlines the key information that you should remember about completing schematic tables.

QUESTIONS ABOUT SCHEMATIC TABLES	
HOW TO IDENTIFY THE QUESTION	A schematic table is given.
WHERE TO FIND THE ANSWER	Because the answer demonstrates an understanding of the major points and critical supporting information, the information needed to answer the question is found throughout the passage.
HOW TO ANSWER THE QUESTION	1. Look at the information that is provided in the schematic table. 2. Read the passage, focusing on the main ideas as they relate to the topics in the schematic table. 3. Read each answer choice, evaluating whether it is *true* information according to the passage, *false* information according to the passage, or *not discussed* in the passage. 4. Eliminate any answers that are *false* or *not discussed*. 5. Match the *true* answer choices to the correct category in the schematic table. 6. Partial credit is possible, and your answers may appear in any order.
HOW TO SCORE THE RESPONSE	A schematic table question may have 5 or 7 correct answers. A question with 5 correct answers is worth 3 points. 1. You get 3 points for 5 correct answers. 2. You get 2 points for 4 correct answers. 3. You get 1 point for 3 correct answers. 4. You get 0 points for 2, 1, or 0 correct answers. A question with 7 correct answers is worth 4 points. 1. You get 4 points for 7 correct answers. 2. You get 3 points for 6 correct answers. 3. You get 2 points for 5 correct answers. 4. You get 1 point for 4 correct answers. 5. You get 0 points for 3, 2, 1, or 0 correct answers. The answers may be in any order in the correct box to be correct.

READING EXERCISE 10: Study each passage, and complete the schematic table that follows by matching the answer choice to its appropriate position in the table. Some answer choices do not belong in the table because they express ideas that are not presented in the passage or are minor ideas in the passage.

PASSAGE ONE (Question 1)

Paragraph

Sand Dunes

1   Sandy deserts contain enormous volumes of sand eroded from mountains and carried to the deserts by wind or water. The huge quantities of sand that make up sandy deserts are blown about into dunes of various shapes.

2   Ridge dunes form where there are large amounts of sand, generally in the interiors of deserts, and winds blow in one direction. Under these conditions, parallel ridges of sand, known as transverse dunes, form at right angles to the wind.

3   When the direction of the wind changes so that it comes from different directions, star-shaped dunes form from the massive amounts of sand in desert interiors. Star-shaped dunes are relatively stable dunes that reach incredible heights, up to 80 meters high in some deserts, and are quite common in massive deserts such as the Sahara.

4   Crescent dunes form on the edges of deserts where there is less sand and where the winds blow mainly in one direction. These dunes, which are also known as barchan dunes, are less stable than star-shaped dunes and can shift as much as 20 meters per year as winds blow over the outer curves of the crescent in the direction of the pointed ends.

Directions:	Select the appropriate ideas from the answer choices, and match them to the appropriate type of dune. TWO of the answer choices will not be used. **This question is worth 3 points** (3 points for 5 correct answers, 2 points for 4 correct answers, 1 point for 3 correct answers, and 0 points for 2, 1, or 0 correct answers).
ridge dunes	• •
star-shaped dunes	•
crescent dunes	• •

Answer Choices (choose 5 to complete the table):

(1) Form when winds from various directions blow over small amounts of sand

(2) Form when winds from one direction blow over small amounts of sand

(3) Form when winds from various directions blow over large volumes of sand

(4) Form when winds from one direction blow over large volumes of sand

(5) Are circular dunes in the middle of deserts

(6) Are ridges of sand in the middle of deserts

(7) Are generally not found in the middle of deserts

PASSAGE TWO *(Question 2)*

Paragraph

A Surprising Connection

1   It can be quite surprising to understand that the words "buckaroo" and "vaccine" are actually derived from the same source inasmuch as a buckaroo is a casual way of identifying a cowboy and a vaccine is a substance that can be used to prevent disease.

2   The word "buckaroo" might not be easily recognizable at first as a borrowing into English of the Spanish word *vaquero,* which in Spanish refers to a cowboy. The initial letter "v" in Spanish is pronounced with two lips rather than the pronunciation with the upper front teeth and lower lip of an English "v" and can sound more like the letter "b" than the letter "v" to an English speaker; thus, the English variation of the Spanish word begins with a "b" rather than a "v." The English word also begins with the syllable "buck," which is somewhat similar in sound to the first syllable of the Spanish word and is also an easily identifiable word itself in English.

3   The Spanish word *vaquero* comes from *vacca,* the Latin word for "cow." Another word from the same Latin source is "vaccine." In the late eighteenth century, the English physician Edward Jenner discovered that inoculation with a form of cowpox was effective in preventing the dreaded disease smallpox. French chemist Louis Pasteur, who was himself experimenting with a number of varieties of inoculation, used the word "vaccination" for preventative inoculation in general and the word "vaccine" for the substance inoculated in honor of Jenner's earlier contribution to the development of vaccines.

Directions:	Select the appropriate phrases from the answer choices and match them to the pairs of words to which they relate. TWO of the answer choices will not be used. **This question is worth 3 points** (3 points for 5 correct answers, 2 points for 4 correct answers, 1 point for 3 correct answers, and 0 points for 2, 1, or 0 correct answers).
"buckaroo" and *vaquero*	• •
"buckaroo" and "vaccine"	•
vacca **and "vaccine"**	• •

Answer Choices (choose 5 to complete the table):

(1) Are from different languages (Latin and English)

(2) Have the same meaning

(3) Are both Spanish words

(4) Refer to different things (an animal and a substance)

(5) Are found in the same language

(6) Have meanings referring to preventative medicine

(7) Are used in different languages (Spanish and English)

PASSAGE THREE *(Question 3)*

Paragraph

Carnivorous Plants

▶1   Unlike the majority of plants that create their nourishment from sunlight, such as the flowering hyacinth or the leafy coleus or the garden-variety dandelion, a limited number of plants are able to enhance their diet by fortifying it with insects and other small animals to supplement the food that they have produced from sunlight. These carnivorous plants can be categorized as those without moving traps that lure their intended victims and then trap them on a sticky surface or drown them in a pool of fluid and those with active traps—moving parts that ensnare prey—such as the sundew.

▶2   Butterworts are harmless-looking plants with circles of flat and sticky leaves. If an insect is unfortunate enough to land on one of the seemingly inviting leaves, it sticks to the surface of the leaf and eventually dies and is digested by the plant.

▶3   The pitcher plant is a plant that is shaped like a pitcher and has fluid at the bottom. Insects are attracted to the pitcher plant by a nectar around the rim of the pitcher opening; when an insect lands on the rim, it cannot maintain its balance on the slippery surface of the rim and falls into the opening and drowns in the fluid.

▶4   Bladderworts are water plants with traps on their leaves that resemble tiny bubbles. A small animal may swim by the plant, totally oblivious to the danger posed by the harmless-looking bladderwort. If the small animal comes too close to the plant, the bubbles open without warning and the animal is pulled inside the plant and digested.

▶5   Probably the best known of the carnivorous plants is the Venus flytrap. This plant features unusual leaf tips that look like an inviting place for an insect to rest and offers the enticement of promised food. If an unwary ladybug or dragonfly settles on the leaves of the Venus flytrap, the two leaves suddenly snap shut, trapping the insect and creating a delicious meal for the plant.

> **Directions:** Select the appropriate phrases from the answer choices, and match them to the type of carnivorous plant to which they relate. TWO of the answer choices will not be used. **This question is worth 3 points** (3 points for 5 correct answers, 2 points for 4 correct answers, 1 point for 3 correct answers, and 0 points for 2, 1, or 0 correct answers).

those with active traps	• • •
those with inactive traps	• •

Answer Choices (choose 5 to complete the table):

(1) Butterworts

(2) Bladderworts

(3) Dragonflies

(4) Pitcher plants

(5) Venus flytraps

(6) Dandelions

(7) Sundews

PASSAGE FOUR (Question 4)

Paragraph

William Faulkner

1   Author William Faulkner is today recognized as one of America's greatest writers on the basis of a body of novels that so convincingly portray the culture of the South in the years following the Civil War, with its citizens overcome by grief and defeat and trying to cling to old values while struggling to take their place in a changing world. The acclaim that today is Faulkner's, however, was slow in coming.

2   Though Faulkner was praised by some critics and reviewers during the first part of his career, his novels did not sell well and he was considered a fairly marginal author. For the first few decades of his career, he made his living writing magazine articles and working as a screenwriter rather than as a novelist. Throughout this period, he continued to write, though his novels, sometimes noted for the stirring portrait that they presented of life in the post-Civil War South, were generally relegated to the category of strictly regional writing and were not widely appreciated.

3   Beginning in 1946, Faulkner's career took an unexpected and dramatic turn as Faulkner came to be recognized as considerably more than a regional writer. *The Portable Faulkner* was published in that year by Viking Press; two years later he was elected to the prestigious National Academy of Arts and Letters; he was awarded the Nobel Prize for literature in 1949. Over the next decade, his work was recognized in various ways, including a National Book Award and two Pulitzer Prizes, and he became a novelist in residence at the University of Virginia. His success led to a degree of affluence that enabled him to take up the life of a southern gentleman, including horseback riding and fox hunting. Ironically, he died as a result of an accident related to these gentlemanly pursuits, succumbing as a result of injuries suffered during a fall from a horse.

Directions:	Select the appropriate phrases from the answer choices, and match them to the phase of William Faulkner's career to which they relate. TWO of the answer choices will not be used. **This question is worth 4 points** (4 points for 7 correct answers, 3 points for 6 correct answers, 2 points for 5 correct answers, 1 point for 4 correct answers, and 0 points for 3, 2, 1, or 0 correct answers).

Faulkner in the first phase of his career	• • •
Faulkner in the second phase of his career	• • • •

Answer Choices (choose 7 to complete the table):

(1) Was considered one of America's greatest writers

(2) Received a small amount of critical acclaim

(3) Died as a result of a horseback-riding incident

(4) Received numerous awards and acclaim

(5) Was considered merely a regional writer

(6) Wrote novels about various American regions

(7) Made his living as a novelist

(8) Made his living with writing other than novels

(9) Had plenty of time for leisure activities

Paragraph

Species

1   Millions of different species exist on the earth. These millions of species, which have evolved over billions of years, are the result of two distinct but simultaneously occurring processes: the processes of **speciation** and **extinction**.

2   One of the processes that affects the number of species on earth is **speciation**, which results when one species diverges into two distinct species as a result of disparate natural selection in separate environments. Geographic isolation is one common mechanism that fosters speciation; speciation as a result of geographic isolation occurs when two populations of a species become separated for long periods of time into areas with different environmental conditions. After the two populations are separated, they evolve independently; if this divergence continues long enough, members of the two distinct populations eventually become so different genetically that they are two distinct species rather than one. The process of speciation may occur within hundreds of years for organisms that reproduce rapidly, but for most species the process of speciation can take thousands to millions of years. One example of speciation is the early fox, which over time evolved into two distinct species, the gray fox and the arctic fox. The early fox separated into populations which evolved differently in response to very different environments as the populations moved in different directions, one to colder northern climates and the other to warmer southern climates. The northern population adapted to cold weather by developing heavier fur, shorter ears, noses, and legs, and white fur to camouflage itself in the snow. The southern population adapted to warmer weather by developing lighter fur and longer ears, noses, and legs and keeping its darker fur for better camouflage protection.

3   Another of the processes that affects the number of species on earth is **extinction**, which refers to the situation in which a species ceases to exist. When environmental conditions change, a species needs to adapt to the new environmental conditions, or it may become extinct. Extinction of a species is not a rare occurrence but is instead a rather commonplace one: it has, in fact, been estimated that more than 99 percent of the species that have ever existed have become extinct. Extinction may occur when a species fails to adapt to evolving environmental conditions in a limited area, a process known as background extinction. In contrast, a broader and more abrupt extinction, known as mass extinction, may come about as a result of a catastrophic event or global climatic change. When such a catastrophic event or global climatic change occurs, some species are able to adapt to the new environment, while those that are unable to adapt become extinct. From geological and fossil evidence, it appears that at least five great mass extinctions have occurred; the last mass extinction occurred approximately 65 million years ago, when the dinosaurs became extinct after 140 million years of existence on earth, marking the end of the Mesozoic Era and the beginning of the Cenozoic Era.

4   The fact that millions of species are in existence today is evidence that speciation has clearly kept well ahead of extinction. In spite of the fact that there have been numerous periods of mass extinction, there is clear evidence that periods of mass extinction have been followed by periods of dramatic increases in new species to fill the void created by the mass extinctions, though it may take 10 million years or more following a mass extinction for biological diversity to be rebuilt through speciation. When the dinosaurs disappeared 65 million years ago, for example, the evolution and speciation of mammals increased spectacularly over the millions of years that ensued.

1.

Directions:	An introductory sentence for a brief summary of the passage is provided below. Complete the summary by selecting the THREE answer choices that express the most important ideas in the passage. Some sentences do not belong in the summary because they express ideas that are not presented in the passage or are minor ideas in the passage. **This question is worth 2 points** (2 points for 3 correct answers, 1 point for 2 correct answers, and 0 points for 1 or 0 correct answers).
This passage discusses processes affecting the development of millions of species.	
•	
•	
•	

Answer Choices (choose 3 to complete the chart):

(1) Though numerous species have become extinct, far more new species have developed than have been lost.

(2) Only 1 percent of the species that have existed have become extinct.

(3) A single species can develop into distinct species through a process called speciation.

(4) The gray fox and the arctic fox separated into different species early in their development.

(5) Social isolation is a major factor that influences the degree of speciation.

(6) Numerous species become extinct when they fail to adapt to evolving conditions or fail to survive a cataclysmic event.

2.

Directions:	Select the appropriate phrases from the answer choices, and match them to the process to which they relate. TWO of the answer choices will not be used. **This question is worth 3 points** (3 points for 5 correct answers, 2 points for 4 correct answers, 1 point for 3 correct answers, and 0 points for 2, 1, or 0 correct answers).
speciation	• •
extinction	• • •

Answer Choices (choose 5 to complete the table):

(1) Can result from failure to adapt to changing environments

(2) Results in the creation of new species

(3) Results in the merging of different species

(4) Can result from failure to adjust to a cataclysmic event

(5) Can result from separation of populations

(6) Can result from the commingling of different species

(7) Results in the disappearance of a species

READING REVIEW EXERCISE (Skills 1–10): Read the passage.

Paragraph

Decisions

1   In a theoretical model of **decision making**, a decision is defined as the process of selecting one option from among a group of options for implementation. Decisions are formed by a **decision maker**, the one who actually chooses the final option, in conjunction with a **decision unit**, all of those in the organization around the decision maker who take part in the process. In this theoretical model, the members of the decision unit react to an unidentified problem by studying the problem, determining the objectives of the organization, formulating options, evaluating the strengths and weaknesses of each of the options, and reaching a conclusion. Many different factors can have an effect on the decision, including the nature of the problem itself, external forces exerting an influence on the organization, the internal dynamics of the decision unit, and the personality of the decision maker.

2   During recent years, decision making has been studied systematically by drawing from such diverse areas of study as psychology, sociology, business, government, history, mathematics, and statistics. Analyses of decisions often emphasize one of three principal conceptual perspectives (though often the approach that is actually employed is somewhat eclectic).

3   In the oldest of the three approaches, decisions are made by a **rational actor**, who makes a particular decision directly and purposefully in response to a specific threat from the external environment. It is assumed that this rational actor has clear objectives in mind, develops numerous reasonable options, considers the advantages and disadvantages of each option carefully, chooses the best option after careful analysis, and then proceeds to implement it fully. A variation of the rational actor model is a decision maker who is a **satisfier**, one who selects the first satisfactory option rather than continuing the decision-making process until the optimal decision has been reached.

4   A second perspective places an emphasis on the impact of routines on decisions within organizations. It demonstrates how organizational structures and routines such as standard operating procedures tend to limit the decision-making process in a variety of ways, perhaps by restricting the information available to the decision unit, by restricting the breadth of options among which the decision unit may choose, or by inhibiting the ability of the organization to implement the decision quickly and effectively once it has been taken. Pre-planned routines and standard operating procedures are essential to coordinate the efforts of large numbers of people in massive organizations. However, these same routines and procedures can also have an inhibiting effect on the ability of the organization to arrive at optimal decisions and implement them efficiently. In this sort of decision-making process, organizations tend to take not the optimal decision but the decision that best fits within the permitted operating parameters outlined by the organization.

5   A third conceptual perspective emphasizes the internal dynamics of the decision unit and the extent to which decisions are based on political forces within the organization. This perspective demonstrates how bargaining among individuals who have different interests and motives and varying levels of power in the decision unit leads to eventual compromise that is not the preferred choice of any of the members of the decision unit.

6   Each of these three perspectives on the decision-making process demonstrates a different point of view on decision making, a different lens through which the decision-making process can be observed. It is safe to say that decision making in most organizations shows marked influences from each perspective; i.e., an organization strives to get as close as possible to the rational model in its decisions, yet the internal routines and dynamics of the organization come into play in the decision.

Refer to this version of the passage to answer the following questions.

Paragraph

Decisions

1   In a theoretical model of **decision making**, a decision is defined as the process of selecting one option from among a group of options for implementation. **4A** Decisions are formed by a **decision maker**, the one who actually chooses the final option, in conjunction with a **decision unit**, all of those in the organization around the decision maker who take part in the process. **4B** In this theoretical model, the members of the decision unit react to an unidentified problem by studying the problem, determining the objectives of the organization, formulating options, evaluating the strengths and weaknesses of each of the options, and reaching a conclusion. **4C** Many different factors can have an effect on the decision, including the nature of the problem itself, external forces exerting an influence on the organization, the internal dynamics of the decision unit, and the personality of the decision maker. **4D**

2   During recent years, decision making has been studied systematically by drawing from such diverse areas of study as psychology, sociology, business, government, history, mathematics, and statistics. Analyses of decisions often emphasize one of three principal conceptual perspectives (though often the approach that is actually employed is somewhat eclectic).

3   In the oldest of the three approaches, decisions are made by a **rational actor**, who makes a particular decision directly and purposefully in response to a specific threat from the external environment. It is assumed that this rational actor has clear objectives in mind, develops numerous reasonable options, considers the advantages and disadvantages of each option carefully, chooses the best option after careful analysis, and then proceeds to implement it fully. A variation of the rational actor model is a decision maker who is a **satisfier**, one who selects the first satisfactory option rather than continuing the decision-making process until the optimal decision has been reached.

4   A second perspective places an emphasis on the impact of routines on decisions within organizations. It demonstrates how organizational structures and routines such as standard operating procedures tend to limit the decision-making process in a variety of ways, perhaps by restricting the information available to the decision unit, by restricting the breadth of options among which the decision unit may choose, or by inhibiting the ability of the organization to implement the decision quickly and effectively once it has been taken. Pre-planned routines and standard operating procedures are essential to coordinate the efforts of large numbers of people in massive organizations. However, these same routines and procedures can also have an inhibiting effect on the ability of the organization to arrive at optimal decisions and implement them efficiently. In this sort of decision-making process, organizations tend to take not the optimal decision but the decision that best fits within the permitted operating parameters outlined by the organization.

5   A third conceptual perspective emphasizes the internal dynamics of the decision unit and the extent to which decisions are based on political forces within the organization. This perspective demonstrates how bargaining among individuals who have different interests and motives and varying levels of power in the decision unit leads to eventual compromise that is not the preferred choice of any of the members of the decision unit.

6   Each of these three perspectives on the decision-making process demonstrates a different point of view on decision making, a different lens through which the decision-making process can be observed. It is safe to say that decision making in most organizations shows marked influences from each perspective; i.e., an organization strives to get as close as possible to the rational model in its decisions, yet the internal routines and dynamics of the organization come into play in the decision.

Questions

1. It can be inferred from the information in paragraph 1 that the theoretical decision-making process
   - Ⓐ involves only the decision maker
   - Ⓑ requires the contemplation of numerous options
   - Ⓒ is made without the decision unit
   - Ⓓ does not work in real situations

2. The phrase "in conjunction with" in paragraph 1 could best be replaced by
   - Ⓐ along with
   - Ⓑ tied to
   - Ⓒ apart from
   - Ⓓ connected to

3. All of the following are listed in paragraph 1 as having an effect on decisions EXCEPT
   - Ⓐ evaluation of the problem
   - Ⓑ focus on objectives
   - Ⓒ generation of options
   - Ⓓ open-ended discussions

4. Look at the four squares [■] that indicate where the following sentence could be added to the passage.

   Additionally, when a decision must be made in a crisis situation, both stress and the speed at which events are progressing can have an effect, often a negative one, on the decision process.

   Where will the sentence best fit? Click on a square [■] to add the sentence to the passage.

5. The word "eclectic" in paragraph 2 is closest in meaning to
   - Ⓐ bizarre
   - Ⓑ personal
   - Ⓒ mixed
   - Ⓓ organized

6. It can be inferred from paragraph 3 that a rational actor would be least likely to
   - Ⓐ deal with a specific threat
   - Ⓑ work in a random fashion
   - Ⓒ ponder various options
   - Ⓓ consider disadvantages of options

7. The word "it" in paragraph 3 refers to
   - Ⓐ each option
   - Ⓑ the best option
   - Ⓒ careful analysis
   - Ⓓ variation

8. Why does the author mention "a satisfier, one who selects the first satisfactory option rather than continuing the decision-making process until the optimal decision has been reached" in paragraph 3?
   - Ⓐ A satisfier shows contrasting behavior to a rational actor.
   - Ⓑ A satisfier exhibits more common behavior than a rational actor.
   - Ⓒ A satisfier is the predecessor of a rational actor.
   - Ⓓ A satisfier shares some characteristics with a rational actor.

9. The word "places" in paragraph 4 could best be replaced by
   - Ⓐ locates
   - Ⓑ puts
   - Ⓒ finds
   - Ⓓ sets

10. Which of the sentences below best expresses the essential information in the highlighted sentence in paragraph 4? *Incorrect* choices change the meaning in important ways or leave out essential information.
    - Ⓐ Set routines within organizations tend to constrain decisions.
    - Ⓑ The restriction of information limits the number of options in a decision.
    - Ⓒ Organizations need to set up strict procedures to maximize the effectiveness of decisions.
    - Ⓓ Procedures are needed to ensure that decisions are implemented quickly and effectively.

11. The word "dynamics" in paragraph 5 is closest in meaning to

   (A) explosions

   (B) emotions

   (C) philosophies

   (D) interactions

12. According to paragraph 5, what is the end result of political bargaining within an organization?

   (A) No decision is ever reached.

   (B) Differing interests and motives are changed.

   (C) No one is completely satisfied with the final outcome.

   (D) The members of the decision unit leave the unit.

13.

Directions: An introductory sentence for a brief summary of the passage is provided below. Complete the summary by selecting the THREE answer choices that express the most important ideas in the passage. Some sentences do not belong in the summary because they express ideas that are not presented in the passage or are minor ideas in the passage. **This question is worth 2 points** (2 points for 3 correct answers, 1 point for 2 correct answers, and 0 points for 1 or 0 correct answers).
This passage presents different models for analyzing the process of decision making.
•
•
•

Answer Choices (choose 3 to complete the chart):

(1) One model looks at how satisfied all participants are after a given decision has been made.

(2) One model looks at how organizational structure and procedures influence a decision and how much a decision has been limited by these procedures.

(3) One model looks at how much a decision-making process has been manipulated and limited by factions within the organization.

(4) One model looks at how rational actors are able to work within organizational structures and routines to achieve optimal solutions.

(5) One model looks at how the decision-making process differs in diverse areas such as psychology, sociology, business, government, history, mathematics, and statistics.

(6) One model looks at how well a decision maker has analyzed a problem and possible solutions to achieve the optimal solution.

READING POST-TEST

30 minutes

Reading

Section Directions

This section tests your ability to understand an English academic reading passage.

Most questions are worth one point each. Some questions are worth more than one point. The directions for these questions will state how many points each is worth.

You will now start the Reading section. You have **30 minutes** to read one passage and answer the questions about it.

Read the passage.

Aquatic Schools

Paragraph

▶1   Many species of fish, particularly smaller fish, travel in schools, moving in tight formations, often with the precision of the most highly disciplined military unit on parade. Some move in synchronized hordes, while others move in starkly geometric forms. In addition to the varieties of shapes of schools of fish, there are countless varieties of schooling behaviors. Some fish coalesce into schools and then spread out in random patterns, while others move into close formations at specific times, such as feeding times, but are more spread out at other times. Some move in schools composed of members of all age groups, while others move in schools predominantly when they are young but take up a more solitary existence as they mature. Though this behavior is quite a regular, familiar phenomenon, there is much that is not completely known about it, particularly the exact function that it serves and what mechanisms fish use to make it happen.

▶2   Numerous hypotheses have been proposed and tested concerning the purpose of schooling behavior in fish. Schooling certainly promotes the survival of the species, but questions arise as to the way the schooling enables fish to have a better chance of surviving. Certainly, the fact that fish congregate together in schools helps to ensure their survival in that schooling provides numerous types of protection for the members of the school. One form of protection derives from the sheer numbers in the school. When a predator attacks a school containing a huge number of fish, the predator will be able to consume only a small percentage of the school. Whereas some of the members of the school will be lost to the predator, the majority of the school will be able to survive. Another form of protection comes from the special coloration and markings of different types of fish. Certain types of coloration or markings such as stripes or patterns in vibrant and shiny colors create a visual effect when huge numbers of the fish are clustered together, making it more difficult for a potential predator to focus on specific members of the school. A final form of protection comes from a special sense that fish possess, a sense that is enhanced when fish swim in schools. This special sense is related to a set of lateral line organs that consist of rows of pores leading to fluid-filled canals. These organs are sensitive to minute vibrations in the water. The thousands of sets of those special organs in a school of fish together can prove very effective in warning the school about an approaching threat.

▶3   It is also unclear exactly how fish manage to maintain their tight formations. Sight seems to play a role in the ability of fish to move in schools, and some scientists believe that, at least in some species, sight may play the principal role. However, many experiments indicate that more than sight is involved. Some fish school quite well in the dark or in murky water where visibility is extremely limited. This indicates that senses other than eyesight must be involved in enabling the schooling behavior. The lateral line system most likely plays a significant role in the ability of fish to school. Because these lateral line organs are sensitive to the most minute vibrations and currents, this organ system may be used by fish to detect movements among members of their school even when eyesight is limited or unavailable.

Refer to this version of the passage to answer the questions that follow.

Paragraph

Aquatic Schools

1   Many species of fish, particularly smaller fish, travel in schools, moving in tight formations often with the precision of the most highly disciplined military unit on parade. **5A** Some move in synchronized hordes, while others move in starkly geometric forms. **5B** In addition to the varieties of shapes of schools of fish, there are countless varieties of schooling behaviors. **5C** Some fish coalesce into schools and then spread out in random patterns, while others move into close formations at specific times, such as feeding times, but are more spread out at other times. **5D** Some move in schools composed of members of all age groups, while others move in schools predominantly when they are young but take up a more solitary existence as they mature. Though this behavior is quite a regular, familiar phenomenon, there is much that is not completely known about it, particularly the exact function that it serves and what mechanisms fish use to make it happen.

2   Numerous hypotheses have been proposed and tested concerning the purpose of schooling behavior in fish. Schooling certainly promotes the survival of the species, but questions arise as to the way the schooling enables fish to have a better chance of surviving. Certainly, the fact that fish congregate together in schools helps to ensure their survival in that schooling provides numerous types of protection for the members of the school. One form of protection derives from the sheer numbers in the school. When a predator attacks a school containing a huge number of fish, the predator will be able to consume only a small percentage of the school. Whereas some of the members of the school will be lost to the predator, the majority of the school will be able to survive. Another form of protection comes from the special coloration and markings of different types of fish. Certain types of coloration or markings such as stripes or patterns in vibrant and shiny colors create a visual effect when huge numbers of the fish are clustered together, making it more difficult for a potential predator to focus on specific members of the school. A final form of protection comes from a special sense that fish possess, a sense that is enhanced when fish swim in schools. This special sense is related to a set of lateral line organs that consist of rows of pores leading to fluid-filled canals. These organs are sensitive to minute vibrations in the water. The thousands of sets of those special organs in a school of fish together can prove very effective in warning the school about an approaching threat.

3   **16A** It is also unclear exactly how fish manage to maintain their tight formations. **16B** Sight seems to play a role in the ability of fish to move in schools, and some scientists believe that, at least in some species, sight may play the principal role. **16C** However, many experiments indicate that more than sight is involved. Some fish school quite well in the dark or in murky water where visibility is extremely limited. **16D** This indicates that senses other than eyesight must be involved in enabling the schooling behavior. The lateral line system most likely plays a significant role in the ability of fish to school. Because these lateral line organs are sensitive to the most minute vibrations and currents, this organ system may be used by fish to detect movements among members of their school even when eyesight is limited or unavailable.

Questions

1. The author mentions "the most highly disciplined military unit on parade" in paragraph 1 in order to

   Ⓐ describe the aggressive nature of a school of fish

   Ⓑ provide an example of a way that military units travel

   Ⓒ create a mental image of the movement of a school of fish

   Ⓓ contrast the movement of a military unit with that of a school of fish

2. The word "hordes" in paragraph 1 is closest in meaning to

   Ⓐ shapes
   Ⓑ masses
   Ⓒ pairs
   Ⓓ patterns

3. All of the following are stated in paragraph 1 about schooling EXCEPT that

   Ⓐ it is quite common
   Ⓑ it can involve large numbers of fish
   Ⓒ it can involve a number of different fish behaviors
   Ⓓ it is fully understood

4. Which fish would be least likely to be in a school?

   Ⓐ A large, older fish
   Ⓑ A smaller, colorful fish
   Ⓒ A young, hungry fish
   Ⓓ A tiny, shiny fish

5. Look at the four squares [■] that indicate where the following sentence could be added to paragraph 1.

   These may take the shape, for example, of wedges, triangles, spheres, or ovals.

   Where would the sentence best fit? Click on a square [■] to add the sentence to the passage. β

6. The word "it" in paragraph 1 refers to

   Ⓐ existence
   Ⓑ behavior
   Ⓒ fish
   Ⓓ function

7. Which of the sentences below best expresses the essential information in the first highlighted sentence in paragraph 2? *Incorrect* choices change the meaning in important ways or leave out essential information.

   Ⓐ After an attack, the fish that survive tend to move into schools.

   Ⓑ The survival of fish depends upon their ability to bring new members into the school.

   Ⓒ Many facts about the way that fish congregate in schools have been studied.

   Ⓓ Fish travel in schools to protect themselves in various ways.

8. The phrase "sheer numbers" in paragraph 2 could best be replaced by

   Ⓐ solitude
   Ⓑ interlude
   Ⓒ multitude
   Ⓓ similitude

9. It can be inferred from the passage that, when a predator attacks,

   Ⓐ it cannot possibly consume all members of a school if the school is large enough

   Ⓑ it rarely manages to catch any fish that are part of a school

   Ⓒ it is usually successful in wiping out the entire school

   Ⓓ it attacks only schools that lack sense organs

10. It is stated in paragraph 2 that

   Ⓐ fish in schools rarely have distinct markings

   Ⓑ schooling fish tend to have muted coloration

   Ⓒ the effect of coloration is multiplied when fish are massed together

   Ⓓ the bright coloration makes it easier for predators to spot fish

11. The word "minute" in paragraph 2 is closest in meaning to
    Ⓐ timely
    Ⓑ tiny
    Ⓒ careful
    Ⓓ instant

12. Which of the sentences below best expresses the essential information in the second highlighted sentence in paragraph 2? *Incorrect* choices change the meaning in important ways or leave out essential information.
    Ⓐ There are thousands of ways that special organs warn fish about a predator.
    Ⓑ When the fish in a school work together, they can use their sense organs to scare off any approaching threat.
    Ⓒ The fish in a large school use their lateral line organs to send out warnings of the arrival of the school.
    Ⓓ Because so many fish are in a school, all of their sense organs work well together to provide warnings.

13. The author begins paragraph 3 with "It is also unclear" in order to indicate that
    Ⓐ contradictory information is about to be presented
    Ⓑ it is necessary to clarify a previously made point
    Ⓒ a second issue is about to be presented
    Ⓓ it is unclear how a problem can be resolved

14. According to paragraph 3,
    Ⓐ fish cannot see well
    Ⓑ sight is the only sense used by fish to remain in schools
    Ⓒ not all fish use sight to remain in schools
    Ⓓ fish can see quite well in the dark

15. The word "murky" in paragraph 3 is closest in meaning to
    Ⓐ cloudy
    Ⓑ warm
    Ⓒ clear
    Ⓓ deep

16. Look at the four squares [■] that indicate where the following sentence could be added to paragraph 3.

    The purpose of schooling behavior is not the only aspect of schooling that is not fully understood.

    Where would the sentence best fit? Click on a square [■] to add the sentence to the passage.

17. The word "This" in paragraph 3 refers to the ability of fish to
    Ⓐ see well in dark water
    Ⓑ stay in schools when they cannot see well
    Ⓒ swim in water where the visibility is low
    Ⓓ use their sight to stay in schools

18. It is NOT stated in the passage that the lateral line system
    Ⓐ contains lines of pores
    Ⓑ can detect movement in the water
    Ⓒ quite possibly helps fish to remain in schools
    Ⓓ in fish is similar to sense organs in other animals

19.

Directions:	An introductory sentence for a brief summary of the passage is provided below. Complete the summary by selecting the THREE answer choices that express the most important ideas in the passage. Some sentences do not belong in the summary because they express ideas that are not presented in the passage or are minor ideas in the passage. **This question is worth 2 points** (2 points for 3 correct answers, 1 point for 2 correct answers, 0 points for 1 or 0 correct answers).

This passage discusses schooling behavior in certain fish.

- 3
- 5
- 6

Answer Choices (choose 3 to complete the chart):

(1) Fish most likely move in schools in various types of water.

(2) Scholars are quite confident in their understanding of schooling behavior.

(3) Fish move in schools by using various senses.

(4) Fish may move in schools at various times of the day or night.

(5) Fish most likely move in schools in various ways.

(6) Much is not known about schooling behaviors.

20.

Directions:	Select the appropriate sentences from the answer choices, and match them to the hypotheses to which they relate. TWO of the answer choices will not be used. **This question is worth 3 points** (3 points for 5 correct answers, 2 points for 4 correct answers, 1 point for 3 correct answers, 0 points for 2, 1, or 0 correct answers).

hypotheses related to purpose	• 1 • 2 • 45
hypotheses related to manner	• 3 • 7

Answer Choices (choose 5 to complete the table):

(1) Coloration provides protection.

(2) Lateral sense organs enable some fish to school.

(3) Sight provides protection.

(4) Coloration enables some fish to move.

(5) Large numbers provide protection.

(6) Sight enables some fish to school.

(7) Lateral sense organs provide protection.

Turn to pages 185–188 to *diagnose* your errors and *record* your results.

READING MINI-TEST 1

PAUSE TEST   SECTION EXIT   VOLUME   HELP   OK   NEXT

Reading

Section Directions

This section tests your ability to understand an English academic reading passage.

All questions except the last one are worth one point each. The last question is worth more than one point. The directions for the last question will state how many points it is worth.

You will now start the Reading section. You have **20 minutes** to read one passage and answer the questions about it.

Read the passage.

Migration

1   A widely held theory today is that the ancestors of today's Native American peoples traveled to the Western Hemisphere from Asia between 25,000 and 30,000 years ago, which was around the same time that Japan was being settled by Stone Age inhabitants. There is dental evidence and blood-type evidence to support this theory. A dental pattern that is found among most ancient human fossils in the Americas is consistent with the dental pattern of ancient human fossils in northeastern Asia. In blood type, the fact that blood type B is almost nonexistent among Native American populations but exists in Asian populations leads to the conclusion that migrations to the Americas from Asia took place before the evolution of blood type B, which is believed to have occurred around 30,000 years ago. In addition to the dental and blood-type evidence, more general evolutionary evidence suggests that it took more than 20,000 years for the variety of physical traits common to Native American populations to evolve, and linguists broadly concur that the development of the approximately 500 distinct languages of the Native Americans would require approximately 25,000 years.

2   The proposed migration from Asia to the Americas took place during the Ice Age that characterized the Pleistocene epoch. During that period of time, there were huge glaciers holding enormous volumes of water, and, because of the huge glaciers, sea levels were as much as 100 meters lower than they are today. The reduced sea levels meant that Asia and North America were linked with a 750-mile-wide landmass, named Beringia after the Bering Straits that now cover it, and consisted of treeless grassland with warm summers and cold dry winters. Because of the geographical features of Beringia during the Pleistocene epoch, it was an environment well-suited to the large mammals of the time, such as mammoth, mastodon, bison, horse, and reindeer, as well as to the Stone Age hunters who depended on these animals for their existence. The Stone Age inhabitants of the area used these animals not only for food but also for shelter, clothing, and weapons; they were able to spread out and expand their hunting areas as their populations grew, and their populations most likely grew at a very high rate because of the huge amount of territory available for expansion.

3   In spite of the evidence, not all anthropologists are convinced that the migrations from Asia to the Americas took place as early as 25,000 to 30,000 years ago. There is general agreement that the migrations took place, but some believe that the migrations took place much later. No fossilized human bones have been found in what used to be Beringia; finding human bones dating from 25,000 to 30,000 years ago would be strong proof of the dates when the migrations took place. However, because what was once Beringia is submerged beneath ocean waters, it may be a formidable task to uncover fossil evidence of migration from Asia to the Americas through Beringia.

Refer to this version of the passage to answer the questions that follow.

Paragraph

Migration

1   A widely held theory today is that the ancestors of today's Native American peoples traveled to the Western Hemisphere from Asia between 25,000 and 30,000 years ago, which was around the same time that Japan was being settled by Stone Age inhabitants. There is dental evidence and blood-type evidence to support this theory. A dental pattern that is found among most ancient human fossils in the Americas is consistent with the dental pattern of ancient human fossils in northeastern Asia. In blood type, the fact that blood type B is almost nonexistent among Native American populations but exists in Asian populations leads to the conclusion that migrations to the Americas from Asia took place before the evolution of blood type B, which is believed to have occurred around 30,000 years ago. In addition to the dental and blood-type evidence, more general evolutionary evidence suggests that it took more than 20,000 years for the variety of physical traits common to Native American populations to evolve, and linguists broadly concur that the development of the approximately 500 distinct languages of the Native Americans would require approximately 25,000 years.

2   The proposed migration from Asia to the Americas took place during the Ice Age that characterized the Pleistocene epoch. During that period of time, there were huge glaciers holding enormous volumes of water, and, because of the huge glaciers, sea levels were as much as 100 meters lower than they are today. The reduced sea levels meant that Asia and North America were linked with a 750-mile-wide landmass, named Beringia after the Bering Straits that now cover it, and consisted of treeless grassland with warm summers and cold dry winters. Because of the geographical features of Beringia during the Pleistocene epoch, it was an environment well-suited to the large mammals of the time, such as mammoth, mastodon, bison, horse, and reindeer, as well as to the Stone Age hunters who depended on these animals for their existence. The Stone Age inhabitants of the area used these animals not only for food but also for shelter, clothing, and weapons; they were able to spread out and expand their hunting areas as their populations grew, and their populations most likely grew at a very high rate because of the huge amount of territory available for expansion.

3   **11A** In spite of the evidence, not all anthropologists are convinced that the migrations from Asia to the Americas took place as early as 25,000 to 30,000 years ago. **11B** There is general agreement that the migrations took place, but some believe that the migrations took place much later. **11C** No fossilized human bones have been found in what used to be Beringia; finding human bones dating from 25,000 to 30,000 years ago would be strong proof of the dates when the migrations took place. However, because what was once Beringia is submerged beneath ocean waters, it may be a formidable task to uncover fossil evidence of migration from Asia to the Americas through Beringia. **11D**

Questions

1. The word "held" in paragraph 1 could best be replaced by
   - Ⓐ accepted
   - Ⓑ possessed
   - Ⓒ contained
   - Ⓓ carried

2. The word "support" in paragraph 1 could best be replaced by
   - Ⓐ hold
   - Ⓑ finance
   - Ⓒ confirm
   - Ⓓ stiffen

3. Which of the following is NOT provided as evidence to support the hypothesis that the migration discussed in the passage occurred 25,000 to 30,000 years ago?
   - Ⓐ Dental patterns common to Asians and Native Americans
   - Ⓑ Variations in blood types between Asians and Native Americans
   - Ⓒ The number of Native American languages in existence today
   - Ⓓ The human bones found in Beringia

4. The phrase "broadly concur" in paragraph 1 is closest in meaning to
   - Ⓐ have the contrary idea
   - Ⓑ have extensive debates
   - Ⓒ openly question
   - Ⓓ are in general agreement

5. Which of the sentences below best expresses the essential information in the highlighted sentence in paragraph 2? *Incorrect* choices change the meaning in important ways or leave out essential information.
   - Ⓐ Since the Ice Age, the amount of water in the oceans has decreased dramatically.
   - Ⓑ During the Ice Age, sea levels were low because of how much water was frozen.
   - Ⓒ Glaciers have grown tremendously since the last Ice Age.
   - Ⓓ During the Ice Age, huge glaciers displaced a lot of water, causing the oceans to rise.

6. It is stated in the passage that Beringia
   - Ⓐ was the source of the name Bering Straits
   - Ⓑ used to be covered with trees
   - Ⓒ is now submerged
   - Ⓓ was unable to support animal life

7. The phrase "well-suited to" in paragraph 2 is closest in meaning to
   - Ⓐ equal to
   - Ⓑ appropriate for
   - Ⓒ flattering to
   - Ⓓ modified for

8. The word "they" in paragraph 2 refers to
   - Ⓐ Stone Age inhabitants
   - Ⓑ animals
   - Ⓒ weapons
   - Ⓓ their hunting areas

9. It is implied in the passage that the Stone Age inhabitants of Beringia were most likely
   - Ⓐ dependent on agriculture
   - Ⓑ poor hunters
   - Ⓒ involved in raising livestock
   - Ⓓ mobile

10. The author begins paragraph 3 with the expression "In spite of" to show that the fact that some anthropologists were not convinced by the evidence was
    - Ⓐ unexpected
    - Ⓑ a natural conclusion
    - Ⓒ unsurprising
    - Ⓓ logical

11. Look at the four squares [■] that indicate where the following sentence could be added to paragraph 3.

    Some, in fact, hypothesize that the migrations took place around 15,000 B.C.

    Where would the sentence best fit? Click on a square [■] to add the sentence to the passage.

12. The word "formidable" in paragraph 3 is closest in meaning to

   Ⓐ superior

   Ⓑ maddening

   Ⓒ powerful

   Ⓓ difficult

13.

Directions: An introductory sentence for a brief summary of the passage is provided below. Complete the summary by selecting the THREE answer choices that express the most important ideas in the passage. Some sentences do not belong in the summary because they express ideas that are not presented in the passage or are minor ideas in the passage. **This question is worth 2 points** (2 points for 3 correct answers, 1 point for 2 correct answers, and 0 points for 1 or 0 correct answers).
This passage discusses a theory of migration from the Eastern Hemisphere to the Western Hemisphere 25,000 to 30,000 years ago.
•
•
•

Answer Choices (choose 3 to complete the chart):

(1) There are geographical reasons to support this theory.

(2) A number of fossils from the Pleistocene epoch have been found in Beringia.

(3) There are physiological reasons to support this theory.

(4) A study of blood types indicates that blood type B is rare among Native Americans.

(5) There are sociological reasons to support this theory.

(6) There are linguistic theories to support this theory.

> Turn to pages 185–188 to *diagnose* your errors and *record* your results.

READING MINI-TEST 2

Reading
Section Directions

This section tests your ability to understand an English academic reading passage.

All questions except the last one are worth one point each. The last question is worth more than one point. The directions for the last question will state how many points it is worth.

You will now start the Reading section. You have **20 minutes** to read one passage and answer the questions about it.

Read the passage.

Birth Order

▶**1**   A considerable body of research has demonstrated a correlation between birth order and aspects such as temperament and behavior, and some psychologists believe that birth order significantly affects the development of personality. Psychologist Alfred Adler was a pioneer in the study of the relationship between birth order and personality. A key point in his research and in the hypothesis that he developed based on it was that it was not the actual numerical birth position that affected personality; instead, it was the similar responses in large numbers of families to children in specific birth order positions that had an effect. For example, first-borns, who have their parents to themselves initially and do not have to deal with siblings in the first part of their lives, tend to have their first socialization experiences with adults and therefore tend to find the process of peer socialization more difficult. In contrast, later-born children have to deal with siblings from the first moment of their lives and therefore tend to have stronger socialization skills.

▶**2**   Numerous studies since Adler's have been conducted on the effect of birth order and personality. These studies have tended to classify birth order types into four different categories: first-born, second-born and/or middle, last, and only child.

▶**3**   Studies have consistently shown that first-born children tend to exhibit similar positive and negative personality traits. First-borns have consistently been linked with academic achievement in various studies; in one study, the number of National Merit scholarship winners who are first-borns was found to be equal to the number of second- and third-borns combined. First-borns have been found to be more responsible and assertive than those born in other birth-order positions and tend to rise to positions of leadership more often than others; more first-borns have served in the U.S. Congress and as U.S. presidents than have those born in other birth-order positions. However, studies have shown that first-borns tend to be more subject to stress and were considered problem children more often than later-borns.

▶**4**   Second-born and/or middle children demonstrate markedly different tendencies from first-borns. They tend to feel inferior to the older child or children because it is difficult for them to comprehend that their lower level of achievement is a function of age rather than ability, and they often try to succeed in areas other than those in which their older sibling or siblings excel. They tend to be more trusting, accepting, and focused on others than the more self-centered first-borns, and they tend to have a comparatively higher level of success in team sports than do first-borns or only children, who more often excel in individual sports.

▶**5**   The last-born child is the one who tends to be the eternal baby of the family and thus often exhibits a strong sense of security. Last-borns collectively achieve the highest degree of social success and demonstrate the highest levels of self-esteem of all the birth-order positions. They often exhibit less competitiveness than older brothers and sisters and are more likely to take part in less competitive group games or in social organizations such as sororities and fraternities.

▶**6**   Only children tend to exhibit some of the main characteristics of first-borns and some of the characteristics of last-borns. Only children tend to exhibit the strong sense of security and self-esteem exhibited by last-borns while, like first-borns, they are more achievement oriented and more likely than middle- or last-borns to achieve academic success. However, only children tend to have the most problems establishing close relationships and exhibit a lower need for affiliation than other children.

Refer to this version of the passage to answer the questions that follow.

Birth Order

Paragraph

1   A considerable body of research has demonstrated a correlation between birth order and aspects such as temperament and behavior, and some psychologists believe that birth order significantly affects the development of personality. Psychologist Alfred Adler was a pioneer in the study of the relationship between birth order and personality. A key point in his research and in the hypothesis that he developed based on it was that it was not the actual numerical birth position that affected personality; instead, it was the similar responses in large numbers of families to children in specific birth order positions that had an effect. For example, first-borns, who have their parents to themselves initially and do not have to deal with siblings in the first part of their lives, tend to have their first socialization experiences with adults and therefore tend to find the process of peer socialization more difficult. In contrast, later-born children have to deal with siblings from the first moment of their lives and therefore tend to have stronger socialization skills.

2   Numerous studies since Adler's have been conducted on the effect of birth order and personality. These studies have tended to classify birth order types into four different categories: first-born, second-born and/or middle, last, and only child.

3   Studies have consistently shown that first-born children tend to exhibit similar positive and negative personality traits. First-borns have consistently been linked with academic achievement in various studies; in one study, the number of National Merit scholarship winners who are first-borns was found to be equal to the number of second- and third-borns combined. First-borns have been found to be more responsible and assertive than those born in other birth-order positions and tend to rise to positions of leadership more often than others; more first-borns have served in the U.S. Congress and as U.S. presidents than have those born in other birth-order positions. However, studies have shown that first-borns tend to be more subject to stress and were considered problem children more often than later-borns.

4   **7A** Second-born and/or middle children demonstrate markedly different tendencies from first-borns. **7B** They tend to feel inferior to the older child or children because it is difficult for them to comprehend that their lower level of achievement is a function of age rather than ability, and they often try to succeed in areas other than those in which their older sibling or siblings excel. **7C** They tend to be more trusting, accepting, and focused on others than the more self-centered first-borns, and they tend to have a comparatively higher level of success in team sports than do first-borns or only children, who more often excel in individual sports. **7D**

5   The last-born child is the one who tends to be the eternal baby of the family and thus often exhibits a strong sense of security. Last-borns collectively achieve the highest degree of social success and demonstrate the highest levels of self-esteem of all the birth-order positions. They often exhibit less competitiveness than older brothers and sisters and are more likely to take part in less competitive group games or in social organizations such as sororities and fraternities.

6   Only children tend to exhibit some of the main characteristics of first-borns and some of the characteristics of last-borns. Only children tend to exhibit the strong sense of security and self-esteem exhibited by last-borns while, like first-borns, they are more achievement oriented and more likely than middle- or last-borns to achieve academic success. However, only children tend to have the most problems establishing close relationships and exhibit a lower need for affiliation than other children.

Questions

1. The word "body" in paragraph 1 could best be replaced by
   Ⓐ corpse
   Ⓑ amount
   Ⓒ organization
   Ⓓ skeleton

2. What is stated in paragraph 1 about Adler?
   Ⓐ He was one of the first to study the effect of birth order on personality.
   Ⓑ He believed that it was the actual birth order that affected personality.
   Ⓒ He had found that the responses by family members had little to do with personality.
   Ⓓ He was the only one to study birth order.

3. The author includes the idea that "These studies have tended to classify birth order types into four different categories" in paragraph 2 in order to
   Ⓐ announce what ideas will be presented in the following paragraphs
   Ⓑ show how other studies differed from Adler's
   Ⓒ explain how Adler classified his work
   Ⓓ describe the various ways that different studies have categorized birth order groups

4. The word "traits" in paragraph 3 is closest in meaning to
   Ⓐ stresses
   Ⓑ marks
   Ⓒ characteristics
   Ⓓ fears

5. Which of the sentences below best expresses the essential information in the highlighted sentence in paragraph 3? *Incorrect* choices change the meaning in important ways or leave out essential information.
   Ⓐ In spite of certain characteristics that first-borns possess, many of them become leaders.
   Ⓑ An interesting fact that is difficult to explain is that many first-borns have served in high government positions.
   Ⓒ Because first-borns tend to be very assertive, they are uncomfortable serving in government positions.
   Ⓓ Several examples support the idea that first-borns have characteristics that make them leaders.

6. The word "accepting" in paragraph 4 is closest in meaning to
   Ⓐ tolerant
   Ⓑ affectionate
   Ⓒ admissible
   Ⓓ respectable

7. Look at the four squares [■] that indicate where the following sentence could be added to paragraph 4.

   Thus, second-borns tend to be better at soccer, football, volleyball, and baseball than at tennis, diving, gymnastics, or archery.

   Where would the sentence best fit? Click on a square [■] to add the sentence to the passage.

8. Which of the following is NOT true, according to the passage?
   Ⓐ First-borns tend to do well in individual sports.
   Ⓑ Middle children tend to have a preference for team sports.
   Ⓒ Last-borns tend to prefer games with fierce competition.
   Ⓓ Only children tend to prefer individual over team sports.

9. The phrase "more achievement oriented" in paragraph 6 is closest in meaning to

Ⓐ more directly involved

Ⓑ more focused on accomplishments

Ⓒ more skilled as leaders

Ⓓ more aware of surroundings

10. Which of the following would be most likely to have a successful career but few close friendships?

Ⓐ A second-born

Ⓑ A middle child

Ⓒ A last-born

Ⓓ An only child

11.

Directions:	The answer choices below are each used to describe one of the birth order groups. Complete the chart by matching appropriate answer choices to the birth order groups they are used to describe. TWO of the answer choices will not be used. **This question is worth 4 points** (4 points for 7 correct answers, 3 points for 6 correct answers, 2 points for 5 correct answers, 1 point for 4 correct answers, and 0 points for 3, 2, 1, or 0 correct answers).

first-borns	• • •
second-borns and middle children	• •
last-borns	• •

Answer Choices (choose 7 to complete the table):

(1) Tendency to feel secure and to achieve social success

(2) Tendency to concentrate on others rather than self

(3) Tendency to bear responsibility better than others

(4) Tendency to do well in school and as leaders

(5) Tendency to do poorly academically while excelling at individual sports

(6) Tendency not to be highly competitive

(7) Tendency to withdraw from others because of feelings of inferiority

(8) Tendency to feel stressed

(9) Tendency to feel inferior to siblings

Turn to pages 185–188 to *diagnose* your errors and *record* your results.

READING MINI-TEST 3

PAUSE TEST   SECTION EXIT   VOLUME   HELP   OK   NEXT

Reading
Section Directions

This section tests your ability to understand an English academic reading passage.

All questions except the last one are worth one point each. The last question is worth more than one point. The directions for the last question will state how many points it is worth.

You will now start the Reading section. You have **20 minutes** to read one passage and answer the questions about it.

Read the passage.

Ketchup

▶**1**   The sauce that is today called ketchup (or catsup) in Western cultures is a tomato-based sauce that is quite distinct from the Eastern ancestors of this product. A sauce called *ke-tiap* was in use in China at least as early as the seventeenth century, but the Chinese version of the sauce was made of pickled fish, shellfish, and spices. The popularity of this Chinese sauce spread to Singapore and Malaysia, where it was called *kechap.* The Indonesian sauce *ketjab* derives its name from the same source as the Malaysian sauce but is made from very different ingredients. The Indonesian *ketjab* is made by cooking black soy beans, fermenting them, placing them in a salt brine for at least a week, cooking the resulting solution further, and sweetening it heavily; this process results in a dark, thick, and sweet variation of soy sauce.

▶**2**   Early in the eighteenth century, sailors from the British navy came across this exotic sauce on voyages to Malaysia and Singapore and brought samples of it back to England on return voyages. English chefs tried to recreate the sauce but were unable to do so exactly because key ingredients were unknown or unavailable in England; chefs ended up substituting ingredients such as mushrooms and walnuts in an attempt to recreate the special taste of the original Asian sauce. Variations of this sauce became quite the rage in eighteenth-century England, appearing in a number of recipe books and featured as an exotic addition to menus from the period.

▶**3**   The English version did not contain tomatoes, and it was not until the end of the eighteenth century that tomatoes became a main ingredient, in the ketchup of the newly created United States. It is quite notable that tomatoes were added to the sauce in that tomatoes had previously been considered quite dangerous to health. The tomato had been cultivated by the Aztecs, who had called it *tomatl*; however, early botanists had recognized that the tomato was a member of the *Solanacaea* family, which does include a number of poisonous plants. The leaves of the tomato plant are poisonous, though of course the fruit is not.

▶**4**   Thomas Jefferson, who cultivated the tomato in his gardens at Monticello and served dishes containing tomatoes at lavish feasts, often receives credit for changing the reputation of the tomato. Soon after Jefferson had introduced the tomato to American society, recipes combining the newly fashionable tomato with the equally fashionable and exotic sauce known as *ketchap* began to appear. By the middle of the nineteenth century, both the tomato and tomato ketchup were staples of the American kitchen.

▶**5**   Tomato ketchup, popular though it was, was quite time-consuming to prepare. In 1876, the first mass-produced tomato ketchup, a product of German-American Henry Heinz, went on sale and achieved immediate success. From tomato ketchup, Heinz branched out into a number of other products, including various sauces, pickles, and relishes. By 1890, his company had expanded to include sixty-five different products but was in need of a marketing slogan. Heinz settled on the slogan "57 Varieties" because he liked the way that the digits 5 and 7 looked in print, in spite of the fact that this slogan understated the number of products that he had at the time.

Refer to this version of the passage to answer the questions that follow.

Paragraph

Ketchup

1   The sauce that is today called ketchup (or catsup) in Western cultures is a tomato-based sauce that is quite distinct from the Eastern ancestors of this product. A sauce called *ke-tiap* was in use in China at least as early as the seventeenth century, but the Chinese version of the sauce was made of pickled fish, shellfish, and spices. The popularity of this Chinese sauce spread to Singapore and Malaysia, where it was called *kechap.* The Indonesian sauce *ketjab* derives its name from the same source as the Malaysian sauce but is made from very different ingredients. The Indonesian *ketjab* is made by cooking black soy beans, fermenting them, placing them in a salt brine for at least a week, cooking the resulting solution further, and sweetening it heavily; this process results in a dark, thick, and sweet variation of soy sauce.

2   Early in the eighteenth century, sailors from the British navy came across this exotic sauce on voyages to Malaysia and Singapore and brought samples of it back to England on return voyages. English chefs tried to recreate the sauce but were unable to do so exactly because key ingredients were unknown or unavailable in England; chefs ended up substituting ingredients such as mushrooms and walnuts in an attempt to recreate the special taste of the original Asian sauce. Variations of this sauce became quite the rage in eighteenth-century England, appearing in a number of recipe books and featured as an exotic addition to menus from the period.

3   The English version did not contain tomatoes, and it was not until the end of the eighteenth century that tomatoes became a main ingredient, in the ketchup of the newly created United States. It is quite notable that tomatoes were added to the sauce in that tomatoes had previously been considered quite dangerous to health. The tomato had been cultivated by the Aztecs, who had called it *tomatl*; however, early botanists had recognized that the tomato was a member of the *Solanacaea* family, which does include a number of poisonous plants. The leaves of the tomato plant are poisonous, though of course the fruit is not.

4   **10A** Thomas Jefferson, who cultivated the tomato in his gardens at Monticello and served dishes containing tomatoes at lavish feasts, often receives credit for changing the reputation of the tomato. **10B** Soon after Jefferson had introduced the tomato to American society, recipes combining the newly fashionable tomato with the equally fashionable and exotic sauce known as *ketchap* began to appear. **10C** By the middle of the nineteenth century, both the tomato and tomato ketchup were staples of the American kitchen. **10D**

5   Tomato ketchup, popular though it was, was quite time-consuming to prepare. In 1876, the first mass-produced tomato ketchup, a product of German-American Henry Heinz, went on sale and achieved immediate success. From tomato ketchup, Heinz branched out into a number of other products, including various sauces, pickles, and relishes. By 1890, his company had expanded to include sixty-five different products but was in need of a marketing slogan. Heinz settled on the slogan "57 Varieties" because he liked the way that the digits 5 and 7 looked in print, in spite of the fact that this slogan understated the number of products that he had at the time.

Questions

1. The word "ancestors" in paragraph 1 is closest in meaning to
   - Ⓐ predecessors
   - Ⓑ descendents
   - Ⓒ creators
   - Ⓓ ingredients

2. It is NOT stated in paragraph 1 that
   - Ⓐ the Chinese sauce was in existence in the seventeenth century
   - Ⓑ the Malaysian sauce was similar to the Chinese sauce
   - Ⓒ the Chinese sauce was made from seafood and spices
   - Ⓓ the Indonesian sauce was similar to the Chinese sauce

3. The word "it" in paragraph 1 refers to
   - Ⓐ a salt brine
   - Ⓑ a week
   - Ⓒ the resulting solution
   - Ⓓ this process

4. The expression "came across" in paragraph 2 could best be replaced by
   - Ⓐ traversed
   - Ⓑ discovered
   - Ⓒ transported
   - Ⓓ described

5. It can be inferred from paragraph 2 that mushrooms and walnuts were
   - Ⓐ difficult to find in England
   - Ⓑ not part of the original Asian recipe
   - Ⓒ not native to England
   - Ⓓ transported to England from Asia

6. The word "rage" in paragraph 2 could best be replaced by
   - Ⓐ anger
   - Ⓑ distinction
   - Ⓒ misunderstanding
   - Ⓓ fashion

7. The author mentions "The English version" at the beginning of paragraph 3 in order to
   - Ⓐ indicate what will be discussed in the coming paragraph
   - Ⓑ explain why tomatoes were considered dangerous
   - Ⓒ make a reference to the topic of the previous paragraph
   - Ⓓ provide an example of a sauce using tomatoes

8. According to paragraph 3, the tomato plant
   - Ⓐ was considered poisonous by the Aztecs
   - Ⓑ is related to some poisonous plants
   - Ⓒ has edible leaves
   - Ⓓ has fruit that is sometimes quite poisonous

9. The word "staples" in paragraph 4 could best be replaced by
   - Ⓐ standard elements
   - Ⓑ strong attachments
   - Ⓒ necessary utensils
   - Ⓓ rare alternatives

10. Look at the four squares [■] that indicate where the following sentence could be added to paragraph 4.

    It turned from very bad to exceedingly good.

    Where would the sentence best fit? Click on a square [■] to add the sentence to the passage.

11. The expression "branched out" in paragraph 5 is closest in meaning to
    - Ⓐ contracted
    - Ⓑ stemmed
    - Ⓒ converted
    - Ⓓ expanded

12. Which of the sentences below best expresses the essential information in the highlighted sentence in paragraph 5? *Incorrect* choices change the meaning in important ways or leave out essential information.

Ⓐ Heinz selected a certain slogan even though it was inaccurate because he liked the look of it.

Ⓑ Heinz was eventually able to settle a dispute about which slogan would be the best for his company.

Ⓒ Heinz was unable to print out the actual number of varieties, so he printed out a different number.

Ⓓ Heinz's company actually had far fewer products than the slogan indicated that it did.

13.

Directions: An introductory sentence for a brief summary of the passage is provided below. Complete the summary by selecting the THREE answer choices that express the most important ideas in the passage. Some sentences do not belong in the summary because they express ideas that are not presented in the passage or are minor ideas in the passage. **This question is worth 2 points** (2 points for 3 correct answers, 1 point for 2 correct answers, and 0 points for 1 or 0 correct answers).
This passage discusses the history of a sauce known as ketchup.
•
•
•

Answer Choices (choose 3 to complete the chart):

(1) An English variation of the sauce, without tomatoes, became popular after sailors returned home with samples.

(2) A plant called the *tomatl* is known to have been cultivated by the Aztecs.

(3) Ketchup was produced in a time-consuming way in Germany.

(4) The sauce was first developed in Asia, without tomatoes.

(5) The sauce known as *ketjab* was a variation of the Chinese sauce that contained tomatoes.

(6) Americans added the exotic tomato to the sauce and later mass-produced it.

Turn to pages 185–188 to *diagnose* your errors and *record* your results.

READING MINI-TEST 4

Reading

Section Directions

This section tests your ability to understand an English academic reading passage.

All questions except the last one are worth one point each. The last question is worth more than one point. The directions for the last question will state how many points it is worth.

You will now start the Reading section. You have **20 minutes** to read one passage and answer the questions about it.

Read the passage.

Paragraph

Estuaries

1   Fresh water from land enters the ocean through rivers, streams, and groundwater flowing through valleys. These valleys that channel fresh water from land to the salty ocean, which range from extremely narrow stream-cut channels to remarkably broad lagoons behind long barrier islands, are called **estuaries**.

2   A number of types of estuaries are commercially vital. Many commercially important estuaries are the mouths of major rivers. The powerful flow of water in major rivers maintains channels that are deep enough for navigation by ocean-bound vessels, and the rivers themselves provide transportation of goods to points farther inland. In addition, estuaries formed as a result of tectonic or glacial activity are sometimes sufficiently deep to provide ports for oceangoing vessels. The types of estuaries that are not viable as ports of call for ocean commerce are those that are not wide enough, not deep enough, and not powerful enough to prevent the buildup of sediment.

3   Estuary systems, which vary to reflect the geology of the coasts where they are found, can be broadly categorized as one of two different types. One type of estuary system is the type that is found in **flooded coastal plains**, the broad land areas that extend out to the continental shelves, on the Atlantic coasts of North and South America, Europe, and Africa, for example. The other category of estuary system encompasses the **mountainous coasts**, with their rugged topography, such as those found along the Pacific coasts of North and South America.

4   Today, much of the eastern coast of the United States is a flooded coastal plain. During the last Ice Age, much of what is today the submerged continental shelf was exposed as an extended part of the continent. Intricate river systems composed of main rivers and their tributaries cut valleys across the plains to the edge of the shelf, where they released the fresh water that they carried into the ocean. Then, as the ice melted at the end of the Ice Age, rising waters extended inland over the lower areas, creating today's broad drowned river valleys. On today's flooded coastal plains, the water is comparatively shallow and huge amounts of sand and sediment are deposited. These conditions foster the growth of extensive long and narrow offshore deposits, many of which are exposed above the water as sandspits or barrier islands. These deposits are constantly being reshaped, sometimes extremely slowly and sometimes quite rapidly, by the forces of water and wind. It is common along flooded coastal plains for drowned river valleys to empty into lagoons that have been created behind the sandspits and barrier islands rather than emptying directly into the ocean. These lagoons support vigorous biological activity inasmuch as they are shallow, which causes them to heat up quickly, and they are fed by a constant inflow of nutrient-rich sediments.

5   Unlike the flooded coastal plains, the mountainous coasts have a more rugged and irregular topography with deeper coastal waters. There is less sand and sediment, and external systems of barrier islands are not as pervasive as they are on flooded coastal plains because the mountainous topography blocks the flow of sediments to the coast and because the deeper ocean water inhibits the growth of barrier islands, and without the protection of barrier beaches, mountainous coasts are more exposed to direct attack by the erosive forces of waves. Different geological processes contribute to the rugged topography along mountain coasts. The tectonic activity that creates the mountains along a mountainous coast can cause large blocks of the Earth's crust to fall below sea level; San Francisco Bay in California and the Strait of Juan de Fuca in Washington state in the north formed in this way. In the northern latitudes, coastal fjords were created as glaciers cut impressive u-shaped valleys through mountains and now carry fresh water from the land to the ocean.

Refer to this version of the passage to answer the questions that follow.

Paragraph

Estuaries

1   Fresh water from land enters the ocean through rivers, streams, and groundwater flowing through valleys. These valleys that channel fresh water from land to the salty ocean, which range from extremely narrow stream-cut channels to remarkably broad lagoons behind long barrier islands, are called **estuaries**.

2   A number of types of estuaries are commercially vital. Many commercially important estuaries are the mouths of major rivers. The powerful flow of water in major rivers maintains channels that are deep enough for navigation by ocean-bound vessels, and the rivers themselves provide transportation of goods to points farther inland. In addition, estuaries formed as a result of tectonic or glacial activity are sometimes sufficiently deep to provide ports for oceangoing vessels. The types of estuaries that are not viable as ports of call for ocean commerce are those that are not wide enough, not deep enough, and not powerful enough to prevent the buildup of sediment.

3   Estuary systems, which vary to reflect the geology of the coasts where they are found, can be broadly categorized as one of two different types. One type of estuary system is the type that is found in **flooded coastal plains**, the broad land areas that extend out to the continental shelves, on the Atlantic coasts of North and South America, Europe, and Africa, for example. The other category of estuary system encompasses the **mountainous coasts**, with their rugged topography, such as those found along the Pacific coasts of North and South America.

4   Today, much of the eastern coast of the United States is a flooded coastal plain. During the last Ice Age, much of what is today the submerged continental shelf was exposed as an extended part of the continent. Intricate river systems composed of main rivers and their tributaries cut valleys across the plains to the edge of the shelf, where they released the fresh water that they carried into the ocean. Then, as the ice melted at the end of the Ice Age, rising waters extended inland over the lower areas, creating today's broad drowned river valleys. On today's flooded coastal plains, the water is comparatively shallow and huge amounts of sand and sediment are deposited. **6A** These conditions foster the growth of extensive long and narrow offshore deposits, many of which are exposed above the water as sandspits or barrier islands. **6B** These deposits are constantly being reshaped, sometimes extremely slowly and sometimes quite rapidly, by the forces of water and wind. **6C** It is common along flooded coastal plains for drowned river valleys to empty into lagoons that have been created behind the sandspits and barrier islands rather than emptying directly into the ocean. **6D** These lagoons support vigorous biological activity inasmuch as they are shallow, which causes them to heat up quickly, and they are fed by a constant inflow of nutrient-rich sediments.

5   Unlike the flooded coastal plains, the mountainous coasts have a more rugged and irregular topography with deeper coastal waters. There is less sand and sediment, and external systems of barrier islands are not as pervasive as they are on flooded coastal plains because the mountainous topography blocks the flow of sediments to the coast and because the deeper ocean water inhibits the growth of barrier islands, and without the protection of barrier beaches, mountainous coasts are more exposed to direct attack by the erosive forces of waves. Different geological processes contribute to the rugged topography along mountain coasts. The tectonic activity that creates the mountains along a mountainous coast can cause large blocks of the Earth's crust to fall below sea level; San Francisco Bay in California and the Strait of Juan de Fuca in Washington state in the north formed in this way. In the northern latitudes, coastal fjords were created as glaciers cut impressive u-shaped valleys through mountains and now carry fresh water from the land to the ocean.

Questions

1. The phrase "commercially vital" in paragraph 2 is closest in meaning to
   - Ⓐ understandably lucky
   - Ⓑ by-products of business
   - Ⓒ the essence of professionality
   - Ⓓ important to trade

2. The word "viable" in paragraph 2 is closest in meaning to
   - Ⓐ workable
   - Ⓑ valuable
   - Ⓒ identifiable
   - Ⓓ verifiable

3. The passage indicates that all of the following are estuaries with commercial potential as ports of call EXCEPT
   - Ⓐ estuaries at the mouths of powerful rivers
   - Ⓑ estuaries formed from tectonic activity
   - Ⓒ estuaries formed by glaciers
   - Ⓓ estuaries on flooded coastal plains

4. According to the passage, drowned river valleys
   - Ⓐ are covered with ice
   - Ⓑ are covered with shallow water
   - Ⓒ are covered with deep water
   - Ⓓ are land areas with rivers cutting through

5. The word "foster" in paragraph 4 is closest in meaning to
   - Ⓐ encourage
   - Ⓑ deter
   - Ⓒ adopt
   - Ⓓ relate

6. Look at the four squares [■] that indicate where the following sentence could be added to paragraph 4.

   Some changes to the deposits can take place gradually over decades, while other changes can be quite radical changes in a period of only a few hours as the result of major storm activity.

   Where would the sentence best fit? Click on a square [■] to add the sentence to the passage.

7. Which of the sentences below best expresses the essential information in the highlighted sentence in paragraph 4? *Incorrect* choices change the meaning in important ways or leave out essential information.
   - Ⓐ Biological activity contributes to the formation of lagoons by heating them up and providing a source of food.
   - Ⓑ Lagoons become more and more shallow as they heat up and flow into the ocean.
   - Ⓒ A lot of life exists in lagoons for two reasons: the low water level and the steady source of new residue.
   - Ⓓ The flow of sediments into lagoons causes biological activity, which in turn causes the lagoons to heat up.

8. The author begins paragraph 5 with the phrase "Unlike the flooded coastal plains" in order to
   - Ⓐ indicate that a thorough discussion of flooded coastal plains follows
   - Ⓑ show that flooded coastal plains and mountainous coasts have some similarities in spite of their differences
   - Ⓒ clarify the ideas of flooded coastal plains that were previously presented
   - Ⓓ indicate that the discussion is moving from one type of estuary system to the other

9. The phrase "this way" in paragraph 5 refers to
   - Ⓐ geological processes contributing to rugged topography
   - Ⓑ the sea level rising along the mountainous coast
   - Ⓒ large blocks of crust sinking as a result of tectonic activity
   - Ⓓ glaciers cutting valleys through mountains

10. It is implied in the passage that fjords
    - Ⓐ are a type of mountainous estuary system
    - Ⓑ are found throughout the world
    - Ⓒ were formed in the same way as the San Francisco Bay
    - Ⓓ have as much sediment as flooded coastal plains

11.

Directions: The answer choices below are each used to describe one of the different types of estuary systems. Complete the table by matching appropriate answer choices to the estuary system they are used to describe. TWO of the answer choices will not be used. **This question is worth 4 points** (4 points for 7 correct answers, 3 points for 6 correct answers, 2 points for 5 correct answers, 1 point for 4 correct answers, and 0 points for 3, 2, 1, or 0 correct answers).	
estuary systems on flooded coastal plains	• • • •
estuary systems on mountainous coasts	• • •

Answer Choices (choose 7 to complete the table):

(1) Lead into deeper bodies of water

(2) Have huge amounts of deposits

(3) Are never commercially viable

(4) Were created by tectonic or glacial activity

(5) Are covered with shallow water

(6) Are not protected by barrier beaches

(7) Are the primary way that fresh water is channeled to the ocean

(8) Were created on part of a submerged continent

(9) Are protected by barrier beaches

Turn to pages 185–188 to *diagnose* your errors and *record* your results.

READING MINI-TEST 5

PAUSE TEST　　SECTION EXIT　　　　　　　　　　　　　　　　　　　　VOLUME　HELP　OK　NEXT

Reading
Section Directions

This section tests your ability to understand an English academic reading passage.

All questions except the last one are worth one point each. The last question is worth more than one point. The directions for the last question will state how many points it is worth.

You will now start the Reading section. You have **20 minutes** to read one passage and answer the questions about it.

Read the passage.

Schizophrenia

➊   Schizophrenia is in reality a cluster of psychological disorders in which a variety of behaviors are exhibited and which are classified in various ways. Though there are numerous behaviors that might be considered schizophrenic, common behaviors that manifest themselves in severe schizophrenic disturbances are thought disorders, delusions, and emotional disorders.

➋   Because schizophrenia is not a single disease but is in reality a cluster of related disorders, schizophrenics tend to be classified into various subcategories. The various subcategories of schizophrenia are based on the degree to which the various common behaviors are manifested in the patient as well as other factors such as the age of the schizophrenic patient at the onset of symptoms and the duration of the symptoms. Five of the more common subcategories of schizophrenia are simple, hebephrenic, paranoid, catatonic, and acute.

➌   The main characteristic of simple schizophrenia is that it begins at a relatively early age and manifests itself in a slow withdrawal from family and social relationships with a gradual progression toward more severe symptoms over a period of years. Someone suffering from simple schizophrenia may early on simply be apathetic toward life, may maintain contact with reality a great deal of the time, and may be out in the world rather than hospitalized. Over time, however, the symptoms, particularly thought and emotional disorders, increase in severity.

➍   Hebephrenic schizophrenia is a relatively severe form of the disease that is characterized by severely disturbed thought processes as well as highly emotional and bizarre behavior. Those suffering from hebephrenic schizophrenia have hallucinations and delusions and appear quite incoherent; their behavior is often extreme and quite inappropriate to the situation, perhaps full of unwarranted laughter, or tears, or obscenities that seem unrelated to the moment. This type of schizophrenia represents a rather severe and ongoing disintegration of personality that makes this type of schizophrenic unable to play a role in society.

➎   Paranoid schizophrenia is a different type of schizophrenia in which the outward behavior of the schizophrenic often seems quite appropriate; this type of schizophrenic is often able to get along in society for long periods of time. However, a paranoid schizophrenic suffers from extreme delusions of persecution, often accompanied by delusions of grandeur. While this type of schizophrenic has strange delusions and unusual thought processes, his or her outward behavior is not as incoherent or unusual as a hebephrenic's behavior. A paranoid schizophrenic can appear alert and intelligent much of the time but can also turn suddenly hostile and violent in response to imagined threats.

➏   Another type of schizophrenia is the catatonic variety, which is characterized by alternating periods of extreme excitement and stupor. There are abrupt changes in behavior, from frenzied periods of excitement to stuporous periods of withdrawn behavior. During periods of excitement, the catatonic schizophrenic may exhibit excessive and sometimes violent behavior; during the periods of stupor, the catatonic schizophrenic may remain mute and unresponsive to the environment.

➐   A final type of schizophrenia is acute schizophrenia, which is characterized by a sudden onset of schizophrenic symptoms such as confusion, excitement, emotionality, depression, and irrational fear. The acute schizophrenic, unlike the simple schizophrenic, shows a sudden onset of the disease rather than a slow progression from one stage of it to the other. Additionally, the acute schizophrenic exhibits various types of schizophrenic behaviors during different episodes, sometimes exhibiting the characteristics of hebephrenic, catatonic, or even paranoid schizophrenia. In this type of schizophrenia, the patient's personality seems to have completely disintegrated.

Refer to this version of the passage to answer the questions that follow.

Paragraph

Schizophrenia

1   Schizophrenia is in reality a cluster of psychological disorders in which a variety of behaviors are exhibited and which are classified in various ways. Though there are numerous behaviors that might be considered schizophrenic, common behaviors that manifest themselves in severe schizophrenic disturbances are thought disorders, delusions, and emotional disorders.

2   Because schizophrenia is not a single disease but is in reality a cluster of related disorders, schizophrenics tend to be classified into various subcategories. The various subcategories of schizophrenia are based on the degree to which the various common behaviors are manifested in the patient as well as other factors such as the age of the schizophrenic patient at the onset of symptoms and the duration of the symptoms. Five of the more common subcategories of schizophrenia are simple, hebephrenic, paranoid, catatonic, and acute.

3   **5A** The main characteristic of simple schizophrenia is that it begins at a relatively early age and manifests itself in a slow withdrawal from family and social relationships with a gradual progression toward more severe symptoms over a period of years. **5B** Someone suffering from simple schizophrenia may early on simply be apathetic toward life, may maintain contact with reality a great deal of the time, and may be out in the world rather than hospitalized. **5C** Over time, however, the symptoms, particularly thought and emotional disorders, increase in severity. **5D**

4   Hebephrenic schizophrenia is a relatively severe form of the disease that is characterized by severely disturbed thought processes as well as highly emotional and bizarre behavior. Those suffering from hebephrenic schizophrenia have hallucinations and delusions and appear quite incoherent; their behavior is often extreme and quite inappropriate to the situation, perhaps full of unwarranted laughter, or tears, or obscenities that seem unrelated to the moment. This type of schizophrenia represents a rather severe and ongoing disintegration of personality that makes this type of schizophrenic unable to play a role in society.

5   Paranoid schizophrenia is a different type of schizophrenia in which the outward behavior of the schizophrenic often seems quite appropriate; this type of schizophrenic is often able to get along in society for long periods of time. However, a paranoid schizophrenic suffers from extreme delusions of persecution, often accompanied by delusions of grandeur. While this type of schizophrenic has strange delusions and unusual thought processes, his or her outward behavior is not as incoherent or unusual as a hebephrenic's behavior. A paranoid schizophrenic can appear alert and intelligent much of the time but can also turn suddenly hostile and violent in response to imagined threats.

6   Another type of schizophrenia is the catatonic variety, which is characterized by alternating periods of extreme excitement and stupor. There are abrupt changes in behavior, from frenzied periods of excitement to stuporous periods of withdrawn behavior. During periods of excitement, the catatonic schizophrenic may exhibit excessive and sometimes violent behavior; during the periods of stupor, the catatonic schizophrenic may remain mute and unresponsive to the environment.

7   A final type of schizophrenia is acute schizophrenia, which is characterized by a sudden onset of schizophrenic symptoms such as confusion, excitement, emotionality, depression, and irrational fear. The acute schizophrenic, unlike the simple schizophrenic, shows a sudden onset of the disease rather than a slow progression from one stage of it to the other. Additionally, the acute schizophrenic exhibits various types of schizophrenic behaviors during different episodes, sometimes exhibiting the characteristics of hebephrenic, catatonic, or even paranoid schizophrenia. In this type of schizophrenia, the patient's personality seems to have completely disintegrated.

Questions

1. The passage states that schizophrenia
   - Ⓐ is a single psychological disorder
   - Ⓑ always involves delusions
   - Ⓒ is a group of various psychological disorders
   - Ⓓ always develops early in life

2. The phrase "manifested in" in paragraph 2 is closest in meaning to
   - Ⓐ internalized within
   - Ⓑ demonstrated by
   - Ⓒ created in
   - Ⓓ maintained by

3. Which of the sentences below best expresses the essential information in the highlighted sentence in paragraph 3? *Incorrect* choices change the meaning in important ways or leave out essential information.
   - Ⓐ Simple schizophrenia generally starts at an early age and slowly worsens.
   - Ⓑ All types of schizophrenics withdraw from their families as their disease progresses.
   - Ⓒ Those suffering from simple schizophrenia tend to move more and more slowly over the years.
   - Ⓓ It is common for simple schizophrenia to start at an early age and remain less severe than other types of schizophrenia.

4. The word "apathetic" in paragraph 3 is closest in meaning to
   - Ⓐ sentimental
   - Ⓑ logical
   - Ⓒ realistic
   - Ⓓ emotionless

5. Look at the four squares [■] that indicate where the following sentence could be added to paragraph 3.

   At this point, hospitalization will most likely be deemed necessary.

   Where would the sentence best fit? Click on a square [■] to add the sentence to the passage.

6. The word "unwarranted" in paragraph 4 is closest in meaning to
   - Ⓐ inappropriate
   - Ⓑ uncontrolled
   - Ⓒ insensitive
   - Ⓓ underestimated

7. The phrase "get along" in paragraph 5 could best be replaced by
   - Ⓐ mobilize
   - Ⓑ negotiate
   - Ⓒ manage
   - Ⓓ travel

8. The author uses the word "While" in paragraph 5 in order to show that paranoid schizophrenics
   - Ⓐ think in a way that is materially different from the way that they act
   - Ⓑ have strange delusions at the same time that they have unusual thought patterns
   - Ⓒ can think clearly in spite of their strange behavior
   - Ⓓ exhibit strange behaviors as they think unusual thoughts

9. It is implied in paragraph 5 that a paranoid schizophrenic would be most likely to
   - Ⓐ break into unexplained laughter
   - Ⓑ believe that he is a great leader
   - Ⓒ withdraw into a stuporous state
   - Ⓓ improve over time

10. The word "mute" in paragraph 6 is closest in meaning to
    - Ⓐ asleep
    - Ⓑ quiet
    - Ⓒ deaf
    - Ⓓ frightened

11. The word "it" in paragraph 7 refers to
    - Ⓐ the disease
    - Ⓑ a slow progression
    - Ⓒ one stage
    - Ⓓ the other

12. It is NOT indicated in the passage that which of the following suffers from delusions?

  Ⓐ A hebephrenic schizophrenic
  Ⓑ A paranoid schizophrenic
  Ⓒ A catatonic schizophrenic
  Ⓓ An acute schizophrenic

13.

> **Directions:** An introductory sentence for a brief summary of the passage is provided below. Complete the summary by selecting the THREE answer choices that express the most important ideas in the passage. Some sentences do not belong in the summary because they express ideas that are not presented in the passage or are minor ideas in the passage. **This question is worth 2 points** (2 points for 3 correct answers, 1 point for 2 correct answers, and 0 points for 1 or 0 correct answers).

This passage discusses characteristics of schizophrenia.

•
•
•

Answer Choices (choose 3 to complete the chart):

(1) Schizophrenia is a single disease with a single set of symptoms.

(2) The onset of schizophrenia may be slow or fast.

(3) Schizophrenics always suffer from delusions.

(4) Families of schizophrenics are generally unaware of the problem.

(5) A schizophrenic may or may not be able to function socially for periods of time.

(6) Schizophrenia is a group of diseases rather than a single disease.

Turn to pages 185–188 to *diagnose* your errors and *record* your results.

READING MINI-TEST 6

Reading
Section Directions

This section tests your ability to understand an English academic reading passage.

All questions except the last one are worth one point each. The last question is worth more than one point. The directions for the last question will state how many points it is worth.

You will now start the Reading section. You have **20 minutes** to read one passage and answer the questions about it.

Read the passage.

Exxon Valdez

1   In the late 1980s, a disaster involving the *Exxon Valdez,* an oil tanker tasked with transporting oil from southern Alaska to the West Coast of the United States, caused a considerable amount of damage to the environment of Alaska. Crude oil from Alaska's North Slope fields near Prudhoe Bay on the north coast of Alaska is carried by pipeline to the port of Valdez on the southern coast and from there is shipped by tanker to the West Coast. On March 24, 1989, the *Exxon Valdez,* a huge oil tanker more than three football fields in length, went off course in a 16-kilometer-wide channel in Prince William Sound near Valdez, Alaska, hitting submerged rocks and causing a tremendous oil spill. The resulting oil slick spread rapidly and coated more than 1,600 kilometers (1,000 miles) of coastline. Though actual numbers can never be known, it is believed that at least a half million birds, thousands of seals and otters, quite a few whales, and an untold number of fish were killed as a result.

2   Decades before this disaster, environmentalists had predicted just such an enormous oil spill in this area because of the treacherous nature of the waters due to the submerged reefs, icebergs, and violent storms there. They had urged that oil be transported to the continental United States by land-based pipeline rather than by oil tanker or by undersea pipeline to reduce the potential damage to the environment posed by the threat of an oil spill. Alyeska, a consortium of the seven oil companies working in Alaska's North Slope fields, argued against such a land-based pipeline on the basis of the length of time that such a pipeline would take to construct and on the belief, or perhaps wishful thinking, that the probability of a tanker spill in the area was extremely low.

3   Government agencies charged with protecting the environment were assured by Alyeska and Exxon that such a pipeline was unnecessary because appropriate protective measures had been taken, that within five hours of any accident there would be enough equipment and trained workers to clean up any spill before it managed to cause much damage. However, when the *Exxon Valdez* spill actually occurred, Exxon and Alyeska were unprepared, in terms of both equipment and personnel, to deal with the spill. Though it was a massive spill, appropriate personnel and equipment available in a timely fashion could have reduced the damage considerably. Exxon ended up spending billions of dollars on the clean-up itself and, in addition, spent further billions in fines and damages to the state of Alaska, the federal government, commercial fishermen, property owners, and others harmed by the disaster. The total cost to Exxon was more than $8 billion.

4   A step that could possibly have prevented this accident even though the tanker did run into submerged rocks would have been a double hull on the tanker. Today, almost all merchant ships have double hulls, but only a small percentage of oil tankers do. Legislation passed since the spill requires all new tankers to be built with double hulls, but many older tankers have received dispensations to avoid the $25 million cost per tanker to convert a single hulled tanker to one with a double hull. However, compared with the $8.5 billion cost of the *Exxon Valdez* catastrophe, it is a comparatively paltry sum.

Refer to this version of the passage to answer the questions that follow.

Paragraph

Exxon Valdez

1   In the late 1980s, a disaster involving the *Exxon Valdez,* an oil tanker tasked with transporting oil from southern Alaska to the West Coast of the United States, caused a considerable amount of damage to the environment of Alaska. Crude oil from Alaska's North Slope fields near Prudhoe Bay on the north coast of Alaska is carried by pipeline to the port of Valdez on the southern coast and from there is shipped by tanker to the West Coast. On March 24, 1989, the *Exxon Valdez,* a huge oil tanker more than three football fields in length, went off course in a 16-kilometer-wide channel in Prince William Sound near Valdez, Alaska, hitting submerged rocks and causing a tremendous oil spill. The resulting oil slick spread rapidly and coated more than 1,600 kilometers (1,000 miles) of coastline. Though actual numbers can never be known, it is believed that at least a half million birds, thousands of seals and otters, quite a few whales, and an untold number of fish were killed as a result.

2   **8A** Decades before this disaster, environmentalists had predicted just such an enormous oil spill in this area because of the treacherous nature of the waters due to the submerged reefs, icebergs, and violent storms there. **8B** They had urged that oil be transported to the continental United States by land-based pipeline rather than by oil tanker or by undersea pipeline to reduce the potential damage to the environment posed by the threat of an oil spill. **8C** Alyeska, a consortium of the seven oil companies working in Alaska's North Slope fields, argued against such a land-based pipeline on the basis of the length of time that such a pipeline would take to construct and on the belief, or perhaps wishful thinking, that the probability of a tanker spill in the area was extremely low. **8D**

3   Government agencies charged with protecting the environment were assured by Alyeska and Exxon that such a pipeline was unnecessary because appropriate protective measures had been taken, that within five hours of any accident there would be enough equipment and trained workers to clean up any spill before it managed to cause much damage. However, when the *Exxon Valdez* spill actually occurred, Exxon and Alyeska were unprepared, in terms of both equipment and personnel, to deal with the spill. Though it was a massive spill, appropriate personnel and equipment available in a timely fashion could have reduced the damage considerably. Exxon ended up spending billions of dollars on the clean-up itself and, in addition, spent further billions in fines and damages to the state of Alaska, the federal government, commercial fishermen, property owners, and others harmed by the disaster. The total cost to Exxon was more than $8 billion.

4   A step that could possibly have prevented this accident even though the tanker did run into submerged rocks would have been a double hull on the tanker. Today, almost all merchant ships have double hulls, but only a small percentage of oil tankers do. Legislation passed since the spill requires all new tankers to be built with double hulls, but many older tankers have received dispensations to avoid the $25 million cost per tanker to convert a single hulled tanker to one with a double hull. However, compared with the $8.5 billion cost of the *Exxon Valdez* catastrophe, it is a comparatively paltry sum.

Questions

1. What is stated in paragraph 1 about the oil industry in Alaska?

   Ⓐ The oil fields are in the southern part of Alaska.

   Ⓑ Oil is carried from the oil fields to Valdez by tanker.

   Ⓒ Oil arrives in Valdez by pipeline and departs by ship.

   Ⓓ Oil is transported from Valdez to the U.S. mainland through a pipeline.

2. The word "coated" in paragraph 1 could best be replaced by

   Ⓐ covered

   Ⓑ warmed

   Ⓒ filled

   Ⓓ blackened

3. "An untold number" in paragraph 1 is most likely a number

   Ⓐ that has not been discussed

   Ⓑ that is so high that it cannot be counted

   Ⓒ that is of little importance to anyone

   Ⓓ that has been hidden away from the public

4. The word "They" in paragraph 2 refers to

   Ⓐ decades

   Ⓑ environmentalists

   Ⓒ waters

   Ⓓ reefs

5. Which point is NOT made by the environmentalists mentioned in paragraph 2?

   Ⓐ That a huge oil spill in the waters off Alaska was possible

   Ⓑ That the waters off the coast of Alaska were dangerous for ships

   Ⓒ That oil tankers should not be used to transport oil from Alaska

   Ⓓ That an undersea pipeline was preferable to a land-based pipeline

6. In paragraph 2, "a consortium" is most likely

   Ⓐ a board

   Ⓑ a leader

   Ⓒ an association

   Ⓓ a contract

7. The author uses the expression "wishful thinking" in paragraph 2 in order to

   Ⓐ emphasize the idea that the belief was misguided

   Ⓑ emphasize the desire that the pipeline would be built

   Ⓒ emphasize the hope that an oil spill could be cleaned up quickly

   Ⓓ emphasize the wish that a lot of oil would be discovered

8. Look at the four squares [■] that indicate where the following sentence could be added to paragraph 2.

   Unfortunately, the line of reasoning proved incorrect, with disastrous results.

   Where would the sentence best fit? Click on a square [■] to add the sentence to the passage.

9. What can be inferred from paragraph 3 about the preparations for a potential oil spill?

   Ⓐ Government agencies assured the oil companies that the environment was protected.

   Ⓑ The oil companies had equipment and staff ready to deal with a spill within five hours of a spill.

   Ⓒ Neither Exxon nor Alyeska had prepared adequately for a tanker accident.

   Ⓓ Exxon had spent billions of dollars preparing for a potential oil spill.

10. The word "fashion" in paragraph 3 could best be replaced by

    Ⓐ style

    Ⓑ direction

    Ⓒ hour

    Ⓓ manner

11. Which of the sentences below best expresses the essential information in the highlighted sentence in paragraph 4? *Incorrect* choices change the meaning in important ways or leave out essential information.

Ⓐ In spite of the legislation requiring double hulls on all ships, many ship owners have paid millions of dollars to avoid installing double hulls.

Ⓑ Although new tankers are legally required to have double hulls, not all older tankers have been required to do so.

Ⓒ Laws have been passed requiring all tankers, both old and new, to have double hulls.

Ⓓ It is very expensive to build double-hulled tankers, so most new tankers do not have double hulls.

12. The word "paltry" in paragraph 4 is closest in meaning to

Ⓐ insignificant

Ⓑ unbelievable

Ⓒ inaccurate

Ⓓ enormous

13.

Directions: An introductory sentence for a brief summary of the passage is provided below. Complete the summary by selecting the THREE answer choices that express the most important ideas in the passage. Some sentences do not belong in the summary because they express ideas that are not presented in the passage or are minor ideas in the passage. **This question is worth 2 points** (2 points for 3 correct answers, 1 point for 2 correct answers, and 0 points for 1 or 0 correct answers).

The passage discusses the tragedy of the *Exxon Valdez* and factors that could have prevented or lessened the damage.
•
•
•

Answer Choices (choose 3 to complete the chart):

(1) Higher fines and damage payments for Exxon

(2) Appropriate preparations by oil companies for tanker spills

(3) A land-based oil pipeline from southern Alaska to the West Coast

(4) Additional dispensations for single-hulled tankers

(5) The use of double-hulled ships to transport oil

(6) A land-based oil pipeline from the North Slope fields to Valdez

Turn to pages 185–188 to *diagnose* your errors and *record* your results.

READING MINI-TEST 7

PAUSE TEST | SECTION EXIT

VOLUME | HELP | OK | NEXT

Reading

Section Directions

This section tests your ability to understand an English academic reading passage.

All questions except the last one are worth one point each. The last question is worth more than one point. The directions for the last question will state how many points it is worth.

You will now start the Reading section. You have **20 minutes** to read one passage and answer the questions about it.

Read the passage.

Plate Tectonics

1 According to the theory of plate tectonics, the upper portion of the Earth's lithosphere, which contains the heavier oceanic and the lighter continental crusts, consists of a series of rigid plates that are in constant motion. This theory provides a cohesive model to explain the integrated actions of continental drift, seafloor spreading, and mountain formation.

2 The Earth's plates are estimated to have an average depth of approximately 60 miles (or 100 kilometers), but they are believed to vary considerably in size. Some are estimated to be continental or even hemispheric in size, while others are believed to be much smaller. Though the actual boundaries and sizes and shapes of the plates are not known for sure, it has been postulated that there are six major plates and somewhere around the same number of smaller ones. Most of the plates consist of both *sial* (continental) and *sima* (oceanic) crust. They are in constant movement, though they move at an extremely slow pace, and these movements cause frequent interactions between plates.

3 At this time, scientists have identified three different types of boundaries between plates. At a **divergent** boundary, plates are moving away from each other. This type of boundary occurs at an oceanic ridge, where new material is being added to the seafloor from deeper within the Earth. Shallow earthquakes and underwater volcanoes are associated with this type of plate activity. At a **convergent** boundary, plates are moving toward each other and collide, causing vast folding and crumpling along the edges of the plates. In addition to the folding and crumpling, one of the plates slowly folds under the other. Though this subduction is slow, it can nonetheless be quite catastrophic as the crustal material of the submerging plate gradually melts into the fiery hot depths below. The area where subduction occurs is usually an area where the crust is relatively unstable and is characterized by numerous deep earthquakes and a significant amount of volcanic activity. The boundaries between convergent plates are generally found around the edges of ocean basins and are sometimes associated with deep ocean trenches. A third type of boundary is a **transcurrent** boundary, which involves two plates sliding past each other laterally, without the folding and crumpling that occurs at a convergent boundary. This third type of boundary is thought to be far less common than the other two types of boundaries.

4 The concept of plate tectonics provides an understanding of the massive rearrangement of the Earth's crust that has apparently taken place. It is now generally accepted that the single supercontinent known as Pangaea indeed existed, that Pangaea subsequently broke apart into two giant pieces, Gondwanaland in the south and Laurasia in the north, and that the continents attached to the various crustal plates separated and drifted in various directions. As the plates drifted, they may have diverged, which was associated with the spread of the seafloor, or they may have converged, which resulted in collision, subduction, and mountain building.

5 The majority of the Earth's major mountain ranges are found in zones where plates converge. The Himalayas, which are the world's highest mountains, along with the central Asian mountains of varying heights associated with them, were formed by the crumpling and folding of two massive plates that collided at a convergent boundary. The landmass that is today known as India was originally part of Gondwanaland, the giant supercontinent in the Southern Hemisphere, but it broke off from Gondwanaland approximately 200 million years ago and drifted north to collide with part of Laurasia, the giant supercontinent in the Northern Hemisphere, to create the world's tallest mountains.

Refer to this version of the passage to answer the questions that follow.

Plate Tectonics

Paragraph

1   According to the theory of plate tectonics, the upper portion of the Earth's lithosphere, which contains the heavier oceanic and the lighter continental crusts, consists of a series of rigid plates that are in constant motion. This theory provides a cohesive model to explain the integrated actions of continental drift, seafloor spreading, and mountain formation.

2   The Earth's plates are estimated to have an average depth of approximately 60 miles (or 100 kilometers), but they are believed to vary considerably in size. Some are estimated to be continental or even hemispheric in size, while others are believed to be much smaller. Though the actual boundaries and sizes and shapes of the plates are not known for sure, it has been postulated that there are six major plates and somewhere around the same number of smaller ones. Most of the plates consist of both *sial* (continental) and *sima* (oceanic) crust. They are in constant movement, though they move at an extremely slow pace, and these movements cause frequent interactions between plates.

3   At this time, scientists have identified three different types of boundaries between plates. At a **divergent** boundary, plates are moving away from each other. This type of boundary occurs at an oceanic ridge, where new material is being added to the seafloor from deeper within the Earth. Shallow earthquakes and underwater volcanoes are associated with this type of plate activity. At a **convergent** boundary, plates are moving toward each other and collide, causing vast folding and crumpling along the edges of the plates. In addition to the folding and crumpling, one of the plates slowly folds under the other. Though this subduction is slow, it can nonetheless be quite catastrophic as the crustal material of the submerging plate gradually melts into the fiery hot depths below. The area where subduction occurs is usually an area where the crust is relatively unstable and is characterized by numerous deep earthquakes and a significant amount of volcanic activity. The boundaries between convergent plates are generally found around the edges of ocean basins and are sometimes associated with deep ocean trenches. A third type of boundary is a **transcurrent** boundary, which involves two plates sliding past each other laterally, without the folding and crumpling that occurs at a convergent boundary. This third type of boundary is thought to be far less common than the other two types of boundaries.

4   The concept of plate tectonics provides an understanding of the massive rearrangement of the Earth's crust that has apparently taken place. It is now generally accepted that the single supercontinent known as Pangaea indeed existed, that Pangaea subsequently broke apart into two giant pieces, Gondwanaland in the south and Laurasia in the north, and that the continents attached to the various crustal plates separated and drifted in various directions. As the plates drifted, they may have diverged, which was associated with the spread of the seafloor, or they may have converged, which resulted in collision, subduction, and mountain building.

5   **11A** The majority of the Earth's major mountain ranges are found in zones where plates converge. **11B** The Himalayas, which are the world's highest mountains, along with the central Asian mountains of varying heights associated with them, were formed by the crumpling and folding of two massive plates that collided at a convergent boundary. **11C** The landmass that is today known as India was originally part of Gondwanaland, the giant supercontinent in the Southern Hemisphere, but it broke off from Gondwanaland approximately 200 million years ago and drifted north to collide with part of Laurasia, the giant supercontinent in the Northern Hemisphere, to create the world's tallest mountains. **11D**

Questions

1. The word "cohesive" in paragraph 1 is closest in meaning to
   - Ⓐ unified
   - Ⓑ contemporary
   - Ⓒ tenacious
   - Ⓓ lengthy

2. It can be inferred from paragraph 2 that
   - Ⓐ none of the plates has a depth of more than 100 kilometers
   - Ⓑ each of the plates has approximately the same dimensions
   - Ⓒ some plates are relatively stationary
   - Ⓓ there are most likely around 6 minor plates

3. The word "postulated" in paragraph 2 is closest in meaning to
   - Ⓐ postponed
   - Ⓑ hypothesized
   - Ⓒ proven
   - Ⓓ forgotten

4. The author uses the expression "At this time" at the beginning of paragraph 3 in order to indicate that
   - Ⓐ more types of boundaries might be found in the future
   - Ⓑ interactions are currently occurring between plates
   - Ⓒ all possible types of boundaries have already been located
   - Ⓓ the major plates are all currently moving away from each other

5. The word "subduction" in paragraph 3 is closest in meaning to
   - Ⓐ strong attack
   - Ⓑ lateral movement
   - Ⓒ sudden melting
   - Ⓓ downward force

6. According to the passage, subduction
   - Ⓐ occurs rapidly
   - Ⓑ has little effect
   - Ⓒ causes one of the plates to sink and melt
   - Ⓓ generally takes place in stable areas

7. It is NOT stated in paragraph 4 that it is generally accepted that
   - Ⓐ there used to be a giant continent
   - Ⓑ the giant continent broke into parts
   - Ⓒ Gondwanaland moved to the south and Laurasia moved to the north
   - Ⓓ the continents moved in various directions

8. The word "drifted" in paragraph 4 is closest in meaning to
   - Ⓐ broke down
   - Ⓑ moved slowly
   - Ⓒ were formed
   - Ⓓ lifted up

9. The word "them" in paragraph 5 refers to
   - Ⓐ zones
   - Ⓑ the Himalayas
   - Ⓒ central Asian mountains
   - Ⓓ two massive plates

10. Which of the sentences below best expresses the essential information in the highlighted sentence in paragraph 5? *Incorrect* choices change the meaning in important ways or leave out essential information.
    - Ⓐ India was formed when a landmass from the Southern Hemisphere broke off and collided with a landmass in the Northern Hemisphere.
    - Ⓑ Gondwanaland drifted north 200 million years ago to merge with Laurasia.
    - Ⓒ India was formed 200 million years ago when two giant supercontinents drifted north and collided.
    - Ⓓ The world's tallest mountains used to be in India, but they broke off from India and drifted to the north.

11. Look at the four squares [■] that indicate where the following sentence could be added to paragraph 5.

    Mountain building is clearly explained through the concept of plate tectonics.

    Where would the sentence best fit? Click on a square [■] to add the sentence to the passage.

12.

Directions: The answer choices below are each used to describe one of the types of boundaries. Complete the table by matching appropriate answer choices to the boundaries they are used to describe. TWO of the answer choices will not be used. **This question is worth 3 points** (3 points for 5 correct answers, 2 points for 4 correct answers, 1 point for 3 correct answers, and 0 points for 2, 1, or 0 correct answers).	

divergent boundary	• •
convergent boundary	• •
transcurrent boundary	•

Answer Choices (choose 5 to complete the table):

(1) Occurs when two plates remain stationary in relation to each other

(2) Occurs when plates moving toward each other do not collide

(3) Occurs when plates move away from each other

(4) Occurs when plates moving toward each other collide

(5) Can result in the creation of mountains

(6) Causes the continents to shift

(7) Can result in the spreading of the seafloor

Turn to pages 185–188 to *diagnose* your errors and *record* your results.

READING MINI-TEST 8

Reading

Section Directions

This section tests your ability to understand an English academic reading passage.

All questions except the last one are worth one point each. The last question is worth more than one point. The directions for the last question will state how many points it is worth.

You will now start the Reading section. You have **20 minutes** to read one passage and answer the questions about it.

Read the passage.

Limners

The earliest known American painters, who were active in the latter part of the seventeenth century and the early part of the eighteenth century, were described in documents, journals, and letters of the time as limners. Most of the paintings created by limners were portraits, and they were unsigned because the finished pieces did not belong to the limners who created them but were instead the possessions of the subjects in the portraits. The portraits today are named after the subjects portrayed in them, and a particular artist is known only as the creator of a particular portrait; thus a particular portrait is named *Mrs. Elizabeth Freake and Baby Mary* after the people in the portrait, and the limner who created the portrait is known only as the Freake Limner. Art historians who specialize in art from this era have been able to identify clusters of portraits painted by each of a number of limners but, in many cases, do not know the name of the actual limner.

As can be seen from the fact that portraits created by limners went unsigned, limners were regarded more as artisans or skilled tradesmen than as artists. They earned their living as many artisans and tradesmen did at the time, as itinerant workers moving from town to town offering their services to either those who could pay or, more likely, to those who had goods or services to offer in return. They were able to paint portraits for those desiring to have a tangible representation of a family member for posterity; they also took on a variety of other types of painting jobs to stay employed, such as painting the walls of buildings, painting signs for businesses, and painting furniture.

3

Some of the early portraitists most likely received their education in art or trained as artisans in Europe prior to their arrival in America and then trained others in America in their craft; because they were working in undeveloped or minimally developed colonial areas, their lives were quite difficult. They had little access to information about the world of art and little access to art supplies, so they needed to mix their own paints and make their own brushes and stretched canvasses. They also needed to be prepared to take on whatever painting jobs were needed to survive.

There seem to be two broad categories of painting styles used by the portraitists, the style of the New England limners and the style of the New York limners. The style of the New England limners was a decorative style with flat characters, characters that seemed to lack mass and volume. This is not because the New England limners had no knowledge of painting techniques but was instead because the New England limners were using the style of Tudor painting that became popular during the reign of Queen Elizabeth I, a style that included characters with a flat woodenness yet with the numerous highly decorative touches and frills popular in the English court.

The New York limners had a rather different style from the New England limners, and this was because New York had a different background from the rest of New England. Much of New England had been colonized by the English, and thus the basis for the style of the New England limners was the Tudor style that had been popularized during the reign of the Tudor queen Elizabeth I. However, the Dutch had settled the colony of New Amsterdam, and though New Amsterdam became an English colony in 1664 and was renamed New York, the Dutch character and influence was strongly in place during the era of the limners. The New York limners, as a result, were influenced by the Dutch artists of the time rather than the Tudor artists. Dutch art, unlike the more flowery Tudor art, was considerably more sober and prosaic. In addition, the New York limners lacked the flat portrayals of characters of the New England limners and instead made use of light and shade to create more lifelike portraits.

Refer to this version of the passage to answer the questions that follow.

Limners

Paragraph

1   The earliest known American painters, who were active in the latter part of the seventeenth century and the early part of the eighteenth century, were described in documents, journals, and letters of the time as limners. Most of the paintings created by limners were portraits, and they were unsigned because the finished pieces did not belong to the limners who created them but were instead the possessions of the subjects in the portraits. The portraits today are named after the subjects portrayed in them, and a particular artist is known only as the creator of a particular portrait; thus a particular portrait is named *Mrs. Elizabeth Freake and Baby Mary* after the people in the portrait, and the limner who created the portrait is known only as the Freake Limner. Art historians who specialize in art from this era have been able to identify clusters of portraits painted by each of a number of limners but, in many cases, do not know the name of the actual limner.

2   As can be seen from the fact that portraits created by limners went unsigned, limners were regarded more as artisans or skilled tradesmen than as artists. They earned their living as many artisans and tradesmen did at the time, as itinerant workers moving from town to town offering their services to either those who could pay or, more likely, to those who had goods or services to offer in return. They were able to paint portraits for those desiring to have a tangible representation of a family member for posterity; they also took on a variety of other types of painting jobs to stay employed, such as painting the walls of buildings, painting signs for businesses, and painting furniture.

3   **9A** Some of the early portraitists most likely received their education in art or trained as artisans in Europe prior to their arrival in America and then trained others in America in their craft; because they were working in undeveloped or minimally developed colonial areas, their lives were quite difficult. **9B** They had little access to information about the world of art and little access to art supplies, so they needed to mix their own paints and make their own brushes and stretched canvasses. **9C** They also needed to be prepared to take on whatever painting jobs were needed to survive. **9D**

4   There seem to be two broad categories of painting styles used by the portraitists, the style of the New England limners and the style of the New York limners. The style of the New England limners was a decorative style with flat characters, characters that seemed to lack mass and volume. This is not because the New England limners had no knowledge of painting techniques but was instead because the New England limners were using the style of Tudor painting that became popular during the reign of Queen Elizabeth I, a style that included characters with a flat woodenness yet with the numerous highly decorative touches and frills popular in the English court.

5   The New York limners had a rather different style from the New England limners, and this was because New York had a different background from the rest of New England. Much of New England had been colonized by the English, and thus the basis for the style of the New England limners was the Tudor style that had been popularized during the reign of the Tudor queen Elizabeth I. However, the Dutch had settled the colony of New Amsterdam, and though New Amsterdam became an English colony in 1664 and was renamed New York, the Dutch character and influence was strongly in place during the era of the limners. The New York limners, as a result, were influenced by the Dutch artists of the time rather than the Tudor artists. Dutch art, unlike the more flowery Tudor art, was considerably more sober and prosaic. In addition, the New York limners lacked the flat portrayals of characters of the New England limners and instead made use of light and shade to create more lifelike portraits.

Questions

1. The word "pieces" in paragraph 1 could best be replaced by
   - Ⓐ parts
   - Ⓑ works
   - Ⓒ ideas
   - Ⓓ fragments

2. The word "them" in paragraph 1 refers to
   - Ⓐ limners
   - Ⓑ portraits
   - Ⓒ possessions
   - Ⓓ subjects

3. Which of the sentences below best expresses the essential information in the highlighted sentence in paragraph 1? *Incorrect* choices change the meaning in important ways or leave out essential information.
   - Ⓐ Art historians have been able to identify characteristics in paintings indicating that the paintings were created by limners.
   - Ⓑ Artists from the era of limners painted clusters of portraits without knowing whom they were painting.
   - Ⓒ People studying art have been able to identify clusters of artists who had painted portraits of the same subjects.
   - Ⓓ Certain groups of portraits are known to have been painted by the same limner, though the limner's name is often not known.

4. The word "itinerant" in paragraph 2 is closest in meaning to
   - Ⓐ successful
   - Ⓑ uneducated
   - Ⓒ wandering
   - Ⓓ professional

5. It is NOT mentioned in paragraph 2 that a limner might
   - Ⓐ work as a carpenter
   - Ⓑ receive pay for a painting
   - Ⓒ offer his services in return for other services
   - Ⓓ paint a house

6. The word "posterity" in paragraph 2 is closest in meaning to
   - Ⓐ prominent display
   - Ⓑ future generations
   - Ⓒ social acceptance
   - Ⓓ delayed gratification

7. It can be inferred from paragraph 3 that limners
   - Ⓐ would not possibly have had any formal training
   - Ⓑ were quite knowledgeable about the world of art
   - Ⓒ were held in high esteem by the population
   - Ⓓ were not all formally trained artists

8. The phrase "take on" in paragraph 3 could best be replaced by
   - Ⓐ accept
   - Ⓑ attack
   - Ⓒ admit
   - Ⓓ allow

9. Look at the four squares [■] that indicate where the following sentence could be added to paragraph 3.

   Few limners were formally trained artists.

   Where would the sentence best fit? Click on a square [■] to add the sentence to the passage.

10. Why does the author state that "the Dutch had settled the colony of New Amsterdam" in a passage about limners?
    - Ⓐ To provide background information about the New England limners
    - Ⓑ To indicate why the Tudor style of painting was possible
    - Ⓒ To give a reason for the highly flowery Dutch paintings
    - Ⓓ To explain why the style of the New York limners differed from that of the New England limners

11. The word "prosaic" in paragraph 5 is closest in meaning to

Ⓐ realistic
Ⓑ poetic
Ⓒ lively
Ⓓ strict

12.

Directions:	The answer choices below are each used to describe one of the groups of limners. Complete the table by matching appropriate answer choices to the groups of limners they are used to describe. TWO of the answer choices will not be used. **This question is worth 3 points** (3 points for 5 correct answers, 2 points for 4 correct answers, 1 point for 3 correct answers, and 0 points for 2, 1, or 0 correct answers).

only the New York limners	• •
only the New England limners	• •
both the New York and New England limners	•

Answer Choices (choose 5 to complete the table):

(1) Used a Tudor style of painting

(2) Painted for Queen Elizabeth I

(3) Were influenced by the Dutch style of painting

(4) Did not sign portraits

(5) Had flat characters and lots of ornamentation

(6) Had flat characters with little ornamentation

(7) Had more lifelike characters and less ornamentation

Turn to pages 185–188 to *diagnose* your errors and *record* your results.

READING COMPLETE TEST 1

PAUSE TEST SECTION EXIT

VOLUME HELP OK NEXT

Reading

Section Directions

This section tests your ability to understand an English academic reading passage.

All questions except the last one are worth one point each. The last question is worth more than one point. The directions for the last question will state how many points it is worth.

You will now start the Reading section. You have **20 minutes** to read one passage and answer the questions about it.

READING 1

Read the passage.

Prehistoric Astronomers

1   Prehistoric peoples most certainly took note of the recurring patterns of movements in the sky of such celestial bodies as the Sun, the Moon, the planets, and the stars, and they most certainly noted that events in their world, such as seasonal fluctuations in weather, which in turn had an effect on the lives of the plants and animals in their world, were often correlated with the movements of the celestial bodies. Because it was important for prehistoric people to have knowledge, for example, of when it was the best time to plant crops or when game herds would be migrating, early farmers and hunters took a great interest in the movements of celestial bodies. An understanding of the relationship between the movements of celestial bodies and recurring patterns of events on Earth was of paramount importance in many cultures; thus, many cultures in widely separated areas of the world developed methods for monitoring astronomical events.

2   The field of archeoastronomy, which combines knowledge and expertise from the fields of archeology and astronomy, is dedicated to the study of the astronomical knowledge of prehistoric cultures. Archeoastronomers who have been studying prehistoric cultures in North America have discovered various devices that made it possible for prehistoric people to study and record astronomical events. An alignment of stones in Wyoming that is known as the Bighorn Medicine Wheel, the remnants of a circular-shaped structure created with wooden posts at Cahoki in Illinois, and specially designed windows in structures of the Southwest that allowed the rays of the Sun to hit designated marks on inside walls are all believed to be constructions that serve the function of monitoring and measuring astronomical events.

3   One particular construction, which is located in the Chaco Canyon area of the state of New Mexico, has been the subject of considerable attention and discussion among archeologists and astronomers. This construction, which is at least 700 years old, consists of large slabs of rock located on top of the flat surface of a high butte that seem to form an observatory of sorts. What makes it appear to experts to be an observatory is that the slabs of rock are positioned so that shafts of sunlight fall between them and hit spiral markings carved into the side of a cliff. As the Sun changes positions with the progression of the seasons, the shafts of light fall in different places on the markings in the cliff wall. Using this system, it must have been possible for early inhabitants of the area to predict upcoming seasonal changes and the events based on them.

4   One question that has been the focus of considerable discussion is whether the stones were actually placed in their current location by early inhabitants of the region or whether the forces of nature created the arrangement. While some scientists argue that the stones could not have fallen in the current arrangement by mere happenstance and must have been purposefully positioned, others find it harder to believe that the huge stones could have been moved and easier to believe that the marks on the cliff wall were placed to reflect the positions where the slabs had fallen naturally. Whether or not the slabs were positioned by the local population, the structure correlating the positions of the slabs and the markings on the cliff wall represents a remarkably sophisticated method of following astronomical events.

Refer to this version of the passage to answer the questions that follow.

Paragraph

Prehistoric Astronomers

1   Prehistoric peoples most certainly took note of the recurring patterns of movements in the sky of such celestial bodies as the Sun, the Moon, the planets, and the stars, and they most certainly noted that events in their world, such as seasonal fluctuations in weather, which in turn had an effect on the lives of the plants and animals in their world, were often correlated with the movements of the celestial bodies. Because it was important for prehistoric people to have knowledge, for example, of when it was the best time to plant crops or when game herds would be migrating, early farmers and hunters took a great interest in the movements of celestial bodies. An understanding of the relationship between the movements of celestial bodies and recurring patterns of events on Earth was of paramount importance in many cultures; thus, many cultures in widely separated areas of the world developed methods for monitoring astronomical events.

2   **7A** The field of archeoastronomy, which combines knowledge and expertise from the fields of archeology and astronomy, is dedicated to the study of the astronomical knowledge of prehistoric cultures. **7B** Archeoastronomers who have been studying prehistoric cultures in North America have discovered various devices that made it possible for prehistoric people to study and record astronomical events. **7C** An alignment of stones in Wyoming that is known as the Bighorn Medicine Wheel, the remnants of a circular-shaped structure created with wooden posts at Cahoki in Illinois, and specially designed windows in structures of the Southwest that allowed the rays of the Sun to hit designated marks on inside walls are all believed to be constructions that serve the function of monitoring and measuring astronomical events. **7D**

3   One particular construction, which is located in the Chaco Canyon area of the state of New Mexico, has been the subject of considerable attention and discussion among archeologists and astronomers. This construction, which is at least 700 years old, consists of large slabs of rock located on top of the flat surface of a high butte that seem to form an observatory of sorts. What makes it appear to experts to be an observatory is that the slabs of rock are positioned so that shafts of sunlight fall between them and hit spiral markings carved into the side of a cliff. As the Sun changes positions with the progression of the seasons, the shafts of light fall in different places on the markings in the cliff wall. Using this system, it must have been possible for early inhabitants of the area to predict upcoming seasonal changes and the events based on them.

4   One question that has been the focus of considerable discussion is whether the stones were actually placed in their current location by early inhabitants of the region or whether the forces of nature created the arrangement. While some scientists argue that the stones could not have fallen in the current arrangement by mere happenstance and must have been purposefully positioned, others find it harder to believe that the huge stones could have been moved and easier to believe that the marks on the cliff wall were placed to reflect the positions where the slabs had fallen naturally. Whether or not the slabs were positioned by the local population, the structure correlating the positions of the slabs and the markings on the cliff wall represents a remarkably sophisticated method of following astronomical events.

Questions

1. The word "correlated" in paragraph 1 could best be replaced by
   Ⓐ in disagreement
   Ⓑ in coordination
   Ⓒ in touch
   Ⓓ in spirit

2. It is NOT mentioned in paragraph 1 that prehistoric peoples were interested in
   Ⓐ the movements of the stars
   Ⓑ changes in the weather
   Ⓒ migration patterns of certain animals
   Ⓓ the evolution of various plants

3. The word "paramount" in paragraph 1 could best be replaced by
   Ⓐ tall
   Ⓑ dependable
   Ⓒ supreme
   Ⓓ computed

4. Which of the following would an archeoastronomer be most likely to study?
   Ⓐ Plans to send a spacecraft to Mars
   Ⓑ Potential remnants of an early civilization's lunar calendar
   Ⓒ Tools used by a prehistoric tribe to prepare food
   Ⓓ Geographic formations on the Moon

5. The author mentions "An alignment of stones in Wyoming," "a circular-shaped structure . . . at Cahoki," and "specially designed windows in structures of the Southwest" in paragraph 2 in order to
   Ⓐ provide proof that archeoastronomers have been studying prehistoric cultures
   Ⓑ provide support for the idea that North American cultures built creative structures
   Ⓒ provide evidence that certain astronomical events have not changed over time
   Ⓓ provide examples of ways that prehistoric peoples monitored occurrences in the sky

6. The word "serve" in paragraph 2 could best be replaced by
   Ⓐ fulfill
   Ⓑ provide
   Ⓒ assist
   Ⓓ demonstrate

7. Look at the four squares [■] that indicate where the following sentence could be added to paragraph 2.

   This apparent understanding of certain aspects of astronomy by certain prehistoric cultures is of great academic interest today.

   Where would the sentence best fit? Click on a square [■] to add the sentence to the passage.

8. What is stated in paragraph 3 about the construction in Chaco Canyon?
   Ⓐ It was created from a single piece of stone.
   Ⓑ It prevents sunlight from entering the area.
   Ⓒ It was built before the fourteenth century.
   Ⓓ It is located in a canyon.

9. The phrase "of sorts" in paragraph 3 is closest in meaning to
   Ⓐ of opportunity
   Ⓑ of some kind
   Ⓒ of the past
   Ⓓ of fate

10. The word "them" in paragraph 3 refers to
    Ⓐ experts
    Ⓑ slabs
    Ⓒ shafts
    Ⓓ markings

11. Which of the sentences below best expresses the essential information in the highlighted sentence in paragraph 4? *Incorrect* choices change the meaning in important ways or leave out essential information.

Ⓐ One issue is whether the stones were positioned by nature or by people.

Ⓑ Early inhabitants often discussed where the stones should be placed.

Ⓒ The current location of the stones was chosen because it provides the most natural setting.

Ⓓ There is much discussion about how often early inhabitants moved the stones.

12. The word "happenstance" in paragraph 4 is closest in meaning to

Ⓐ standing
Ⓑ event
Ⓒ order
Ⓓ chance

13.

Directions: An introductory sentence for a brief summary of the passage is provided below. Complete the summary by selecting the THREE answer choices that express the most important ideas in the passage. Some sentences do not belong in the summary because they express ideas that are not presented in the passage or are minor ideas in the passage. **This question is worth 2 points** (2 points for 3 correct answers, 1 point for 2 correct answers, and 0 points for 1 or 0 correct answers).
This passage discusses the study of astronomy as it refers to prehistoric cultures in North America.
•
•
•

Answer Choices (choose 3 to complete the chart):

(1) The structure at Chaco Canyon was most likely used for something other than astronomy.

(2) Prehistoric cultures in North America were not as advanced in their study of astronomy as were cultures in other parts of the world. ➤

(3) One structure used by a certain prehistoric culture to monitor astronomical events was either discovered or created by the culture.

(4) Prehistoric cultures in North America created devices to monitor astronomical events.

(5) The Bighorn Medicine Wheel was constructed with stones. ➤

(6) Prehistoric cultures in North America most likely understood the relationship between astronomy and their daily lives.

TOEFL Reading

PAUSE
TEST

SECTION
EXIT

VOLUME   HELP   OK   NEXT

Reading

Section Directions

In this part of the Reading section, you will read 2 passages. You will have **40 minutes** to read the passages and answer the questions.

Most questions are worth 1 point, but the last question for each passage is worth more than 1 point. The directions for the last question indicate how many points you receive.

READING 2

Read the passage.

Paragraph

Truman and the Railroads

1   The period following World War II was filled with a succession of crises as the United States dealt with the difficulty of postwar reconversion to a peacetime economy. A threatened railroad strike in 1946 was one of many crises that led to a reconsideration of the interrelationships among government, management, and labor.

2   Organized labor, which had fared well during the war years of 1939–1945, faced severe problems because of the swift demobilization of thirteen million service personnel following the war and the destabilizing results of industrial reconversions from wartime to peacetime uses. During late 1945 and early 1946, a record wave of labor disputes and strikes hit the United States, and even more strikes and disputes were expected. At the height of the problems, more than 500 strikes were under way, some of them in industries that were highly critical to the overall U.S. economy, including coal, steel, cars, and oil. When a national strike was threatened by the railroads in the spring of 1946, the government moved into action, believing that the U.S. economy was threatened were it to take place.

3   President Harry S. Truman had dealt rather patiently with the labor problems until the spring of 1946. Throughout his political career, Truman had been a friend of organized labor and had been strongly supported by labor in his elections, and when the railroad strike was first threatened, he called for a sixty-day mediation period while the issues, particularly the main issue of a wage hike for railroad workers, were negotiated between management and labor. By April, eighteen of the twenty unions related to the railroads had arrived at an agreement; however, the remaining unions, which together controlled 280,000 workers and were essential to the operation of the railroads, were dissatisfied and set a date for a strike.

4   The day before the strike deadline, Truman's patience wore thin, and he signed an executive order authorizing government seizure of the railroads. Under threat of having the government take over the operation of the railroads, the two unions in question agreed to a five-day delay in the strike. Truman even suggested an 18.5-cent per hour pay raise for railroad workers. However, as the strike deadline approached, negotiations remained at a stalemate. The strike began as scheduled and had an immediate impact; of the country's 200,000 trains, only a few hundred remained in operation. Infuriated, Truman took to the radio waves and delivered a burning speech to the public; two days later, he delivered a speech to Congress blasting the striking workers and urging Congress to take unprecedented steps to break the strike, including urging approval to draft striking workers into military service. As Truman was delivering the speech, he was handed a note stating that the strike had been settled.

5   Even though the strike was resolved, deep issues had been raised over what role the government should play in disputes between management and labor. Truman's proposal to use the federal government to break a strike by drafting strikers into the armed forces brought this issue to the fore. Although management was pleased with the toughness that Truman had shown and many citizens were pleased that disruption of the economy had been avoided, concern was expressed about the constitutionality of having Congress take such a step. The Labor Management Relations Act (also known as the Taft-Hartley Act), which was enacted in the year following the strike, was an attempt to clarify some of the interrelationships among government, management, and labor.

Refer to this version of the passage to answer the questions that follow.

Truman and the Railroads

Paragraph

1   The period following World War II was filled with a succession of crises as the United States dealt with the difficulty of postwar reconversion to a peacetime economy. A threatened railroad strike in 1946 was one of many crises that led to a reconsideration of the interrelationships among government, management, and labor.

2   Organized labor, which had fared well during the war years of 1939–1945, faced severe problems because of the swift demobilization of thirteen million service personnel following the war and the destabilizing results of industrial reconversions from wartime to peacetime uses. During late 1945 and early 1946, a record wave of labor disputes and strikes hit the United States, and even more strikes and disputes were expected. At the height of the problems, more than 500 strikes were under way, some of them in industries that were highly critical to the overall U.S. economy, including coal, steel, cars, and oil. When a national strike was threatened by the railroads in the spring of 1946, the government moved into action, believing that the U.S. economy was threatened were it to take place.

3   President Harry S. Truman had dealt rather patiently with the labor problems until the spring of 1946. Throughout his political career, Truman had been a friend of organized labor and had been strongly supported by labor in his elections, and when the railroad strike was first threatened, he called for a sixty-day mediation period while the issues, particularly the main issue of a wage hike for railroad workers, were negotiated between management and labor. By April, eighteen of the twenty unions related to the railroads had arrived at an agreement; however, the remaining unions, which together controlled 280,000 workers and were essential to the operation of the railroads, were dissatisfied and set a date for a strike.

4   The day before the strike deadline, Truman's patience wore thin, and he signed an executive order authorizing government seizure of the railroads. **22A** Under threat of having the government take over the operation of the railroads, the two unions in question agreed to a five-day delay in the strike. **22B** Truman even suggested an 18.5-cent per hour pay raise for railroad workers. **22C** However, as the strike deadline approached, negotiations remained at a stalemate. **22D** The strike began as scheduled and had an immediate impact; of the country's 200,000 trains, only a few hundred remained in operation. Infuriated, Truman took to the radio waves and delivered a burning speech to the public; two days later, he delivered a speech to Congress blasting the striking workers and urging Congress to take unprecedented steps to break the strike, including urging approval to draft striking workers into military service. As Truman was delivering the speech, he was handed a note stating that the strike had been settled.

5   Even though the strike was resolved, deep issues had been raised over what role the government should play in disputes between management and labor. Truman's proposal to use the federal government to break a strike by drafting strikers into the armed forces brought this issue to the fore. Although management was pleased with the toughness that Truman had shown and many citizens were pleased that disruption of the economy had been avoided, concern was expressed about the constitutionality of having Congress take such a step. The Labor Management Relations Act (also known as the Taft-Hartley Act), which was enacted in the year following the strike, was an attempt to clarify some of the interrelationships among government, management, and labor.

Questions

14. The phrase "fared well" in paragraph 2 is closest in meaning to
    Ⓐ recovered from illness
    Ⓑ won battles
    Ⓒ made good wages
    Ⓓ experienced good fortune

15. According to paragraph 2, in late 1945 and early 1946
    Ⓐ there were labor problems because too many workers were in the military
    Ⓑ there were labor problems because too many people were leaving the military
    Ⓒ there were 500 strikes in the railroad industry
    Ⓓ there were 500 strikes in critical industries

16. The word "it" in paragraph 2 refers to
    Ⓐ a national strike
    Ⓑ the government
    Ⓒ action
    Ⓓ the U.S. economy

17. The phrase "called for" in paragraph 3 is closest in meaning to
    Ⓐ criticized
    Ⓑ cheered
    Ⓒ proposed
    Ⓓ postponed

18. According to paragraph 3, it is NOT true that the railroad workers
    Ⓐ were all in favor of the strike
    Ⓑ were interested in higher pay
    Ⓒ from two unions set a strike date
    Ⓓ turned down Truman's offer of a pay raise

19. Why does the author mention "280,000 workers" in paragraph 3?
    Ⓐ To indicate how many workers were opposed to the strike
    Ⓑ To demonstrate that the railroads were not really a critical industry
    Ⓒ To support management's claim that a wage increase was not possible
    Ⓓ To illustrate how serious the strike threat was

20. The phrase "wore thin" in paragraph 4 is closest in meaning to
    Ⓐ was extended
    Ⓑ decreased
    Ⓒ lightened
    Ⓓ lost weight

21. The phrase "remained at a stalemate" in paragraph 4 is closest in meaning to
    Ⓐ stayed on target
    Ⓑ proceeded on a friendly basis
    Ⓒ suddenly started up again
    Ⓓ were at a standstill

22. Look at the four squares [■] that indicate where the following sentence could be added to paragraph 4.

    This was an offer that was considerably more generous than previous offers.

    Where would the sentence best fit? Click on a square [■] to add the sentence to the passage.

23. The word "steps" in paragraph 4 could best be replaced by
    Ⓐ paces
    Ⓑ measures
    Ⓒ stairs
    Ⓓ suggestions

24. It can be inferred from paragraph 4 that
    Ⓐ Truman actually drafted striking workers into the military
    Ⓑ Congress passed a law allowing the drafting of striking workers
    Ⓒ it was the threat of drafting strikers that ended the strike
    Ⓓ Truman was actually opposed to drafting workers into the military

25. Which of the sentences below best expresses the essential information in the highlighted sentence in paragraph 5? *Incorrect* choices change the meaning in important ways or leave out essential information.

Ⓐ Though some were pleased that Truman had kept the economy going, there was concern about how he had done it. ˣ

Ⓑ During the strike, the economy was disrupted, and Congress was forced to take steps to fix it.

Ⓒ Because of the effects of the strike on the citizens of the country, it was necessary for Congress to make changes to the Constitution.

Ⓓ Management took tough actions during the strike; as a result, Congress expressed concern about the steps that management had taken. ˣ

26.

Directions: An introductory sentence for a brief summary of the passage is provided below. Complete the summary by selecting the THREE answer choices that express the most important ideas in the passage. Some sentences do not belong in the summary because they express ideas that are not presented in the passage or are minor ideas in the passage. **This question is worth 2 points** (2 points for 3 correct answers, 1 point for 2 correct answers, and 0 points for 1 or 0 correct answers).
This passage discusses harsh steps Truman took with the railroads.
•
•
•

Answer Choices (choose 3 to complete the chart):

(1) He made himself president of the railroad.

(2) He enabled the government to take control of the railroads.

(3) He brought wartime veterans in to work for the railroads.

(4) He suggested putting strikers in the military.

(5) He passed a law making strikes by railroad workers illegal.

(6) He made strong speeches arguing against a railroad strike.

READING 3

Read the passage.

Mathematical Bases

1 The system of numeration that is now most widely used is a base-10 system with the following characteristics: each number from 1 to 10 as well as the powers of 10 (such as one hundred or one thousand) has a distinctive name, and the names of the other numbers tend to be combinations of the names of the numbers from 1 to 10 and the powers of 10. In most Indo-European, Semitic, and Mongolian languages, the numerical systems have a decimal base and conform at least approximately to this theoretical model. The almost universal adoption of the base-10 numerical system was undoubtedly influenced by the fact that humans have ten fingers, since people most likely first learned to count on their fingers. Though the base-10 numerical systems are convenient for reasons of anatomy, they are not as mathematically practical as would be systems based on perhaps 11 or 12. Some mathematicians have suggested that a base-11 system would be preferable to a base-10 system because 11 is a prime number (and is thus divisible only by 1 and 11), while 10 is not a prime number (because it is divisible by 1, 2, 5, and 10); others have suggested that a base-12 system would be preferable to a base-10 system because 12 is divisible by more whole numbers (1, 2, 3, 4, 6, 12) than is 10.

2 Base-10 numerical systems were not the only systems based on anatomical parts: there were also systems based on 5 and 20. While it is difficult to find a number system that is a purely base-5, or quinary, system, it is possible to find number systems that have traces of groupings by fives, and these systems are most likely what remains of older systems that developed from counting the fingers on one hand. In a quinary system, there would be distinct units for numbers 1 through 5, but the words for numbers 6 through 9 are compounds of five-and-one, five-and-two, five-and-three, and so on. Remnants of quinary systems can be found today only in historical records of ancient languages, such as the language of the early Sumerians.

3 Examples of base-20, or vigesimal, systems, which most likely developed from counting by making use of all the digits, are more common than are those of base-5 systems. A number of early cultures, including the Mayans, the Aztecs, and the Celts, developed numerical systems that involved counting by 20s. The Mayan calendar had 20 months of 20 days each, and the Mayans counted years in terms of 20-year periods rather than decades; study of the Aztec numbers for 1 through 20 shows that the names of the first five numbers are related to the fingers of one hand, the names of the next five numbers are related to the fingers of the other hand, the names of the numbers 11 through 16 are related to the toes on one foot, and the names of numbers 16 through 20 are related to the toes on the other foot. In Celtic languages, counting is also done by 20s, and a number of other European languages maintain remnants of this characteristic. In French and Latin, the words for 20 are clearly remnants of a vigesimal system in that they are distinct words not derived from words for "two-tens," which would occur in a purely base-10 system, and the way of expressing the number 80 is by counting by 20s and saying "four-twenties." In English, the way of counting by 20s was to use the word "score"; this method of counting was commonly used by Shakespeare and was still in use at the time of Abraham Lincoln, who opened his famous address at Gettysburg by saying: "Four score and seven years ago. . . ."

4 Some cultures had systems based upon 60, a system with a major drawback in that it requires 60 distinct words for numbers 1 through 60. In Sumerian, Babylonian, Greek, and Arab cultures, for example, the sexagesimal system was a scholarly numerical system. Sexagesimal systems were obviously not developed based on body parts, and numerous theories have been raised to explain how such systems came about, but it is not know conclusively which of these theories is correct. One hypothesis is that 60 was chosen as the base because it is the lowest number with a great many divisors (1, 2, 3, 4, 5, 6, 10, 12, 15, 20, 30, 60). Another theory provides a more natural explanation for the use of 60 as a base: the approximate number of days in a year is 360, which supposedly led to the use of 360 degrees in a circle and was reduced to the more manageable 60, which is one-sixth of 360. A third theory suggests that the use of 60 as a base must have come about as a result of interchange between two different civilizations, one using a decimal (base-10) system and the other using a base-6 system. A weakness of this theory is that there is no historical foundation to support the existence of a base-6 system.

Refer to this version of the passage to answer the questions that follow.

Mathematical Bases

Paragraph

1 The system of numeration that is now most widely used is a base-10 system with the following characteristics: each number from 1 to 10 as well as the powers of 10 (such as one hundred or one thousand) has a distinctive name, and the names of the other numbers tend to be combinations of the names of the numbers from 1 to 10 and the powers of 10. In most Indo-European, Semitic, and Mongolian languages, the numerical systems have a decimal base and conform at least approximately to this theoretical model. The almost universal adoption of the base-10 numerical system was undoubtedly influenced by the fact that humans have ten fingers, since people most likely first learned to count on their fingers. Though the base-10 numerical systems are convenient for reasons of anatomy, they are not as mathematically practical as would be systems based on perhaps 11 or 12. Some mathematicians have suggested that a base-11 system would be preferable to a base-10 system because 11 is a prime number (and is thus divisible only by 1 and 11), while 10 is not a prime number (because it is divisible by 1, 2, 5, and 10); others have suggested that a base-12 system would be preferable to a base-10 system because 12 is divisible by more whole numbers (1, 2, 3, 4, 6, 12) than is 10.

2 Base-10 numerical systems were not the only systems based on anatomical parts: there were also systems based on 5 and 20. While it is difficult to find a number system that is a purely base-5, or quinary, system, it is possible to find number systems that have traces of groupings by fives, and these systems are most likely what remains of older systems that developed from counting the fingers on one hand. In a quinary system, there would be distinct units for numbers 1 through 5, but the words for numbers 6 through 9 are compounds of five-and-one, five-and-two, five-and-three, and so on. Remnants of quinary systems can be found today only in historical records of ancient languages, such as the language of the early Sumerians.

3 Examples of base-20, or vigesimal, systems, which most likely developed from counting by making use of all the digits, are more common than are those of base-5 systems. A number of early cultures, including the Mayans, the Aztecs, and the Celts, developed numerical systems that involved counting by 20s. The Mayan calendar had 20 months of 20 days each, and the Mayans counted years in terms of 20-year periods rather than decades; study of the Aztec numbers for 1 through 20 shows that the names of the first five numbers are related to the fingers of one hand, the names of the next five numbers are related to the fingers of the other hand, the names of the numbers 11 through 16 are related to the toes on one foot, and the names of numbers 16 through 20 are related to the toes on the other foot. In Celtic languages, counting is also done by 20s, and a number of other European languages maintain remnants of this characteristic. In French and Latin, the words for 20 are clearly remnants of a vigesimal system in that they are distinct words not derived from words for "two-tens," which would occur in a purely base-10 system, and the way of expressing the number 80 is by counting by 20s and saying "four-twenties." In English, the way of counting by 20s was to use the word "score"; this method of counting was commonly used by Shakespeare and was still in use at the time of Abraham Lincoln, who opened his famous address at Gettysburg by saying: "Four score and seven years ago. . . ."

Some cultures had systems based upon 60, a system with a major drawback in that it requires 60 distinct words for numbers 1 through 60. **35A** In Sumerian, Babylonian, Greek, and Arab cultures, for example, the sexagesimal system was a scholarly numerical system. **35B** Sexagesimal systems were obviously not developed based on body parts, and numerous theories have been raised to explain how such systems came about, but it is not know conclusively which of these theories is correct. **35C** One hypothesis is that 60 was chosen as the base because it is the lowest number with a great many divisors (1, 2, 3, 4, 5, 6, 10, 12, 15, 20, 30, 60). **35D** Another theory provides a more natural explanation for the use of 60 as a base: the approximate number of days in a year is 360, which supposedly led to the use of 360 degrees in a circle and was reduced to the more manageable 60, which is one-sixth of 360. A third theory suggests that the use of 60 as a base must have come about as a result of interchange between two different civilizations, one using a decimal (base-10) system and the other using a base-6 system. A weakness of this theory is that there is no historical foundation to support the existence of a base-6 system.

Questions

27. Which of the sentences below best expresses the essential information in the highlighted sentence in paragraph 1? *Incorrect* choices change the meaning in important ways or leave out essential information.

Ⓐ It has been suggested that either base 11 or base 12 would be preferable to base 10, for opposite reasons.

Ⓑ The number 10 has fewer divisors than the number 11 but more divisors than the number 12.

Ⓒ All mathematicians agree that a numerical system based on a number with the most divisors would be the best system.

Ⓓ Mathematicians have suggested that either base 11 or base 12 would be better than base 10 because both 11 and 12 are prime numbers.

28. The author begins paragraph 2 by mentioning "Base-10 numerical systems" in order to

Ⓐ introduce a new topic in paragraph 2

Ⓑ indicate that base-10 systems are based on anatomy, while other systems are not

Ⓒ emphasize that base-10 systems were less common than other systems

Ⓓ relate the topic of paragraph 1 to the topic of paragraph 2

29. The word "traces" in paragraph 2 could best be replaced by

Ⓐ remnants
Ⓑ tracks
Ⓒ results
Ⓓ processes

30. The word "digits" in paragraph 3 could best be replaced by

Ⓐ hands
Ⓑ numbers
Ⓒ fingers and toes
Ⓓ measurements

31. The phrase "this characteristic" in paragraph 3 refers to

Ⓐ using Celtic words
Ⓑ counting by 20s
Ⓒ relating the names of numbers to the toes
Ⓓ counting on the toes of one foot

32. The passage indicates that all of the following languages show characteristics of a vigesimal system EXCEPT

Ⓐ Latin
Ⓑ Celtic
Ⓒ English
Ⓓ Greek

33. It can be determined from paragraph 3 that four score and seven is equal to

Ⓐ 47
Ⓑ 87
Ⓒ 327
Ⓓ 749

34. The word "drawback" in paragraph 4 is closest in meaning to

Ⓐ disadvantage
Ⓑ attraction
Ⓒ reversal
Ⓓ interest

35. Look at the four squares [■] that indicate where the following sentence could be added to paragraph 4.

It was one that was used mainly for scientific study and analysis.

Where would the sentence best fit? Click on a square [■] to add the sentence to the passage.

36. The word "interchange" in paragraph 4 is closest in meaning to

Ⓐ barter
Ⓑ absorption
Ⓒ finance
Ⓓ contact

37. The number 25 would most likely be

Ⓐ a distinct number from 1 through 24 in a quinary system
Ⓑ a variation of "five-fives" in a decimal system
Ⓒ a variation of "twenty-plus-five" in a vigesimal system
Ⓓ a variation of "two-tens-plus-five" in a sexagesimal system

38.

Directions:	The answer choices below are each used to describe one of the numerical systems. Complete the table by matching appropriate answer choices to the numerical systems they are used to describe. TWO of the answer choices will not be used. **This question is worth 3 points** (3 points for 5 correct answers, 2 points for 4 correct answers, 1 point for 3 correct answers, and 0 points for 2, 1, or 0 correct answers).
decimal system	• •
vigesimal system	•
sexagesimal system	• •

Answer Choices (choose 5 to complete the table):

(1) Most likely based on the fingers of one hand

(2) The most commonly used system

(3) Most likely based on the fingers and toes

(4) Most likely not based on the fingers and toes

(5) Most likely based on the toes on both feet

(6) Not known to have been used by the masses in any culture

(7) Most likely based on the fingers on both hands

Turn to pages 185–188 to *diagnose* your errors and *record* your results.

READING COMPLETE TEST 2

TOEFL Reading

VOLUME HELP OK NEXT

PAUSE TEST SECTION EXIT

Reading
Section Directions

This section tests your ability to understand an English academic reading passage.

All questions except the last one are worth one point each. The last question is worth more than one point. The directions for the last question will state how many points it is worth.

You will now start the Reading section. You have **20 minutes** to read one passage and answer the questions about it.

READING 1

Read the passage.

Paragraph

Navigational Devices

1   From the earliest of times, sailors have found ways to navigate their ships on the seas and oceans of the world. The earliest sailors navigated by simply following the coastline. Aside from being a rather slow method of navigating, this method was also rather dangerous and limited. It was dangerous in that waters close to the shoreline could be shallow enough to strand a ship or the waters could be full of rocky protrusions capable of sending ships to their graves. When seafarers began sailing out of sight of land more than 4,000 years ago, they used the stars to determine their direction. They calculated the distance traveled from their speed and sailing time, and they drew rough charts and maps to find their way and to exchange information about navigational routes with others. It had also been known as early as 300 B.C. that a sundial casts a longer shadow as it is moved farther north of the equator, and this information was used by sailors from that time to get an idea of how far north of the equator a ship was. All of these methods provided only very rudimentary means of navigating.

2   It was not until more than 3,000 years after sailors set out on the seas that the compass was developed. The premise of a compass is that the magnetized needle of a compass, when it is balanced on a central pivot or left to float on liquid, will always turn to point in the direction of magnetic north. Navigators on Chinese ships were the first ones who were known to use compasses to determine the direction their ships were heading, as early as 1100.

3   Numerous inventions were created to determine a ship's latitude. With the invention of the astrolabe in the fourteenth century, sailors were able to measure the Sun's height with better accuracy than with a sundial, and they were able to use the information provided by the astrolabe to determine how far north of the equator they were. An astrolabe was a metal circle with a sighting rule that rotated in the circle; the rule could be aligned with the Sun, and measurements on the ring indicated the Sun's height. Other devices followed that were better able to determine the Sun's height and thus provide an idea of the ship's latitude. The backstaff, invented in 1595, and the sextant, invented in 1757, were devices that each improved a navigator's ability to determine latitude. The backstaff was a device that required the navigator to face away from the Sun and make a calculation of the shadow in relation to the horizon. The sextant was a measuring device that required the navigator to look into an eyepiece and calculate the Sun's position relative to the horizon and then check printed tables to convert this information into latitude.

4   The missing piece in the navigational puzzle was the ability to calculate longitude, or how far east or west a ship had traveled. The need for a device to calculate longitude was so important to navigators that the English Parliament offered a reward of 20,000 pounds (an extraordinarily large sum at the time, perhaps $10 million in today's currency) to anyone who could invent a method for calculating longitude. In 1759, English clockmaker John Harrison built a chronometer that was accurate enough for navigation. The premise of the device was that the Sun rises two seconds later each day for each kilometer traveled in a westerly direction, so the accurately measured change in time was an accurate way to calculate longitude. Harrison was easily able to convince Parliament that the reward was warranted.

Refer to this version of the passage to answer the questions that follow.

Navigational Devices

Paragraph

1   From the earliest of times, sailors have found ways to navigate their ships on the seas and oceans of the world. The earliest sailors navigated by simply following the coastline. Aside from being a rather slow method of navigating, this method was also rather dangerous and limited. It was dangerous in that waters close to the shoreline could be shallow enough to strand a ship or the waters could be full of rocky protrusions capable of sending ships to their graves. When seafarers began sailing out of sight of land more than 4,000 years ago, they used the stars to determine their direction. They calculated the distance traveled from their speed and sailing time, and they drew rough charts and maps to find their way and to exchange information about navigational routes with others. It had also been known as early as 300 B.C. that a sundial casts a longer shadow as it is moved farther north of the equator, and this information was used by sailors from that time to get an idea of how far north of the equator a ship was. All of these methods provided only very rudimentary means of navigating.

2   It was not until more than 3,000 years after sailors set out on the seas that the compass was developed. The premise of a compass is that the magnetized needle of a compass, when it is balanced on a central pivot or left to float on liquid, will always turn to point in the direction of magnetic north. Navigators on Chinese ships were the first ones who were known to use compasses to determine the direction their ships were heading, as early as 1100.

3   Numerous inventions were created to determine a ship's latitude. With the invention of the astrolabe in the fourteenth century, sailors were able to measure the Sun's height with better accuracy than with a sundial, and they were able to use the information provided by the astrolabe to determine how far north of the equator they were. An astrolabe was a metal circle with a sighting rule that rotated in the circle; the rule could be aligned with the Sun, and measurements on the ring indicated the Sun's height. Other devices followed that were better able to determine the Sun's height and thus provide an idea of the ship's latitude. The backstaff, invented in 1595, and the sextant, invented in 1757, were devices that each improved a navigator's ability to determine latitude. The backstaff was a device that required the navigator to face away from the Sun and make a calculation of the shadow in relation to the horizon. The sextant was a measuring device that required the navigator to look into an eyepiece and calculate the Sun's position relative to the horizon and then check printed tables to convert this information into latitude.

4   The missing piece in the navigational puzzle was the ability to calculate longitude, or how far east or west a ship had traveled. **8A** The need for a device to calculate longitude was so important to navigators that the English Parliament offered a reward of 20,000 pounds (an extraordinarily large sum at the time, perhaps $10 million in today's currency) to anyone who could invent a method for calculating longitude. **8B** In 1759, English clockmaker John Harrison built a chronometer that was accurate enough for navigation. **8C** The premise of the device was that the Sun rises two seconds later each day for each kilometer traveled in a westerly direction, so the accurately measured change in time was an accurate way to calculate longitude. **8D** Harrison was easily able to convince Parliament that the reward was warranted.

Questions

1. The expression "to their graves" in paragraph 1 could best be replaced by
   - Ⓐ to shipyards
   - Ⓑ to the seafloor
   - Ⓒ to be repaired
   - Ⓓ to their destination

2. According to the passage, sailors 4,000 years ago
   - Ⓐ were able to calculate their speed
   - Ⓑ were dependent on stars to tell time
   - Ⓒ never ventured away from the coastline
   - Ⓓ used the compass to navigate

3. The word "rudimentary" in paragraph 1 is closest in meaning to
   - Ⓐ reliable
   - Ⓑ direct
   - Ⓒ established
   - Ⓓ elementary

4. The word "it" in paragraph 2 refers to
   - Ⓐ premise
   - Ⓑ compass
   - Ⓒ needle
   - Ⓓ pivot

5. It is NOT stated in the passage that the astrolabe
   - Ⓐ was used to determine distance from the equator
   - Ⓑ was similar in shape to a sundial
   - Ⓒ had moving parts
   - Ⓓ was a circular-shaped device

6. The word "rule" as used in paragraph 3 is most likely
   - Ⓐ a regulation followed by sailors on a ship
   - Ⓑ a device used to make measurements
   - Ⓒ a law enacted by a government
   - Ⓓ a customary way of acting

7. The author refers to "The missing piece of the navigational puzzle" in paragraph 4 in order to
   - Ⓐ show that navigation was considered an amusing game
   - Ⓑ highlight that the ability to determine longitude was the final problem to be solved
   - Ⓒ indicate that missing ships were difficult to find
   - Ⓓ determine that it was difficult to calculate latitude

8. Look at the four squares [■] that indicate where the following sentence could be added to paragraph 4.

   Though many tried, it took a number of years after the offer was made for someone to succeed.

   Where would the sentence best fit? Click on a square [■] to add the sentence to the passage.

9. Which of the sentences below best expresses the essential information in the highlighted sentence in paragraph 4? *Incorrect* choices change the meaning in important ways or leave out essential information.
   - Ⓐ A chronometer could be used to measure longitude by combining knowledge about the rising Sun and accurate measurement of time.
   - Ⓑ A chronometer could be used to determine when the Sun was going to rise.
   - Ⓒ A chronometer could be used only to calculate longitude if one was traveling in a westerly direction.
   - Ⓓ A chronometer was an inaccurate measure of time because of the movement of the ship.

10. It is implied in the passage that
    - Ⓐ Harrison's device was not very accurate
    - Ⓑ Harrison spent considerable time traveling
    - Ⓒ Harrison received 20,000 pounds from Parliament
    - Ⓓ Harrison's device was better than any other device in determining latitude

11.

Directions:	Various navigational devices were used to resolve different navigational issues. Complete the table by matching appropriate navigational devices to the navigational problems they were used to resolve. TWO of the answer choices will not be used. **This question is worth 4 points** (4 points for 7 correct answers, 3 points for 6 correct answers, 2 points for 5 correct answers, 1 point for 4 correct answers, and 0 points for 3, 2, 1, or 0 correct answers).

direction	• • •
latitude	• • • •

Answer Choices (choose 7 to complete the table):

(1) Astrolabe

(2) Stars

(3) Sextant

(4) Navigational puzzle

(5) Compass

(6) Sundial

(7) Coastline

(8) Reward

(9) Backstaff

PAUSE
TEST

SECTION
EXIT

VOLUME HELP OK NEXT

Reading

Section Directions

In this part of the Reading section, you will read 2 passages. You will have **40 minutes** to read the passages and answer the questions.

Most questions are worth 1 point, but the last question for each passage is worth more than 1 point. The directions for the last question indicate how many points you receive.

READING 2

Read the passage.

Paragraph

The Neanderthals

1   Relatively recent archeological finds have brought about a considerable change in perception about the Neanderthals. Neanderthals had previously been characterized more as primitive grunting beasts than as intelligent and compassionate human ancestors. However, evidence suggests that they may have exhibited more learned skills and social compassion than had previously been thought.

2   The Neanderthals lived during a period that extended from at least 40,000 to 100,000 years ago in a variety of environments ranging from relatively warm and dry to extremely cold areas. The Neanderthals differed from modern man in that they had a stronger and heavier skeleton and facial structure with a more projecting brow, a broader nose, and larger teeth. Casts made of Neanderthal brains by archeologists show little difference in size from those of modern man.

3   It has been known for some time that Neanderthals were rather skilled stone artisans. They are best known for their production of stone tools, which included a large number of scrapers and pointed implements. The techniques that the Neanderthals used to prepare these tools demonstrated a clear and important technological advance over their predecessors. Edges of their stone tools have been studied under microscopes for evidence of how the tools may have been used. Many of the tools seem to have been used for working with wood, both for hacking at large branches and for doing more detailed work on smaller pieces; other tools were clearly used to prepare food, both meat and vegetables; still others, which resemble many of today's suede and leather tools, were used to work with animal skins.

4   A clearer picture of Neanderthals has come about recently as archeologists have determined that, in addition to the known ability to develop and employ tools in a rather skilled way, Neanderthals also exhibited evidence of beliefs and social rituals, aspects of life that were newly introduced by Neanderthals and that provide evidence of humanlike thoughts and feelings. Neanderthal cemeteries have been discovered in places like La Ferrassie in France and Shanidar in Iraq; Neanderthal remains in these cemeteries have provided proof of social organization and ritual in the Neanderthals. One skeleton of a Neanderthal was found with a crushed skull; the blow on the top of the head, perhaps from a falling boulder, had quite obviously been the cause of death. What was interesting was that study of the skeleton showed that while he had been alive this man had been seriously handicapped with a defect that had limited use of the upper right side of his body, that he suffered from arthritis, and that he was blind in one eye. The fact that he had survived well into old age was a strong indication that others had been helping to care for him and to provide him with food rather than allowing him to die because he was no longer fit. Other skeletal remains of Neanderthals show clear examples of burial rituals. Another skeleton of a grown male was found surrounded by pollen from eight different flowers, including ancestors of today's hyacinth, bachelor's button, and hollyhock; experts are convinced that the flowers could not have been growing in the cave where they were found and that they had been arranged around the body in a burial ritual. In a different Neanderthal cemetery, a young child was found buried with a deposit of ibex horns laid out with the body. These discoveries about Neanderthals help to create a picture of Neanderthals as beings with the feelings and emotions that go along with developed social customs and rituals.

Refer to this passage to answer the questions that follow.

Paragraph

The Neanderthals

1   Relatively recent archeological finds have brought about a considerable change in perception about the Neanderthals. Neanderthals had previously been characterized more as primitive grunting beasts than as intelligent and compassionate human ancestors. However, evidence suggests that they may have exhibited more learned skills and social compassion than had previously been thought.

2   **14A** The Neanderthals lived during a period that extended from at least 40,000 to 100,000 years ago in a variety of environments ranging from relatively warm and dry to extremely cold areas. **14B** The Neanderthals differed from modern man in that they had a stronger and heavier skeleton and facial structure with a more projecting brow, a broader nose, and larger teeth. **14C** Casts made of Neanderthal brains by archeologists show little difference in size from those of modern man. **14D**

3   It has been known for some time that Neanderthals were rather skilled stone artisans. They are best known for their production of stone tools, which included a large number of scrapers and pointed implements. The techniques that the Neanderthals used to prepare these tools demonstrated a clear and important technological advance over their predecessors. Edges of their stone tools have been studied under microscopes for evidence of how the tools may have been used. Many of the tools seem to have been used for working with wood, both for hacking at large branches and for doing more detailed work on smaller pieces; other tools were clearly used to prepare food, both meat and vegetables; still others, which resemble many of today's suede and leather tools, were used to work with animal skins.

4   A clearer picture of Neanderthals has come about recently as archeologists have determined that, in addition to the known ability to develop and employ tools in a rather skilled way, Neanderthals also exhibited evidence of beliefs and social rituals, aspects of life that were newly introduced by Neanderthals and that provide evidence of humanlike thoughts and feelings. Neanderthal cemeteries have been discovered in places like La Ferrassie in France and Shanidar in Iraq; Neanderthal remains in these cemeteries have provided proof of social organization and ritual in the Neanderthals. One skeleton of a Neanderthal was found with a crushed skull; the blow on the top of the head, perhaps from a falling boulder, had quite obviously been the cause of death. What was interesting was that study of the skeleton showed that while he had been alive this man had been seriously handicapped with a defect that had limited use of the upper right side of his body, that he suffered from arthritis, and that he was blind in one eye. The fact that he had survived well into old age was a strong indication that others had been helping to care for him and to provide him with food rather than allowing him to die because he was no longer fit. Other skeletal remains of Neanderthals show clear examples of burial rituals. Another skeleton of a grown male was found surrounded by pollen from eight different flowers, including ancestors of today's hyacinth, bachelor's button, and hollyhock; experts are convinced that the flowers could not have been growing in the cave where they were found and that they had been arranged around the body in a burial ritual. In a different Neanderthal cemetery, a young child was found buried with a deposit of ibex horns laid out with the body. These discoveries about Neanderthals help to create a picture of Neanderthals as beings with the feelings and emotions that go along with developed social customs and rituals.

Questions

12. The phrase "brought about" in paragraph 1 is closest in meaning to

Ⓐ carried

Ⓑ raised

Ⓒ led

Ⓓ caused

13. The word "those" in paragraph 2 refers to

Ⓐ teeth

Ⓑ casts

Ⓒ brains

Ⓓ archeologists

14. Look at the four squares [■] that indicate where the following sentence could be added to paragraph 2.

Neanderthals have been found in areas as diverse as desertlike regions of the Middle East and glacial areas of northern Europe.

Where would the sentence best fit? Click on a square [■] to add the sentence to the passage.

15. The word "predecessors" in paragraph 3 is closest in meaning to

Ⓐ ancestors

Ⓑ precedents

Ⓒ survivors

Ⓓ successors

16. It is NOT stated in the passage that Neanderthal tools were used to

Ⓐ chop wood

Ⓑ make woven clothing

Ⓒ prepare things to eat

Ⓓ prepare animal skins for use

17. The word "picture" in paragraph 4 could best be replaced by

Ⓐ fantasy

Ⓑ photograph

Ⓒ conception

Ⓓ sight

18. The author refers to "cemeteries" in paragraph 4 in order to

Ⓐ indicate that Neanderthals buried their dead as their predecessors had

Ⓑ make a point about the use of Neanderthal tools in the construction of cemeteries

Ⓒ demonstrate that Neanderthals were unsuccessful in their attempt to initiate social rituals

Ⓓ provide an example of a Neanderthal social ritual

19. The word "proof" in paragraph 4 is closest in meaning to

Ⓐ evidence

Ⓑ motivation

Ⓒ details

Ⓓ logic

20. Which of the following is stated in the passage about Neanderthal burial sites?

Ⓐ They have all been found in only one place.

Ⓑ They all seem to demonstrate the existence of Neanderthal social structure.

Ⓒ They have all held the remains of old people.

Ⓓ They have all been surrounded by flowers.

21. The word "fit" in paragraph 4 could best be replaced by

Ⓐ healthy

Ⓑ appropriate

Ⓒ necessary

Ⓓ old

22. Which of the sentences below best expresses the essential information in the highlighted sentence in paragraph 4? *Incorrect* choices change the meaning in important ways or leave out essential information.

Ⓐ The large number of flowers found in a particular cave proves that the skeleton was a Neanderthal.

Ⓑ The fact that the flowers could not have grown there indicates that the burial site must have been moved.

Ⓒ Because only pollen and not actual flowers was found, experts believe that there had originally been more than eight types of flowers.

Ⓓ Because of the pollen around one grave, experts believe that the body was buried during a ceremony.

23. An "ibex" in paragraph 4 is most likely a type of

Ⓐ clothing
Ⓑ weapon
Ⓒ animal
Ⓓ gemstone

24.

Directions: An introductory sentence for a brief summary of the passage is provided below. Complete the summary by selecting the THREE answer choices that express the most important ideas in the passage. Some sentences do not belong in the summary because they express ideas that are not presented in the passage or are minor ideas in the passage. **This question is worth 2 points** (2 points for 3 correct answers, 1 point for 2 correct answers, and 0 points for 1 or 0 correct answers).
The passage discusses our understanding of the Neanderthals.
•
•
•

Answer Choices (choose 3 to complete the chart):

(1) The discovery of what are apparently Neanderthal rituals shows that they possessed a degree of social structure.

(2) The language skills of the Neanderthals are not known.

(3) It has been discovered that the brains of Neanderthals were much smaller than those of humans.

(4) It was previously believed that Neanderthals were lacking in intelligence and social structure.

(5) Remnants of Neanderthal cultures have been found in what is today Iraq.

(6) The use of stone tools by the Neanderthals is an indication of the skills that they possessed.

READING 3

Read the passage.

The Silent Era

1   The first thirty-five years of motion picture history are called the silent era, even though films were accompanied by the music of pianists or organists or small orchestras of house musicians, because there was no practical means for recording and playing back recorded dialogue or music in synchronization with the reel of film. Films of this era progressed from very rudimentary to much more elaborate in the years 1894 to 1928 that bookend the era of silent films. The films of this era can quite logically be divided into three phases: the primitive era (1894–1907), the transitional era (1908–1917), and the mature era (1918–1928).

2   The primitive era began when the Kinetograph and the Kinetoscope, inventions created in Thomas Edison's New Jersey laboratory in 1892 to film and to view short sequences respectively, were used to create and present thirty-second vignettes of novelty acts in U.S. and European cities in 1894. An alternative to Edison's equipment, the Cinématographe, was developed by Auguste and Louis Lumière; the Cinématographe was a camera that was lighter than Edison's and could be easily converted into a projector, and it was this machine that turned the motion picture into a worldwide phenomenon. The Lumières held the first public screening of their motion pictures in Paris in 1895. For the next few years, the films created were rather short and primitive: each film consisted of a single shot from a lone stationary viewpoint.

3   The period from 1908 to 1917 was known as the transitional era. In this era, motion pictures changed from a primitive form of recreation to a well-respected part of popular culture. Actors developed in their ability to convey ideas without words, and creative intertitles provided commentary and narrative between sections of frames. Filming techniques were developed, with the introduction of such stylistic devices as alternating close-ups and long shots. Films became much longer, and the repertoire of film topics expanded considerably from the earlier scenes of real life to include film adaptations of popular and classic literature and plays. During this period, newspapers also began carrying reviews of films so that audiences would know which films were worth seeing. By 1917, a major shift in the film industry had occurred. France had been the world's leading exporter of films prior to World War I, but the war had decimated the film industry in France. By 1917, the United States had assumed leadership in the motion-picture industry, and the sleepy town of Hollywood, California, which had been used as a winter shooting site for filmmakers from the East Coast as early as 1907, had become the seat of the filmmaking industry. By 1920, Hollywood boasted a clique of movie stars with worldwide fame, and, as the decade progressed, fan magazines and gossip columns devoted to publicizing both the public and private lives of the stars flourished. The 1920s were also a time of great expansion of the Hollywood studios, as Metro-Goldwyn-Mayer (MGM) was created from a merger to form the largest studio in Hollywood, as Universal, Paramount, and Fox became firmly established as studios, and as the small company Warner Brothers, which was to grow immensely in later decades, introduced a series of films featuring the canine star Rin Tin Tin.

4   However, by the end of the 1920s, the era of silent films ended rather abruptly. Edison and other inventors had introduced technology for creating motion pictures with sound at various times throughout the early decades of the twentieth century, but those early devices could not ensure good enough sound quality and amplification to induce studios to try any of them out. Finally, Warner Brothers took a chance with the 1927 film, *The Jazz Singer,* which starred popular recording artist Al Jolson and featured both singing and talking. When *The Jazz Singer* became a tremendous hit, Warner Brothers and Fox immediately converted to producing motion pictures with sound; the other large studios, believing that talking pictures might be only a passing fad, continued making silent pictures for one more year. When it became clear that talking pictures were the future of film rather than a passing fad, the remaining studios converted to the exclusive production of talking films a year later; by 1929, all of the films produced in Hollywood studios were talking pictures, and the era of silent films was over.

Refer to this version of the passage to answer the questions that follow.

Paragraph

The Silent Era

1   The first thirty-five years of motion picture history are called the silent era, even though films were accompanied by the music of pianists or organists or small orchestras of house musicians, because there was no practical means for recording and playing back recorded dialogue or music in synchronization with the reel of film. Films of this era progressed from very rudimentary to much more elaborate in the years 1894 to 1928 that bookend the era of silent films. The films of this era can quite logically be divided into three phases: the primitive era (1894–1907), the transitional era (1908–1917), and the mature era (1918–1928).

2   The primitive era began when the Kinetograph and the Kinetoscope, inventions created in Thomas Edison's New Jersey laboratory in 1892 to film and to view short sequences respectively, were used to create and present thirty-second vignettes of novelty acts in U.S. and European cities in 1894. **28A** An alternative to Edison's equipment, the Cinématographe, was developed by Auguste and Louis Lumière; the Cinématographe was a camera that was lighter than Edison's and could be easily converted into a projector, and it was this machine that turned the motion picture into a worldwide phenomenon. **28B** The Lumières held the first public screening of their motion pictures in Paris in 1895. **28C** For the next few years, the films created were rather short and primitive: each film consisted of a single shot from a lone stationary viewpoint. **28D**

3   The period from 1908 to 1917 was known as the transitional era. In this era, motion pictures changed from a primitive form of recreation to a well-respected part of popular culture. Actors developed in their ability to convey ideas without words, and creative intertitles provided commentary and narrative between sections of frames. Filming techniques were developed, with the introduction of such stylistic devices as alternating close-ups and long shots. Films became much longer, and the repertoire of film topics expanded considerably from the earlier scenes of real life to include film adaptations of popular and classic literature and plays. During this period, newspapers also began carrying reviews of films so that audiences would know which films were worth seeing. By 1917, a major shift in the film industry had occurred. France had been the world's leading exporter of films prior to World War I, but the war had decimated the film industry in France. By 1917, the United States had assumed leadership in the motion-picture industry, and the sleepy town of Hollywood, California, which had been used as a winter shooting site for filmmakers from the East Coast as early as 1907, had become the seat of the filmmaking industry. By 1920, Hollywood boasted a clique of movie stars with worldwide fame, and, as the decade progressed, fan magazines and gossip columns devoted to publicizing both the public and private lives of the stars flourished. The 1920s were also a time of great expansion of the Hollywood studios, as Metro-Goldwyn-Mayer (MGM) was created from a merger to form the largest studio in Hollywood, as Universal, Paramount, and Fox became firmly established as studios, and as the small company Warner Brothers, which was to grow immensely in later decades, introduced a series of films featuring the canine star Rin Tin Tin.

4   However, by the end of the 1920s, the era of silent films ended rather abruptly. Edison and other inventors had introduced technology for creating motion pictures with sound at various times throughout the early decades of the twentieth century, but those early devices could not ensure good enough sound quality and amplification to induce studios to try any of them out. Finally, Warner Brothers took a chance with the 1927 film, *The Jazz Singer,* which starred popular recording artist Al Jolson and featured both singing and talking. When *The Jazz Singer* became a tremendous hit, Warner Brothers and Fox immediately converted to producing motion pictures with sound; the other large studios, believing that talking pictures might be only a passing fad, continued making silent pictures for one more year. When it became clear that talking pictures were the future of film rather than a passing fad, the remaining studios converted to the exclusive production of talking films a year later; by 1929, all of the films produced in Hollywood studios were talking pictures, and the era of silent films was over.

Questions

25. The author includes the last sentence in paragraph 1 in order to

Ⓐ describe events leading up to the events in the following paragraphs

Ⓑ provide examples showing that there were many different types of silent films

Ⓒ announce the organization of the passage

Ⓓ present a concluding idea to summarize paragraph 1

26. It is implied in paragraph 2 that

Ⓐ the Kinetoscope was invented some time before the Kinetograph

Ⓑ the Kinetoscope was used to view films created with the Kinetograph

Ⓒ the Cinématographe could create films but could not be used to view them

Ⓓ the Cinématographe was used to view films created with the Kinetograph

27. The word "turned" in paragraph 2 could best be replaced by

Ⓐ rotated

Ⓑ accepted

Ⓒ changed

Ⓓ alternated

28. Look at the four squares [■] that indicate where the following sentence could be added to paragraph 2.

They depicted short everyday scenes of people taking part in outdoor activities, laborers working at a construction site, and travellers scurrying through a train station.

Where would the sentence best fit? Click on a square [■] to add the sentence to the passage.

29. It is NOT true according to paragraph 3 that Hollywood

Ⓐ was the leading producer of films before World War I

Ⓑ was used as a winter site for films early in the twentieth century

Ⓒ was a small town prior to the success of the film industry

Ⓓ took over the role of leader in the film industry from France

30. The word "seat" in paragraph 3 could best be replaced by

Ⓐ chair

Ⓑ basis

Ⓒ center

Ⓓ success

31. The word "them" in paragraph 4 refers to

Ⓐ early decades

Ⓑ early devices

Ⓒ sound quality and amplification

Ⓓ studios

32. The phrase "took a chance" in paragraph 4 is closest in meaning to

Ⓐ behaved randomly

Ⓑ lost an opportunity

Ⓒ took a risk

Ⓓ had good fortune

33. According to paragraph 4, *The Jazz Singer*

Ⓐ was produced by Fox Studios

Ⓑ was the last great silent film

Ⓒ featured a famous Hollywood movie star

Ⓓ was extremely successful

34. Which of the sentences below best expresses the essential information in the highlighted sentence in paragraph 4? *Incorrect* choices change the meaning in important ways or leave out essential information.

Ⓐ After studios were sure that pictures with sound were going to be successful, they converted to talking pictures relatively quickly.

Ⓑ The future of film was presented in a series of talking films that were produced in Hollywood for release in 1929.

Ⓒ The era of silent films ended when the exclusive production for making talking pictures was granted to Hollywood studios.

Ⓓ It was clear to studios that talking pictures were only a fad, so they decided not to produce them until sometime in the future.

35.

Directions:	The answer choices listed below each describe one of the eras in the history of silent films. Complete the table by matching appropriate answer choices to the eras they are used to describe. TWO of the answer choices will not be used. **This question is worth 4 points** (4 points for 7 correct answers, 3 points for 6 correct answers, 2 points for 5 correct answers, 1 point for 4 correct answers, and 0 points for 3, 2, 1, or 0 correct answers).

primitive era	• •
transitional era	• •
mature era	• • •

Answer Choices (choose 7 to complete the table):

(1) The era of the introduction of adaptations of novels and plays

(2) The era of Hollywood stars

(3) The era of *The Jazz Singer*

(4) The era of single-shot films

(5) The era of the introduction of close-ups and long shots

(6) The era of fan magazines

(7) The era of talking pictures

(8) The era of short films

(9) The era of Hollywood studios

Turn to pages 185–188 to *diagnose* your errors and *record* your results.

READING DIAGNOSIS AND SCORING

For the Reading test sections in this book, it is possible to do the following:

- *diagnose* errors in the Reading Pre-Test, Reading Post-Test, Reading Mini-Tests, and Reading Complete Tests
- *score* the Reading Pre-Test, Reading Post-Test, Reading Mini-Tests, and Reading Complete Tests
- *record* your test results

DIAGNOSING READING ERRORS

Every time you take a Reading Pre-Test, Reading Post-Test, Reading Mini-Test, or Reading Complete Test, you should use the following chart to diagnose your errors.

Circle the number of each of the questions on the test that you *answered incorrectly* or *were unsure of*. Then you will see which skills you should focus on.

	READING PRE-TEST	READING POST-TEST	READING MINI-TESTS 1	2	3	4	5	6	7	8	READING COMPLETE TEST 1 1-13	14-26	27-38	READING COMPLETE TEST 2 1-11	12-24	25-35
SKILL 1	3 9 16 17	2 8 11 15	1 2 4 7 12	1 4 6 9	1 4 6 9 11	1 2 5	2 4 6 7 10	2 3 6 10 12	1 3 6 8	1 4 6 8 11	1 3 6 9 12	14 17 20 21 23	29 30 34 36	1 3 6	12 15 17 19 21	27 30 32
SKILL 2	11 14	6 17	8		3	9	11	4	9	2	10	16	31	4	13	31
SKILL 3	4 13	7 12	5	5	12	7	3	11	10	3	11	25	27	9	22	34
SKILL 4	8 18	5 16	11	7	10	6	5	8	11	9	7	22	35	8	14	28
SKILL 5	5 15	10 14	6	2	8	4	1	1	5		8	15	33	2	20	33
SKILL 6	1 10	3 18	3	8	2	3	12	5	7	5	2	18	32	5	16	29
SKILL 7	6 7	4 9	9	10	5	10	9	9	2	7	4	24	37	10	23	26
SKILL 8	2 12	1 13	10	3	7	8	8	7	4	10	5	19	28	7	18	25
SKILL 9	20	19	13		13		13	13			13	26			24	
SKILL 10	19	20		11		11			12	12			38	11		35

SCORING THE READING PRE-TEST AND POST-TEST

To determine a scaled score on the Reading Pre-Test or Reading Post-Test, you must first determine the number of points you received in the section. You must determine the number of points you receive on the last two questions before you can determine the total number of points out of a possible 23 points. When you know the total points you received on the Reading Pre-Test or Post-Test, you can refer to the following chart to determine your scaled score out of 30 for this section.

TOTAL POINTS	READING SCALED SCORE	TOTAL POINTS	READING SCALED SCORE
23	30	11	16
22	29	10	14
21	28	9	13
20	26	8	12
19	25	7	11
18	24	6	10
17	23	5	8
16	21	4	7
15	20	3	6
14	19	2	4
13	18	1	2
12	17	0	0

SCORING THE READING MINI-TESTS

To determine a scaled score on a Reading Mini-Test, you must first determine the number of points you received in the section. You must determine the number of points you receive on the last questions before you can determine the total number of points out of a possible 14 points. When you know the total points you received on a Reading Mini-Test, you can refer to the following chart to determine your scaled score out of 30 for this section.

TOTAL POINTS	READING SCALED SCORE	TOTAL POINTS	READING SCALED SCORE
14	30	6	8
13	28	5	7
12	25	4	5
11	22	3	4
10	19	2	2
9	16	1	1
8	14	0	0
7	11		

SCORING THE READING COMPLETE TESTS

To determine a scaled score on a Reading Complete Test section, you must first determine the number of points you received in the section. You must determine the number of points you receive on the last question of each reading passage before you can determine the total number of points out of a possible 42 points. When you know the total points you received on a Reading Complete Test section, you can refer to the following chart to determine your scaled score out of 30 for this section.

TOTAL POINTS	READING SCALED SCORE	TOTAL POINTS	READING SCALED SCORE
42	30	20	9
41	29	19	8
40	28	18	8
39	27	17	7
38	26	16	7
37	25	15	6
36	24	14	6
35	23	13	5
34	22	12	5
33	21	11	4
32	20	10	4
31	19	9	3
30	18	8	3
29	17	7	2
28	16	6	2
27	16	5	1
26	15	4	1
25	14	3	1
24	13	2	0
23	12	1	0
22	11	0	0
21	10		

RECORDING YOUR READING TEST RESULTS

Each time you complete a Reading Pre-Test, a Reading Post-Test, a Reading Mini-Test, or a Reading Complete Test, you should record the results in the chart that follows. In this way, you will be able to keep track of the progress you are making.

READING TEST RESULTS	
READING PRE-TEST	_____ out of 23 possible points **Reading Scaled Score** _____
READING POST-TEST	_____ out of 23 possible points **Reading Scaled Score** _____
READING MINI-TEST 1	_____ out of 14 possible points **Reading Scaled Score** _____
READING MINI-TEST 2	_____ out of 14 possible points **Reading Scaled Score** _____
READING MINI-TEST 3	_____ out of 14 possible points **Reading Scaled Score** _____
READING MINI-TEST 4	_____ out of 14 possible points **Reading Scaled Score** _____
READING MINI-TEST 5	_____ out of 14 possible points **Reading Scaled Score** _____
READING MINI-TEST 6	_____ out of 14 possible points **Reading Scaled Score** _____
READING MINI-TEST 7	_____ out of 14 possible points **Reading Scaled Score** _____
READING MINI-TEST 8	_____ out of 14 possible points **Reading Scaled Score** _____
READING COMPLETE TEST 1	_____ out of 42 possible points **Reading Scaled Score** _____
READING COMPLETE TEST 2	_____ out of 42 possible points **Reading Scaled Score** _____

ANSWER KEY

READING DIAGNOSTIC PRE-TEST Page 1

1. A	5. D	9. D	13. B	17. C
2. C	6. A	10. B	14. C	18. D
3. A	7. D	11. A	15. C	
4. C	8. B	12. D	16. B	

19.
theories attributing aggression to instinct:	(2) (6)
theories attributing aggression to learned behaviors:	(1) (4) (7)

20.
causes of aggression:	(1) (4) (5)

Note: These answers may be in any order.

READING SKILLS

READING EXERCISE 1 Page 12

1. B	6. B	11. C	16. B	21. A
2. D	7. D	12. A	17. C	22. A
3. C	8. A	13. B	18. B	23. A
4. A	9. C	14. D	19. A	24. C
5. B	10. B	15. A	20. D	

READING EXERCISE 2 Page 18

1. C	5. A	9. B	13. B	17. C
2. B	6. B	10. A	14. B	18. A
3. A	7. A	11. C	15. D	
4. A	8. C	12. A	16. B	

READING EXERCISE (Skills 1–2) Page 22

1. A	4. A	7. A	10. B	13. A
2. C	5. B	8. C	11. D	
3. B	6. D	9. D	12. B	

READING EXERCISE 3 Page 27

1. A	4. B	7. A	10. D	13. B
2. D	5. C	8. C	11. D	14. C
3. A	6. D	9. B	12. A	

READING EXERCISE 4 Page 36

1. A	3. B	5. D	7. D	9. C
2. C	4. D	6. D	8. D	

READING EXERCISE (Skills 3–4) Page 40

1. C	3. B	5. B	7. B	9. D
2. A	4. C	6. C	8. D	10. B

READING REVIEW EXERCISE (Skills 1–4) Page 44

1. A	4. B	7. B	10. A	13. D
2. C	5. D	8. A	11. B	
3. B	6. D	9. C	12. C	

READING EXERCISE 5 Page 50

1. D	6. C	11. A	16. A	21. C
2. A	7. A	12. D	17. B	22. D
3. D	8. D	13. C	18. A	
4. C	9. B	14. B	19. C	
5. B	10. C	15. D	20. D	

READING EXERCISE 6 Page 58

1. D	6. C	11. D	16. D	21. C
2. C	7. A	12. A	17. A	22. A
3. A	8. D	13. B	18. B	
4. D	9. C	14. D	19. D	
5. B	10. D	15. C	20. D	

READING EXERCISE (Skills 5–6) Page 62

1. C	4. B	7. B	10. A	13. B
2. C	5. B	8. C	11. D	
3. A	6. D	9. D	12. D	

READING REVIEW EXERCISE (Skills 1–6) Page 65

1. C	4. A	7. D	10. A	13. B
2. B	5. D	8. C	11. D	
3. D	6. B	9. B	12. A	

READING EXERCISE 7 Page 71

1. B	5. A	9. A	13. D	17. B
2. A	6. A	10. C	14. C	18. B
3. D	7. D	11. D	15. B	19. D
4. C	8. C	12. B	16. A	

READING EXERCISE 8 Page 77

1. D	5. B	9. C	13. D	17. D
2. A	6. A	10. B	14. A	18. B
3. C	7. D	11. A	15. B	19. D
4. C	8. D	12. D	16. A	

READING EXERCISE (Skills 7–8) Page 82

1. B	3. D	5. D	7. C	9. B
2. C	4. A	6. A	8. C	10. A

READING REVIEW EXERCISE (Skills 1–8) Page 86

1. B	4. C	7. A	10. A	13. C
2. A	5. C	8. B	11. D	
3. D	6. A	9. D	12. B	

READING EXERCISE 9 Page 93

1.
the ways that plant life is able to develop on islands:	(2) (4) (6)

2.
Ben and Jerry's unconventional company:	(2) (4) (5)

3.
radical shifts in population that the bald eagle has undergone:	(1) (4) (6)

4.
characteristics shared by modernism in art:	(1) (4) (5)

READING EXERCISE 10 Page 100

1.
ridge dunes:	(4) (6)
star-shaped dunes:	(3)
crescent dunes:	(2) (7)

2.
"buckaroo" and *vaquero*:	(2) (7)
"buckaroo" and "vaccine":	(5)
vacca and "vaccine":	(1) (4)

3.
those with active traps:	(2) (5) (7)
those with inactive traps:	(1) (4)

4.
Faulkner in the first phase of his career:	(2) (5) (8)
Faulkner in the second phase of his career:	(1) (4) (7) (9)

READING EXERCISE (Skills 9–10) Page 104

1.
processes affecting the development of millions of species:	(1) (3) (6)

2.
speciation:	(2) (5)
extinction:	(1) (4) (7)

READING REVIEW EXERCISE (Skills 1–10) Page 106

1. B	4. D	7. B	10. A
2. A	5. C	8. A	11. D
3. D	6. B	9. B	12. C

13.
different models for analyzing the process of decision making:	(2) (3) (6)

READING POST-TEST Page 110

1. C	5. B	9. A	13. C	17. B
2. B	6. B	10. C	14. C	18. D
3. D	7. D	11. B	15. A	
4. A	8. C	12. D	16. A	

19.
schooling behavior in certain fish:	(3) (5) (6)

20.
hypotheses related to purpose:	(1) (5) (7)
hypotheses related to manner:	(2) (6)

READING MINI-TEST 1 Page 116

1. A	4. D	7. B	10. A
2. C	5. B	8. A	11. C
3. D	6. C	9. D	12. D

13.
a theory of migration:	(1) (3) (6)

READING MINI-TEST 2 Page 121

1. B	4. C	7. D	10. D
2. A	5. D	8. C	
3. A	6. A	9. B	

11.
first-borns:	(3) (4) (8)
second-borns and middle children:	(2) (9)
last-borns:	(1) (6)

READING MINI-TEST 3 Page 126

1. A	4. B	7. C	10. B
2. D	5. B	8. B	11. D
3. C	6. D	9. A	12. A

13.
the history of a sauce known as ketchup:	(1) (4) (6)

READING MINI-TEST 4 Page 131

1. D	4. B	7. C	10. A
2. A	5. A	8. D	
3. D	6. C	9. C	

11.
estuary systems on flooded coastal plains:	(2) (5) (8) (9)
estuary systems on mountainous coasts:	(1) (4) (6)

READING MINI-TEST 5 Page 136

1. C	4. D	7. C	10. B
2. B	5. D	8. A	11. A
3. A	6. A	9. B	12. C

13.
characteristics of schizophrenia:	(2) (5) (6)

READING MINI-TEST 6 Page 141

1. C	4. B	7. A	10. D
2. A	5. D	8. D	11. B
3. B	6. C	9. C	12. A

13.
the tragedy of the *Exxon Valdez*:	(2) (3) (5)

READING MINI-TEST 7 Page 146

1. A	4. A	7. C	10. A
2. D	5. D	8. B	11. A
3. B	6. C	9. B	

12.
divergent boundary:	(3) (7)
convergent boundary:	(4) (5)
transcurrent boundary:	(2)

READING MINI-TEST 8 Page 151

1. B	4. C	7. D	10. D
2. B	5. A	8. A	11. A
3. D	6. B	9. A	

12.
only the New York limners:	(3) (7)
only the New England limners:	(1) (5)
both the New York and New England limners:	(4)

READING COMPLETE TEST 1 Page 156

READING 1 Page 157

1. B	4. B	7. B	10. B
2. D	5. D	8. C	11. A
3. C	6. A	9. B	12. D

13.
study of astronomy as it refers to prehistoric cultures:	(3) (4) (6)

READING 2 Page 162

14. D	17. C	20. B	23. B
15. B	18. A	21. D	24. C
16. A	19. D	22. C	25. A

26.
Truman and organized labor:	(2) (4) (6)

READING 3 Page 166

27. A	30. C	33. B	36. D
28. D	31. B	34. A	37. C
29. A	32. D	35. B	

38.

decimal system:	(2) (7)
vigesimal system:	(3)
sexagesimal system:	(4) (6)

READING COMPLETE TEST 2 Page 171

READING 1 Page 172

1. B	4. C	7. B	10. C
2. A	5. B	8. B	
3. D	6. B	9. A	

11.

direction:	(2) (5) (7)
latitude:	(1) (3) (6) (9)

READING 2 Page 177

12. D	15. A	18. D	21. A
13. C	16. B	19. A	22. D
14. B	17. C	20. B	23. C

24.

our understanding of Neanderthals:	(1) (4) (6)

READING 3 Page 181

25. C	28. D	31. B	34. A
26. B	29. A	32. C	
27. C	30. C	33. D	

35.

primitive era:	(4) (8)
transitional era:	(1) (5)
mature era:	(2) (6) (9)

Single User License Agreement:

IMPORTANT: READ CAREFULLY

WARNING: BY OPENING THE PACKAGE YOU AGREE TO BE BOUND BY THE TERMS OF THE LICENSE AGREEMENT BELOW

This is a legally binding agreement between You (the user or purchaser) and Pearson Education, Inc. By retaining this license, any software media or accompanying written materials or carrying out any of the permitted activities You agree to be bound by the terms of the license agreement below. If You do not agree to these terms, then promptly return the entire publication (this license and all software, written materials, packaging and any other components received with it) with Your sales receipt to Your supplier for a full refund.

SINGLE USER LICENSE AGREEMENT

❑ **YOU ARE PERMITTED TO:**

✓ Use (load into temporary memory or permanent storage) a single copy of the software on only one computer at a time. If this computer is linked to a network then the software may only be installed in a manner such that it is not accessible to other machines on the network.

✓ Use the software with a class provided it is only installed on one computer

✓ Transfer the software from one computer to another provided that you only use it on one computer at a time

✓ Print out individual screen extracts from the disk for (a) private study or (b) to include in Your essays or classwork with students

✓ Photocopy individual screen extracts for Your schoolwork or classwork with students

❑ **YOU MAY NOT:**

✗ Rent or lease the software or any part of the publication

✗ Copy any part of the documentation, except where specifically indicated otherwise

✗ Make copies of the software, even for backup purposes

✗ Reverse engineer, decompile or disassemble the software or create a derivative product from the contents of the databases or any software included in them

✗ Use the software on more than one computer at a time

✗ Install the software on any networked computer or server in a way that could allow access to it from more than one machine on the network

✗ Include any material or software from the disk in any other product or software materials except as allowed under "You are permitted to"

✗ Use the software in any way not specified above without prior written consent of the Publisher

✗ Print out more than one page at a time

ONE COPY ONLY

This license is for a single user copy of the software. THE PUBLISHER RESERVES THE RIGHT TO TERMINATE THIS LICENSE BY WRITTEN NOTICE AND TO TAKE ACTION TO RECOVER ANY DAMAGES SUFFERED BY THE PUBLISHER IF YOU BREACH ANY PROVISION OF THIS AGREEMENT.

The Publisher owns the software. You only own the disk on which the software is supplied.

LIMITED WARRANTY

The Publisher warrants that the disk or CD-ROM on which the software is supplied is free from defects in materials and workmanship under normal use for ninety (90) days from the date You received them. This warranty is limited to You and is not transferable. The Publisher does not warrant that the functions of the software meet Your requirements or that the media is compatible with any computer system on which it is used or that the operation of the software will be unlimited or error free.

You assume responsibility for selecting the software to achieve Your intended results and for the installation of, the use of, and the results obtained from the software. The entire liability of the Publisher and Your only remedy shall be replacement free of charge of the components that do not meet this warranty.

This limited warranty is void if any damage has resulted from accident, abuse, misapplication, service or modification by someone other than the Publisher. In no event shall the Publisher or its suppliers be liable for any damages whatsoever arising out of installation of the software, even if advised of the possibility of such damages. The Publisher will not be liable for any loss or damage of any nature suffered by any part as a result of reliance upon or reproduction of any errors in the content of the publication.

The Publisher does not limit its liability for death or personal injury caused by its negligence. This license agreement shall be governed by and interpreted and construed in accordance with New York State law.

For technical assistance, you may call (877) 546-5408 or e-mail epsupport@pearsoned.com.